PENALTY STRIKE

The Stackpole Military History Series

THE AMERICAN CIVIL WAR

Cavalry Raids of the Civil War
Ghost, Thunderbolt, and Wizard
Pickett's Charge
Witness to Gettysburg

WORLD WAR I

Doughboy War

WORLD WAR II

After D-Day
Armor Battles of the Waffen-SS, 1943–45
Armoured Guardsmen
Army of the West
Australian Commandos
The B-24 in China
Backwater War
The Battle of Sicily
Beyond the Beachhead
The Brandenburger Commandos
The Brigade
Bringing the Thunder
Coast Watching in World War II
Colossal Cracks
A Dangerous Assignment
D-Day Deception
D-Day to Berlin
Destination Normandy
Dive Bomber!
A Drop Too Many
Eagles of the Third Reich
Eastern Front Combat
Exit Rommel
Fist from the Sky
Flying American Combat Aircraft of World War II
Forging the Thunderbolt
Fortress France
The German Defeat in the East, 1944–45
German Order of Battle, Vol. 1
German Order of Battle, Vol. 2
German Order of Battle, Vol. 3
The Germans in Normandy

Germany's Panzer Arm in World War II
GI Ingenuity
Goodwood
The Great Ships
Grenadiers
Hitler's Nemesis
Infantry Aces
Iron Arm
Iron Knights
Kampfgruppe Peiper at the Battle of the Bulge
Kursk
Luftwaffe Aces
Massacre at Tobruk
Mechanized Juggernaut or Military Anachronism?
Messerschmitts over Sicily
Michael Wittmann, Vol. 1
Michael Wittmann, Vol. 2
Mountain Warriors
The Nazi Rocketeers
On the Canal
Operation Mercury
Packs On!
Panzer Aces
Panzer Aces II
Panzer Commanders of the Western Front
The Panzer Legions
Panzers in Normandy
Panzers in Winter
The Path to Blitzkrieg
Red Star under the Baltic
Retreat to the Reich
Rommel's Desert Commanders
Rommel's Desert War
Rommel's Lieutenants
The Savage Sky
A Soldier in the Cockpit
Soviet Blitzkrieg
Stalin's Keys to Victory
Surviving Bataan and Beyond
T-34 in Action
Tank Tactics
Tigers in the Mud

Triumphant Fox
The 12th SS, Vol. 1
The 12th SS, Vol. 2
The War against Rommel's Supply Lines
War in the Aegean
Wolfpack Warriors

THE COLD WAR / VIETNAM

Cyclops in the Jungle
Expendable Warriors
Flying American Combat Aircraft: The Cold War
Here There Are Tigers
Land with No Sun
Phantom Reflections
Street without Joy
Through the Valley

WARS OF THE MIDDLE EAST

Never-Ending Conflict

GENERAL MILITARY HISTORY

Carriers in Combat
Desert Battles
Guerrilla Warfare

PENALTY STRIKE

The Memoirs of a Red Army Penal Company Commander, 1943–45

Alexander V. Pyl'cyn
Edited by Artem Drabkin
Translated by Bair Irincheev

STACKPOLE
BOOKS

Published in paperback in 2009 by
STACKPOLE BOOKS
5067 Ritter Road
Mechanicsburg, PA 17055
www.stackpolebooks.com

PENALTY STRIKE: THE MEMOIRS OF A RED ARMY PENAL COMPANY COM-
MANDER 1943–45, by Alexander Pyl'cyn, was originally published in hard cover by
Helion & Company Limited, Solihull, West Midlands, England. Copyright © 2006 by
Artem Drabkin. Paperback edition by arrangement with Helion & Company. All
rights reserved.

Cover design by Tracy Patterson

Printed in the United States of America

10 9 8 7 6 5 4 3 2 1

Library of Congress Cataloging-in-Publication Data

Pyl'tsyn, A. V. (Aleksandr Vasil'evich), 1923–
    [Shtrafnoi udar. English]
    Penalty strike : the memoirs of a Red Army penal company commander, 1943–45 /
Alexander V. Pyl'cyn ; edited by Artem Drabkin ; translated by Bair Irincheev.
        p. cm. — (Stackpole military history series)
    Originally published: Solihull, England : Helion, 2006.
    ISBN 978-0-8117-3599-5 (pbk.)
    1. Pyl'tsyn, A. V. (Aleksandr Vasil'evich), 1923– 2. Berlin, Battle of, Berlin, Ger-
many, 1945—Personal narratives, Russian. 3. World War, 1939–1945—Campaigns—
Germany. 4. World War, 1939–1945—Campaigns—Eastern Front. 5. Soviet Union.
Raboche-Krest'ianskaia Krasnaia Armiia—Biography. 6. Soldiers—Soviet Union—
Biography. I. Drabkin, Artem, 1971– II. Title.
    D757.9.B4P9513 2009
    940.54'1247092—dc22
    [B]
                                    2008054752

Contents

1	Beginnings	1
2	Rogachev and the First Experience of Battle	16
3	'Rokossovski's Gang'	35
4	Operation 'Bagration'	50
5	Wounded	67
6	The Narev Bridgehead	82
7	In Defence on the Narev	125
8	Marriage	134
9	The Vistula-Oder Offensive	143
10	Over the Oder to Berlin	162
11	Victory!	190

CHAPTER 1

Beginnings

In 1923 I was born into the family of a railway worker in Russia's Far East. Our home was so close to the railway, that when a train passed by the whole house would shiver, as if it was itself ready to leave on a long journey. We all got so used to this proximity of railway and noise, that when we moved to another house, far away from the railway, we could not get used to the silence, it seemed unnatural to us. My father, Vasily Vasilievich Pylcyn, was born in 1881. He was from Kostroma, but for some reason, either trouble with the police or an unsuccessful marriage, he had to escape to the Far East. He spoke about this matter very vaguely and unwillingly, but he even changed his last name. I believe his real last name was Smirnov. He was a rather learned person for his time. We had a vast library of classic Russian literature in our home. If I remember correctly, he was a foreman of railway workers and then a railway master. He was an extremely skilful craftsman. Sophisticated carved wooden furniture, a fair amount of metal cutlery, and all sorts of wooden barrels for pickling vegetables, were all things he made himself. He was so strict in family life that we children were afraid of his mere look at us, although he never hit us.

Despite the active role that he played in social life, especially in defence voluntary organisations, such as *Osoaviakhim* and others, he was never a member of the Communist party. In 1938 my father was arrested for negligence in repair of a railway. It almost led to the crash of a passenger train. He was sentenced to three years in jail. The sentence was considered by everyone to be just. He returned from jail immediately before the outbreak of the Great Patriotic War. My father had a strange habit of talking aloud to himself. One time he said, out loud, that "Hitler turned out to be smarter than all our genius leaders", and that the main leader, i.e. Stalin, merely "screwed Russia". Someone heard this and informed the authorities. There were plenty of 'woodpeckers', or informers, in those days. My father was again arrested. In the same way as many other people, he was sent from the Far East somewhere to the North, or to Siberia, where he vanished for good.

My mother, Maria Danilovna, was 20 years younger than my father. She was from the family of a simple railway worker. He was Siberian, a real Russian, as they said in those days, *chaldon* Danila Leontievich Karelin. In those days the word *chaldon* was pronounced as *cheldon* in the Far East, and was interpreted by some people as *chelovek's Dona*, a man from Don River, i.e. a Don Cossack. It was much later that I learnt that *chaldon* actually meant 'a real Russian Siberian', not an immigrant from the rest of Russia.

My grandmother, on my mother's side, was Ekaterina Ivanovna. Her maiden name was Smertina. She was from Khakassia. My grandfather would tell us that he 'stole' her from the neighbouring village of Khakassian. My mother's parents were illiterate, although Granny Kate could count money very well, almost without looking. My mother was also illiterate, but knew a great number of sayings and superstitions. I taught her to read and write when I went to the first grade of school,

1

although I could read when I was only four or five years old. I insisted that she attended *likbez*, a 'liquidation of illiteracy' study group, and I 'supervised' her. My mother learnt the basics of literacy well. She could read, slowly but steadily, and write, although with some difficulty. She did not have much time or patience for more. However, that level of literacy was enough for her to learn a trade. She became an automatic-railway-point operator at Kimkan station, when the war broke out and women had to replace men in many trades. She also worked in that office for many years after the war.

Our family was not rich before the war. I think there were no rich families at all in those days. But we survived, even the tragic famine year of 1933, without losing anyone in our family. It was mostly the *taiga* that was supplying us with food. Our father was also a dedicated hunter and supplied us with game. I remember that during the winter it was especially hard. He would go into the *taiga* every weekend and bring back a couple of rabbits, or several squirrels, and sometimes wood-grouse. Thus, we were well supplied, and inclined to squirrel meat, which was quite tasty. As well as all that, father was processing, and turning in to the State, rabbit and squirrel furs, getting flour and sugar in return. Also, he would go on vacation in the autumn and go into the *taiga* to harvest Siberian pine seeds. He would bring whole bags of those seeds home, and extract excellent oil out of them with a press that he made himself.

Mother used remains of the seeds for making 'Siberian pine milk', by boiling them in water. She also used the seeds for adding to flour in making bread. Mother would bake bread from a small amount of flour, mixed with barley acorn 'coffee' that one could buy in shops in those days, and crushed oats. The bread was dark black or brown, but it rescued us from starvation. Our family tradition of harvesting berries, wild fruits, plants and mushrooms, also rescued us. Those pickled and dried preserves protected us from hunger, and from scurvy that was widespread in the Far East in those days. From childhood we were taught to pick up mushrooms and berries, and knew them well. There were not many wild fruits in the Far East, except for wild 'Chinese apples' as they were called. Jokers said that they were sold by 'glasses', not by kilograms, because they were so small. However, there were a lot of berries, from wild strawberry, to honeysuckle and wild grapes.

My father and grandfather knew how to make baskets. They fished in a nearby cold and fast river, not with a fishing rod, but with a specially shaped basket. Sometimes they would bring small fish, with such delicacies as graylings. During the spawning of salmon they would bring humpback salmons, Siberian salmons that weighed up to 6–8 kilograms! Of course, on such days we had plenty of red caviar, although at that time it was readily available from shops. All the seafood was boiled in soup or fried, and also smoked, pickled and dried for winter. Everything was used for food. It was that variety that helped us to survive long and cold winters, and maintained our 'Siberian' health. It is probably due to those reasons that we survived the years of famine better than people in Central Russia or the Ukraine.

Seven children were born into our family, but three of them died very young. It was quite usual in those days. Only four of us lived to see the outbreak of war, two of my older brothers, my younger sister, and me. My father never told us about our ancestors, and I did not know anyone further back than my grandfather Danila and Granny Kate. At that time it was not common to dig up old genealogical connections. You never knew if you would find something unfavourable for you and your family! However, I knew relatives on the side genealogical branches quite well. They were the other children and grandchildren of the Karelin family who lived not far from us. First of all, there was my mother's brother, Petr Danilovich. He was also a railway master and a Communist. Absolutely unexpectedly, he fell under the 'steamroller of arrests' in 1937, and vanished into the endless expanses of Siberia or the Extreme North. He left behind a sick wife and five children. They managed to grow up, get education and survive the war. Many of them are still alive today.

It is only now, seventy years later, that I start to realise there simply could not have been so many 'saboteurs' and 'enemies of the people'. However, I must honestly acknowledge that in the atmosphere of that time, searching for 'enemies of the people', and the arrests, despite the absence of electronic media, often captured the minds of many people, even us schoolchildren. I remember that when we were in the 2nd and 3rd grades, we would look for secret signs of, "off with VKP (b)!" on the covers of our notebooks, and in reproductions of Vasnetsov's paintings in our textbooks. Even if we could not find them, the teachers would tell us that we 'searched for them badly'. Sudden arrests of our relatives, as for example, my uncle, who seemed to be completely innocent, were perceived as 'small mistakes', in the huge country-wide effort to "arrest saboteurs, spies, and any sorts of enemies of the people". The saying, "you cannot make an omelette without breaking eggs", was stressed in the media a lot in those days. The amazing thing is, that in addition to a campaign of searching for 'enemies', the media propagated love towards our country, and ideals of Communism, not only among youth, but also among the entire population of the country. You just have to recall the films and patriotic songs of those days. All of them intensified our love for the Motherland, and the high patriotism with which we entered the 'holy' war against Nazi Germany.

The repression of those years, despite taking away our family members, did not spread out to their relatives. Maybe that was the case only in Russia's Far East. My mother's younger sister Klavdia Danilovna, born in 1915, continued to work as a telegraph operator, a rather responsible office in those days, despite their brother being arrested. She married an engineer, Vasily Alekseevich Baranov, who went to the Front on the very first days of the war, and became a KGB officer after the war. He worked as a KGB officer in Riga, Latvia, till the end of his days, in 1970. Through them I have a cousin Stanislav, who was born in 1938. He graduated from the Border Guard Academy and became a good officer. Before the collapse of the Soviet Union, he became part of the list of 'red witches' in Latvia. Because of threats of repression from the Latvian authorities, he had to leave the Latvian Republic when that became hostile, and simply flee back to Russia.

As I mentioned, I had two brothers. I looked amazingly similar to my older brother who was born in 1918, so that even our friends confused us. We both looked like our mother and our grandfather Danila. Ivan had a lot of different talents. He could play all sorts of musical instruments, including the harmonica, and had an amazing talent for drawing. He was also very good at maths. Immediately after graduation from high school, he was invited to teach mathematics in our village seven-year school. In 1937 he was drafted into the Coastal Defence of the Pacific Fleet. There he taught maths to sailors and soldiers who were still illiterate, and himself received the training of a radio operator. In 1942 he was sent into active service. He was killed in action, in September 1943, while serving in the 5th Shock Army of the Southern Front. "Guards Sergeant Ivan Vasilievich Pylcyn, faithful to his oath, displaying heroism and bravery, fell in battle for our Socialist Motherland on September 18, 1943". That was the official message that my family received with his death certificate.

My second brother Viktor, who was three years older than me, did not have any special talents. The only thing that he inherited from our father was the habit of talking aloud, especially during sleep, and also his rather pedantic manners. After graduation from high school, he worked as a station chief assistant for one year, and was drafted into the Red Army in 1939. He served in an airborne brigade in the Far East. Shortly before the outbreak of the war, his brigade was transferred to the Ukraine. There he had to face the first deadly strikes of the German military machine, and experience the bitterness of retreat. He was wounded in the defence of the Northern Caucasus. Later he fought in Stalingrad, and went missing there in December 1942.

My sister Antonina Vasilievna, who was born in 1927, now lives in St Petersburg, formerly Leningrad. The fact that her father and uncle were arrested in Stalin's era never prevented her from being elected into her village Soviet. Later she moved to Leningrad. There, she worked as a clerk in top secret documentation, at one of the city's recruitment offices for the Army. The fact that my father was arrested did not prevent me from becoming a member of the Communist party. I then progressed from being a simple Red Army man to a Colonel, and served honestly and faithfully a full forty years in the Army. So we both got to see, that 'a son or daughter are not responsible for the deeds of their father'. I guess everyone had a different destiny, and relatives of the arrested ones could still go on with their lives.

I studied in our village school until graduation from the 7th grade. That was where I became a member of the *Komsomol*. From the 8th grade on, I studied in the railway school of Obluch'e, a nearby town. It happened at exactly the time when my father was in jail. My older brother was drafted into the army, so it was impossible for my mother to pay for my dormitory room and studies in the school, given Viktor's low salary. Then I decided to write a letter to the *Narkom*[1] of the Railways, L. M. Kaganovitch. In it I described all the difficulties of our family in getting me educated. I also wrote that my father was serving a term in jail for negligence. Quite soon I, a schoolboy, received a government letter. It contained an order of the *Narkom* that provided all payments for dormitory and studies in my secondary school, up to the moment of graduation. I would also have free railway tickets to and from school. I clearly remember the unique signature on the official letterhead, "L. Kaganovitch", with an oversized letter L for Lazar. So I had three years of studies paid for.

As I learnt later, the husband of my aunt Klavdia Danilovna, took an even more desperate step when he was a kid. He was not admitted for further studies, after the sixth grade, due to the extreme poverty of the family. So he, a fourteen years old teenager, from a god-forsaken village in the Yaroslavl area, went to Moscow himself. He managed to get a meeting with Nadezhda Konstantinovna

1   *Narkom,* Narodny Komissar, People's Commissar, a title equivalent to the title of a Minister

Krupskaya, Lenin's widow, who was at that time serving as Deputy *Narkom* of Education of the Russian Federative Socialistic Republic. As a result, the People's Commissariat of Education issued an order, "Accept Vasily Baranov into seventh-grade school". After that he went into a trade school, and so on! It is amazing that in those days quite a lot of problems were solved in such a simple manner.

Obviously care for children was important then. My sister and I, and our five cousins, the children of my arrested uncle, were cared for and brought up by our mothers. Both of them had lost their husbands. May the memory of those ordinary, hard-working Russian women be treasured forever!

Unlike at our village school, in the railway secondary school in Obluch'e, we had daily defence activities after school. In fact, it was a well organised, military education. We did not have teachers of military science, but we had Sergeants from the Army units stationed in the cities. They visited us regularly and trained us in all military science subjects. Boys and girls alike were eager to study everything related to it. There were some boys who attended air clubs, where they learnt to fly aircraft and jump with parachutes. That gave them an opportunity to enter Air Force Academies immediately after the 9th grade.

The military organisation of the school consisted of platoons, or classes, and companies, i.e. all classes of the same age. For example, three 10th grades comprised a company. Given all the 8th, 9th and 10th grades of the school, we had a 'young army battalion'. Prefects of the classes were platoon leaders. The most diligent of them would be appointed company commander. The oldest student of the 10th grade would be battalion commander. When I was elected secretary of the school *Komsomol* organisation, in the 9th grade, my rank became 'battalion commissar'. Naturally, *Komsomol* leaders of each class were the company's 'political officers'. We took those 'young army' responsibilities very seriously! We would even sew collar-tabs on to our shirts and jackets, with the corresponding rank pips made of squares and bars of tin, and were very proud of them. The manner of address also corresponded, "Comrade young battalion commissar!" In our school, from the youngest upwards, that was how respect for the armed forces was nurtured. There were also many who developed some leadership skills. I recalled this 'young army' experience, with a feeling of appreciation, when I was drafted into the army at the outbreak of the war. All those skills were essential!

We graduated from the 10th grade in 1941, two days before June 22. That date was a fatal one for our entire country. Right after our graduation party we went to a regional centre, in the town of Bira, in order to apply for military academies. In those days, Soviet youth were crazy about the Military Academies for the Air Force, as well as the Tank and Artillery Academies, and so on. I chose Novosibirsk Military Institute of railway engineers, because of the strong traditions of our family, and in gratitude to the railway People's Commissariat for my free education. It was still a military institute, after all. But all our plans and dreams were interrupted by the news of war that we heard there, in Bira. It was where we heard Molotov's speech. Incidentally, the news of war only reached us in the Far East at seven o'clock in the evening, then just noon in Moscow. Immediately, as if a command was given, a long line of men appeared in front of the army recruiting office. It should have been a happy and carefree Sunday night! All those men were longing to join the army. Those arrogant Nazis had gone too far, and we wanted to show them that we were ready to strike back. "A little blood will be shed, when on enemy soil, To the last we destroy hostile forces[2]".

For two days, as fresh school graduates, we did not hear anything about our applications for the military academies. I had immediately changed my mind and written a new application for a tank academy. Then we were told that all the military academies were already full and that we were drafted as regular rank and file men. We were given two days to pack. We quickly went home to pack our belongings. A short farewell to our families and soon military trains were taking us into different areas of the Far East.

I was on the train with several school friends, the train was going west, but our joy was short-lived. Two days later we arrived in the town of Belogorsk, and that was it. The town was a mere 300 kilometres from our homes. There we became part of the newly formed 5th Reserve Rifle Regiment of the 2nd Red Banner Army of the Far East military district. The district was already renamed a Front, but was not yet active. That urgently formed regiment still did not have enough commanders, while trains were bringing in uncountable numbers of drafted enlisted men.

My company was led by junior *politruk* Nikolai Vasilievich Tarasov. I well remember this first commander of my whole military career. He was a tall, slim and already exhausted commander, who still had a lot of wise calmness in his tired eyes. With just two 'squares' in his collar-tabs, he managed to lead a company of over five hundred men. They were mostly men of different ages, without any military training, and many were illiterate. The men were arriving on the first days of mobilisation, especially from small and remote villages in the *taiga*. Tarasov, our first company commander, immediately separated those who had secondary education and those, as he saw from the first glance, who could temporarily act as platoon and squad leaders. I was appointed platoon leader. So, this unmanageable mass of people gradually became settled into some form of military units. On the second day, the commander took us to a *banya*, which was actually a series of tents with showers. There our heads were shaved. Then we washed, and received our uniforms. We put on 'boots too large, caps too big, covering our eyes'. We became so similar looking that we could not even recognise our friends, not to mention that we simply did not know who was in which platoon.

The company was gradually becoming more and more military-like. We were put in a tent camp more than three kilometres from the canteen. All the way to the canteen, our junior *politruk* Tarasov would cheer us up by teaching us ceremonial and marching steps. Meanwhile, we 'platoon leaders' tried our best to assist him, given our level of knowledge and skills. Our company commander, by some miracle, also managed to organise preparations for taking the military oath, and to have personal talks with many of us. I wondered how he had time and energy for all that! Nikolai Vasilievich Tarasov remained the pattern of a real commander, a commissar in the best sense of that word. I would recall him and his decisions a good many times in my life.

We had about 5–6 hours for sleep, while our *politruk* had even less. However, a Lieutenant and a Junior Lieutenant, mobilised from reserve, arrived in our company several days later. Each of them received half a company. I do not

2   A line from a popular march of the 1930s "If tomorrow brings war"

remember the surnames of those two commanders, but I remember that both were rather lively, stocky and very humorous persons. They would address each other by nothing less than "General Lieutenant", and "General Junior Lieutenant".

Several days later we were taken to a firing range, and all those who managed to complete a rifle firing exercise were sworn in. The ritual was not solemn, but I remember even the smallest details. We swore to be faithful to our Motherland, the USSR. That was the only day of its kind in my life. I never swore to any other government or country. God was merciful to me. All forty years of my military service I served under this one and only military oath.

Little by little we became used to the permanent stress and training. After about a month, our company became a more or less fully working military organism. It seemed to us that our commander-*politruk* was proud that this once chaotic mass of people was goose-stepping in the streets of the city. The 'half-company commanders', our Lieutenants, cheered us up with rather rude jokes. "Keep your heads, noses and cheeks up! Look at the girls looking at you! Their smiles say that they would not open their legs to you, but at least think of it!" The jokes always worked!

Time passed, and our company was distributed among regiments and divisions of the "Far East Army, the strong mainstay", as we sang in our marching song. We felt sorry that we had to leave our company commander, who had managed to become our real 'father commander'. He was an example of a truly dedicated, political officer. I am sure that our *politruk* also had a hard time parting from us, a unit in which he invested so much energy, time and goodwill. He left a small part of his heart in each one of us.

My destiny sent me to a scout platoon of the 198th Rifle Regiment, 12th Rifle Division of the 2nd Red Banner Army of the Far East Front, at Blagoveshensk-on-Amur. The most important commander there, for me, was deputy platoon leader Sergeant Zamyatin. I received my first disciplinary punishment from him, 'a personal reprimand'. It happened in the following way. As I was tall, during morning exercise, which was mostly jogging, I was put in front of everyone, even the older soldiers in the platoon. When the Sergeant ordered 'wider step', I would make my steps longer with my long legs, and accelerate. But the 'old hands' of the platoon would snub me, "you will have enough running here, don't run too fast". So of course, I would slow down. After several such incidents the Sergeant stopped the platoon, ordered me to walk out of the formation, and declared a 'personal reprimand', for not following orders. I was quite offended, as I could have run faster, but did not. I did not write back home about the reprimand, as I was rather ashamed of myself. I tried to get this reprimand off me for a long time. It was hanging over me, until a forced march of thirty kilometres, in which I helped a completely exhausted soldier. I took his rifle and literally pulled him by his hand. The Sergeant praised me for the display of mutual help, and publicly cancelled my reprimand. I was so happy!

I rarely saw my platoon leader Lieutenant Zolotov. The platoon was actually led by Zamyatin. I don't remember my regimental commander at all. But I still remember the commander of the division, a short and chubby Georgian officer, General Chanchibadze. By the end of the war he was the commander of the 2nd Guards Army. His resourcefulness and demanding attitude taught us a lot. In general, the 'science of winning' took a lot of sweat from us. Our *gimnastyorka* tunics were so saturated with salt from our sweat that we could stand them on the floor, and they would not fall! I had some disease of my knee joint. My family used to treat it, both with medicines prescribed by the doctor and with medicines made by my grandmother. But then, even under such unbearable stress, the disease vanished and never came back. The army treated men for many diseases, both physical and mental.

Military training on the Far East Front was very intensive. I guess I would be right if I said that the main element of battle training was marching training, not to mention all sorts of forced marches. Those replaced both physical training and many drill exercises. Once they made a forced march that included all scout units of the division, including the scout-company of the division. It was a sixty kilometre cross-country march. Those who were in the Far East would understand what that meant. *Taiga*-covered hills all the way! One also has to remember that, in addition to a rifle or a machine-gun, each soldier had to carry a knapsack or a bag-pack weighing at least thirty kilograms. That forced march was extremely hard, especially for us new conscripts. It was on a hot August day, but our platoon was the first to complete it, barely moving our feet, but with a marching song! Completely exhausted, almost collapsing, in the last kilometre of the march, we started to sing a marching song! With broken voices, without singing the melody correctly, but we sang! With every step, the song grew louder and more cheerful, while the ranks of the platoon became more even and our strides became stronger. The song brought back both power and morale! If I remember, we sang the marching song of the Far East Army, "The Far East Army, the strong mainstay".

The Division commander, who was waiting for the scouts at the end of the route, must have been touched by the song itself, and by the platoon that was marching with good alignment and heads up! He stopped the platoon, expressed his gratitude to the men, and added with his famous Georgian accent, "I am awarding the platoon one pair of new boots!" I should say that by that time most of our boots were worn out. The old hands of the platoon were supposed to have been discharged, but the war changed everything. All their boots were way beyond their life span. So, with this 'one pair of new boots' the platoon significantly improved its situation. Platoon leader Lieutenant Zolotov, his authority now unchallenge-able, gave the new pair to a soldier whose old boots were the most worn out of the whole platoon. His were used as material for patching the boots that could still be repaired. There were a good many pairs to be mended!

I served in that scout platoon until January 1, 1942. On New Year's Eve I was suddenly taken off sentry duty at the Regiment's Banner. That same night, without even giving me a chance to clean my rifle, which was quite rusted, and I felt quite sorry about it, they sent me to the 2nd Vladivostok Infantry Academy. That was the initiative of the local *Komsomol* organisation. At first I was happy that I would see Vladivostok, the city that I had heard so much about, and which was my child-hood dream. However, it turned out that the Academy was located in Komsomolsk-on-Amur.

I studied there for a whole six months. But those six months were exhausting, intensive and filled with the knowledge and skills necessary in warfare. I still recall those cold winter months of studies in the Academy with a special feeling of warmth. I remember all my teachers with a keen feeling of gratitude, starting with the company's Sergeant-major Khasmutdinov. Our cadet platoon leader was the extremely young Lieutenant Lilichkin, our company commander the most elegant Senior Lieutenant Litvinov. He was amazingly immune to the almost arctic sub-zero temperatures of that area. I recall, with awe, my fellow cadets, especially my bed neighbour Nikolai Pahtusov, Andrey Lobkis our company's singer, who could sing even in the hardest frosts, and the always sleepy cadet with glasses, Sergey Vetchinkin. Those cadets, as well as many others, were the ones who would help me out in hard times. But there were also those who I never met again. I cannot help recalling and describing some details of our daily life in the Academy, and the teachers there.

The Academy was stationed in one of the suburbs, called Mylki, not far from the Amur River. The schedule was quite stressful. Morning exercises started two hours before breakfast. Those were normally physical exercises or bayonet training, a daily practice. We did not have any days off, except for the days after we had been awakened during the night and had been on forced march training. In such cases we would receive dry tack instead of breakfast, i.e. canned fish or 'porridge with meat', one can for two men. A breakfast in the canteen normally consisted of buckwheat, oat or barley porridge, a piece of buttered bread, and sweet tea. We were much stressed physically and even this calorie-rich catering was never enough for us. Before lunch we had our training outdoors. Temperatures in January and February were sometimes below −30 degrees. After lunch, when it grew dark, we had two or three hours of classes including topography, theory of ballistics, small arms, battle engineer training, signals and communications, etc. Then we had homework or individual study time. Every night before dinner we had one or two hours of drill or ski training. Luckily for us, our ski route passed close to a small grocery shop. The shopkeeper kept it open late especially for us. Unfortunately, the grocery store had only canned crab meat, which filled all the shelves and window cases. A small can of crab meat only cost 50 *kopek* so we bought it quite often. That was our additional nutrition, which we ate immediately on return to the barracks, or saved it till the next breakfast, in order to mix the crab meat with porridge. It was a good combination and the food was tasty!

Lunch was sufficiently rich in calories. For the first course we had a thick grain or pasta soup, or cabbage soup with meat, with the addition of some vitamins that looked like dried and ground dog-rose hips, as a means to prevent scurvy. For the second course we received a fair portion of porridge or pasta, with meat or pickled Siberian or humpback salmon. It really showed that the Far East was a seafood area! However, they were training us for war, not for parades. Therefore, despite good and calorie-rich rations, extreme sub-zero temperatures and huge physical stress did their job, drying and freezing out those calories from us. Only those who did a duty in the kitchen could eat as much as they wanted. That was probably the reason why those who were punished with extra duty, were never appointed to a kitchen. The only job for them was cleaning the soldiers' toilets!

Feelings of constant hunger caused us to indulge in sweet nostalgic memories of how great the cooking of our mothers and grandmothers was before the war. We normally did that during short smoking breaks. My closest friend in the Academy, Nikolai Pahtusov, was from Nikolaevsk-on-Amur. He really liked talking eloquently of his mother, and her cooking an excellent stuffed goose during important celebrations. He was even rebuked by other cadets, who would interrupt his story by begging him, "Don't make me even hungrier!"

I can very clearly remember our teacher of topography. He was only a Junior Lieutenant Elman, an Estonian officer drafted from reserve. He taught us to find our bearings by the stars, define the phases of the moon, and determine, with only a one-day error, when the full moon or new moon would come. I knew all those tricks from childhood, it was my grandfather Danila who taught me. But I finally received a good theoretical explanation, there in the Academy, from our teacher of topography. He was such an interesting and knowledgeable person. He could implant the necessary knowledge into our heads so that we were all impatiently waiting for his classes. He organised practical '*azimuth*' training. He did it in such a way that the team that could find the shortest, and the best route, would receive some sort of prize, such as a pack of *mahorka* tobacco, or a bottle of *eau-de-cologne*. Those were rather valuable prizes for that time, as we were all short of tobacco, while everyone wanted to have a good fragrance after sweaty and exhausting physical exercises! According to our supply regulations, cadets were not supposed to get any tobacco, while almost all cadets smoked.

There was a prison next to the Academy, behind a wooden fence. The prisoners were getting tobacco and they would sell it to us, 60 *roubles* for a matchbox of tobacco. 60 *roubles* were the monthly wage of a cadet! We gave them money through slits in the fence and they gave us matchboxes back. They were cheating on us young boys quite a lot. In fact those matchboxes only had a small portion of *mahorka*, while the rest was sawdust, dry oak leaves and even dried horse-shit! A parcel with cigarettes from home was a real celebration for all us cadets. 10–12 people, in turn, smoked each cigarette! That was why a pack of *mahorka* was the most precious gift for 'diligence' in service.

I will always remember our teacher of artillery and small arms, Major Babkin. He was a person with great humour, but did not give anyone a chance to take a nap during his classes. If someone was falling asleep after outdoor classes in the frost, he could tell such a joke that the whole platoon or company would explode with laughter, and that would chase away sleep from everyone. He would also arrange competitions for assembling and disassembling the semi-automatic Tokarev rifle (SVT). It was still little known, compared with a regular Mosin-Nagant rifle, or the light Degtyarev machine-gun (RPD), the automatic Simonov rifle (AVS) and other weapons. I cannot remember all of them now.

I spent six months in the Academy, from the first days of 1942 to July 1942, and graduated 'with distinction', i.e. with all excellent grades. I was commissioned, just like seventeen other cadets 'with distinction', as a Lieutenant. That was my first officer rank. Out of more than a hundred cadets, only around seventy graduated without distinction. They had 'good' and 'satisfactory' grades. Those who failed the final exams graduated only as Sergeants.

We received commanders', later renamed officers', IDs and equipment. We had a leather waist belt with shoulder belts, a map case, and a Nagant revolver holster. We were supposed to receive the revolvers once in our units. We were dressed in brand new wool *gimnastyorka* tunics, with new collar-tabs, with two red enamel squares, which we called *kubari* or 'cubes'. They issued us trousers with 'raspberry' piping, visor caps with a raspberry-coloured cap-band, and even long leather boots. We walked around in all those brand new uniforms with great pride, squeaking our new belts and long boots. However, our joy was short-lived! Almost all Junior Lieutenants and Sergeants were sent to the Front, while all Lieutenants were sent to the units in the Far East. A small group of graduates, including me, was appointed platoon leaders in the 29th Independent Rifle Brigade, under Lieutenant Colonel Suin.

Literally from the first day after taking over a platoon I, like all the newly commissioned Lieutenants, started to write official requests for transfer to the Active Army on the Western Fronts. The Brigade's battalions were stationed at Hanka Lake, on the border with Manchuria, which was under Japanese occupation at the time. Our Brigade commander gathered us all and calmly, but convincingly, proved to us that our 'idle' Far East Front could very quickly and unexpectedly become 'very active'!

Winter came. Although we were stationed in the southern part of the Soviet Far East, the frosts were impressive, while constant strong winds made our life especially uncomfortable. For ski marches, which took quite a lot of time, we were issued not only woollen helmet liners with only a hole for eyes and mouth, but also some special sorts of small bags to pack our genitals, so that they would not get frost-bitten! In late 1942, when the German offensive at Stalingrad was stopped, and the threat of a Japanese assault had abated, one company from each battalion was reformed into a replacement company for the Front. They were loaded on trains and sent to the west in the first days of January 1943.

As I later found out, we were sent to form part of the Yugoslavian army, following the pattern of the newly created divisions of *Woisko Polsko,* and the Czechoslovakian Brigade, under Ludvig Svoboda. Our train literally 'flew' all the way to Zima. The steam engines were changed so quickly there was no time to receive hot food from the field kitchen of our regiment that was on the same train with us. We could not even grab a bucket of hot water from the station. However, at Zima station we suddenly stopped. We stood there idle for almost a week. Apparently, the formation with the Yugoslavian units did not work out. Our journey continued at such a 'turtle's' pace that it took us a month to make it to Ufa, the capital of Bashkiria. We passed Ufa, and were unloaded on Alkino station at night.

There we became an organic part of the 59th Reserve Rifle Regiment, 12th Reserve Rifle Brigade, of the Southern Urals Military District. Our most important job in that regiment was the training of new recruits. They were mostly older men, and mostly from the Muslim republics of the Soviet Union. We were teaching them the basics of war science, and formed replacement companies out of them for the Front. Just like other officers, it took me a long time, almost nine months of writing reports and requests, to be sent to the Front. In that town I entered the Communist Party of the Soviet Union. There too, destiny brought me together with a girl who was evacuated from besieged Leningrad. One year later, at the Front, she became my wife for the rest of my life.

We were fed by the *Voentorg.* The menu mostly consisted of sour cabbage soup, probably pickled two years before! For the main course we had the same cabbage, stewed in water! We did not receive any meat, it being replaced by reddish rusty herring, which must also have been pickled ages ago. We heard rumours and jokes that such catering was deliberate, in order to strengthen the patriotism of officers, who would then want to go to the Front just to get better food! I guess it was then that some officers told a joke that the *Voentorg* workers paid for the construction of a plane for the Front, but the pilots refused to fly it with its gift signature '*Voentorg*'. They said that the plane would be shot down immediately by friendly fire! Apparently it was the same way with *kolkhoz* workers too. All of us officers eagerly waited for a duty in the soldiers' canteen. The soldiers were getting completely different food, such as meat soups with pasta, and buckwheat porridge with meat etc. We might get enough good food at least once in two weeks!

It was only in August, or early September, that one of my numerous requests had an effect. Together with a small group of officers, I was sent to IORR, the Independent officer reserve regiment of the Military District, and then to the similar regiment of the Belorussian Front. We were on duty, guarding important areas from possible attacks by the enemy, in the 27th IORR. But that was not the front line that we were all longing for.

One day, in early December 1943, I was summoned for another interview by the regimental staff. It was a Major who interviewed me that time. He was dressed in a sheepskin coat and, despite the warmth of the room, his belts were tightened, as if he was ready to leave and move at any second. His face was almost black from the wind, and I immediately saw that his right ear was damaged. The Major looked through my rather meagre personal file, then asked several questions about my family, and the Academy, and my health. The Major suddenly said, "Very good! You are coming to our Penal Battalion, Lieutenant!" I stuttered with shock and asked, "But why?" I immediately had the memory flashing through my mind that my father had served three years in jail before the war, for negligence that almost led to a railway accident, and then was sent to a camp for unpatriotic speeches at the beginning of the war. Of course everyone knew the formula, "A son is not responsible for his father", but I could not find any other explanation for my transfer to a Penal Battalion.

But the Major's reply was, "You are asking the wrong question, Lieutenant. Not why, but what for. You will lead the *shtrafniks*[3], and help them 'redeem' their guilt to the Motherland. You will need both your knowledge and endurance. You have thirty minutes to pack." In accordance with the saying, 'a beggar only has to tighten his belt to pack', a small group of officers was waiting for the Major only several minutes later. It turned out that he was Chief of Staff of the 8th Independent Penal Battalion, Major Vasily Afanasievich Lozovoi. I started my front line life with him in 1943. I also met him twenty-five years after the war, at a training session of senior officers of the Kiev Military District. By then I was a Colonel and recognised him, also a Colonel, by his damaged right ear.

In December 1943, by which time the battalion had suffered severe losses both in permanent officers and *shtrafniks*, he selected us, eighteen officers ranking from Lieutenant to Major, to replace those losses. He mostly chose experienced *frontoviks* who were returning to the Front from hospitals. I was the only 'green' officer among them. I was surprised, but also proud that I was selected along with experienced *frontovik* officers.

3   *Shtrafnik* is a common name that was used for officers and men serving their sentence in
     a penal battalion, *shtrafnoi battalion*, or *shtrafbat* in Russian

One hour later we were already in a truck, with dipped headlights, racing towards the front line. We could clearly see it, lit up by the explosions of shells, colourful tracers, and illumination flares hanging in the sky. The 8th Detached Penal (Officer) Battalion was lying in defence, under German fire, somewhere out there. They were still unknown to us, but we were to become very close to them. I had some idea about penal battalions, but probably I knew less than the others. At least I knew of the famous Order No. 227 by the People's Commissar of Defence. But the actual state of affairs in the battalion was quite different from my concepts! Unfortunately, I do not have official tables of organisation and equipment for our battalion, and it must have been as far from the TOE as one could imagine.

The former chief of staff of our battalion, General Major F. A. Kiselev, who served in the battalion from its very formation, to its disbandment after the war, described the structure of our battalion in his memoirs. The battalion consisted of permanent and temporary personnel. The temporary personnel were those who were sent to the battalion for committed wrong-doings or crimes, i.e. *shtrafniks*. Incidentally, I had heard that in some penal battalions they addressed the *shtrafniks* with their former military ranks, adding the word 'penal'. For example, a rank of 'penal major' or 'penal private' etc, was used. I do not know whose decision that was. However, in our battalion it was not done. Apparently, the permanent officers did not like to stress the former titles of the *shtrafniks*, and we addressed all temporary personnel of the battalion as "temporary soldier". In turn they addressed us by regular ranks, for example, "Comrade Captain".

General Kiselev wrote in his memoirs, "The permanent personnel of the battalion were staff officers, company commanders, platoon leaders, their political deputies, Sergeant-majors of small units, artillery, supply, catering and financial officers, as well as others. The battalion consisted of a staff, three rifle companies, a submachine-gun company, a machine-gun company, a mortar company, an anti-tank rifle company, a military police platoon, a supply platoon and a signal platoon". As it turned out, the battalion also had a medical platoon with its own battalion's dressing station. Of course, there was a representative of *Smersh*, i.e. *Smert' Shpionam*, or Death to Spies, a special department.

My brother-in-arms Petr Zagumennikov, described the same thing to me in his memoirs of the early days of the battalion. He wrote, that at first each company and each platoon had both officers and political deputies, the *politruks*. Even Petr himself, then a Lieutenant, who arrived in the battalion after his recovery from a wound, was first offered an office of deputy platoon leader, political, as he was then very young, under 19 years old. Petr did not agree, and soon the role of political officer in platoons and companies was abolished. Apparently the initial idea, of having so many officers on each level, was that it would be impossible to lead *shtrafniks* who were temporarily demoted officers, with ranks up to Colonel. It turned out that the problem was illusory, and each company started having only one line deputy, not even a political officer. Platoons started having two deputy platoon leaders, appointed from the *shtrafniks*. However, such a significant decrease of numbers of political officers allowed for having a large staff for the political officer of the battalion. This was the battalion, modified, but based on the experience of the first battles that I was in.

As I only arrived in the battalion in late 1943, I shall describe the pre-1943 battles from the memoirs of two other officers. My brother-in-arms Petr Zagumennikov, started service in the battalion as a permanent officer from the very first days. A former *shtrafnik*, Major Semen Basov, ended up in the very first temporary personnel of the battalion, and took part in its first battles.

The 8th Detached Penal (Officer) Battalion of the Central Front was formed in late April 1943 in the village of Zmievka, not far from the village of Orel. The permanent personnel of the battalion were mostly recruited from officers who had gone through the battle of Stalingrad. The TOE of the battalion was in fact that of a regular rifle regiment. The *kombat*, battalion commander with TOE rank of Colonel, had two line deputies, a chief of staff, and a political deputy, all Lieutenant Colonels, as well as a supply deputy. The Chief of staff had four deputies, G1, G2, G3 and G4, all Majors. Each company had about 200 men or more, and looked rather like a regular rifle battalion. Thus, in terms of numbers the penal battalion was closer to a rifle regiment. The TOE rank of a company commander was Major; and the TOE rank of a platoon leader was Captain.

By July 1943, at the outbreak of the battle of Kursk, the battalion was fully formed and took up its defences in the Ponyri – Maloarkhangelskoe area, in the sector of the 7th Lithuanian Rifle Division. There it received its baptism of fire. In extremely stubborn and tough battles, the battalion managed to hold its positions. Then they broke through the enemy's defences and, towards Trosna, went over to the offensive. Thus, their very first battles demonstrated incomparable stoicism, and showed the ability of the battalion to carry out decisive offensive operations, and then to drive forward despite heavy losses. After the battle of Kursk, the battalion continued its progress. They went through their fiercest battles in the Kursk area, in northern Ukraine, including the battles for Putivl, and further on to the Dnepr River in the vicinity of Chernigov. It was only after those battles that the battalion was given rest and replacements, in the village of Dobryanka. After receiving replacements, the battalion was sent to the Loev bridgehead, on the Sozh River in Belorussia, in order to widen and deepen the bridgehead. Having successfully completed that mission, and liberating the town of Loev, the Penal Battalion went over to the offensive toward Gomel.

At that time the Central Front was renamed the Belorussian Front. The battalion became an organic part of the 48th Army, under General P. L. Romanenko. The battalion fought its way to the town of Rechitsa, where it took part in the completion of the encirclement of Gomel, and the surrounding of the German troops. After the liberation of Gomel, on November 26, 1943, the battalion marched through the town. They reached the village of Pervomaiskoe, in the district of Zhlobin, and took up defensive positions on the left bank of the Dnepr River. Several days later, the Soviet troops went over to the offensive after a two hour long artillery barrage. The battalion advanced some four to five kilometres, but the neighbouring units on the left and the right could not advance, and the battalion's flanks were exposed. The Germans immediately used the opportunity, and started to cut off the battalion with pincer movements. Breaking out of the encirclement, the battalion suffered high losses, and was again put into defensive positions. That was exactly at the time I arrived in the battalion, together with 18 officers from the Front's reserve. There were only three officers left alive from that group by the end of the war, Michael Goldstein, Ivan Matvienko and me. It was exactly like that song, "Just three left standing out of eighteen guys … "

Having arrived in the battalion, I took over a platoon, although later I learnt that I was to be appointed a company commander by the order of the Front. Then I wondered what sort of company commander I would have been, if I had not even led a platoon in battle? My mistake was corrected right there in the battalion. The *kombat*[4] sent for me and asked if I would object to leading a scout platoon. It was my first personal conversation with Lieutenant Colonel Osipov. I was surprised by both his kindness and, to me, inexplicable fatherly care. I was very happy to take that offer. I had served in a scout platoon in the Far East, which meant that the duty there would be at least partially familiar to me! I guess that was why our *kombat* offered me the office. That informal arrangement was formalised by order of the Front Commander, General Rokossovski, as late as the end of March. Apparently, the Front Commander did not have time for such unimportant things.

Then, in late December, during my first days of leading the platoon, I found I did not yet understand all the peculiarities of the penal battalion, and the relationship between *shtrafniks* and officers. The only thing I noticed was that a senior officer would address both subordinate officers and *shtrafniks* with a simple conversational form of 'you'. It did not annoy anyone. On the contrary, this informal address brought everyone closer and did not alienate *shtrafniks* from officers. The vast majority of *shtrafniks* had had much higher ranks before being sent to the penal battalion. They were also older than we were. *Shtrafniks* had former ranks from Junior Lieutenant to Lieutenant Colonel. However, we never had a single Colonel serving as a simple *shtrafnik* in our battalion.

I was amazed by one incident, which took place during my early days in the Penal Battalion. A *shtrafnik* was walking to a field kitchen from the trench line. Another *shtrafnik* caught up with him, as he was walking back to the battalion's HQ, after delivering some message to the front line. The following conversation took place between them. The 'kitchen' guy told the 'staff' guy, "I have a good, golden, German wrist-watch, do you want it to be yours?" – "Do you mean we exchange without looking?" – "No. I lift my hand in the air and you shoot it from 5 – 6 metres. Don't shoot from a greater distance, or you will miss, and don't shoot from a closer one, or there will be traces of gunpowder in the wound". – "OK! But first show me the wrist-watch." When the guy who wanted to be wounded lifted his hand with the golden wrist-watch, the second guy ordered, "And now you lift your other hand in the air, you bastard! Lift it higher! I will show you that not all are such cheap bastards as you!" After that, the *shtrafnik* escorted the second guy to the battalion HQ, like a prisoner. The battalion commander gave the wrist-watch to the 'guard', and the escorted *shtrafnik*, who wanted to simulate being wounded by the enemy, was court-martialled. I do not know what happened to him, but that is not important. The most important part of the story is the relations between fellow *shtrafniks*. It did not matter what their ranks were before they were sent to a penal battalion, if they were captured ones or *frontoviks*. The crucial thing was the attitude of *shtrafniks* themselves to such cunning bastards. There were not many *shtrafniks* like that, but we came across them sometimes.

4   *kombat* – Red Army acronym for *komandir bataliona*, battalion commander

CHAPTER 2

Rogachev and the
First Experience of Battle

Just as we thought in those days, and as I continue to think now, our 8th Detached Penal Battalion played a rather important role in the liberation of the regional town of Rogachev, in the Gomel region of Belorussia. The problem was that numerous attempts by our troops to go over to the offensive, to break through well-fortified German defences on the Dnepr and Drut rivers, and to destroy the Rogachev bridgehead on the Dnepr River, had all failed. The enemy knew that the loss of occupied Belorussia, containing the shortest route to the Baltic States, would have serious consequences. Therefore the Germans continued to man and strengthen their defences in the sector. Belorussia was the shortest route to Poland and Eastern Prussia. That factor had huge importance. It was then that our battalion was sent to join the effort in the destruction of the Rogachev bridgehead, and the capturing of Rogachev.

In the period before the battle, our battalion was resting, and receiving reinforcements in the village of Maiskoe Buda, in the district of Koshelev. There were many fresh personnel arriving in good numbers. Among the newly arrived men were not only *frontovik* officers who had committed some crimes, but also former Red Army officers who ended up in 'encirclements' in the first years of the war, and who did not take part in partisan warfare. We even made a common nickname for all of them, 'encircled ones'. There were also some former Red Army officers who had been liberated from German concentration camps, and who had gone through interrogation in *Smersh* departments. The *Polizei* and other collaborators were not sent to our battalion, they had another destiny.

There are many statements in modern historical literature, that all Soviet POWs were sent into Soviet concentration camps, according to an order of Stalin, and that all POWs were declared 'enemies of the people'. The fact that our Penal Battalion also received replacements from this category of officers means that those statements are an over-generalisation. It is known that former POW officers who had not 'stained' themselves by collaboration with the enemy, were sent to penal battalions. However, they were sent to penal battalions not by sentences of courts-martial, but by resolutions of some commissions that were governed only by the Stavka Order No 270, of August 16, 1941. That Order stated that "surrender to the enemy equalled state treason". The problem was that those commissions did not care about who surrendered to the Germans voluntarily, or were taken prisoner, or wounded, or in other tragic circumstances. If the first ones deserved punishment for state treason and breaking of their oath, the latter ones had no guilt before our nation. I think it was unjust to blame all former POWs for treason, but that's the way it was. I guess those commissions did not have time to find out the real circumstances of all POWs. Apparently, when the penal battalions and companies were only being formed in 1942–1943, and they urgently needed personnel, there were not enough officers sentenced by courts-martial to man the new penal battalions. Thus they had to create those strange commissions which speeded up the process for the sake of fulfilling "The order of People's Commissar of Defence, Comrade Stalin". Of course, they did not care about the different fates of the POWs. It seems as if it was 'profitable' for the Army to have such commissions, given the circumstances of those days. But the word 'profit' is tricky, so many unjust deeds were done in the name of 'profit'.

Besides that, some officers were sent to penal battalions without any court-martial or commission, merely by order of Corps and Army commanders. Our battalion had quite a lot of former POWs sent to us by resolutions of such commissions, and the personal orders of commanders of different ranks. I think that, in some situations, such orders by high-ranking commanders could be justified. In our situation, it was due to the need for fast replacements, after high losses that the battalion had suffered in heavy fighting at Zhlobin. In those days, our battalion received so many replacements that it was more like a rifle regiment. Platoons had up to 50 men, companies were sometimes as big as 300 men, and the battalion itself had sometimes up to 850 'active bayonets', as they were called in those days. We were three times larger than a regular rifle battalion of the Red Army.

The Rogachev-Zhlobin offensive operation of the Belorussian Front, lasted from February 21 to 26, 1944, as all official books about the Great Patriotic War state. However, the operation started earlier for us. Late on the night of February 17, the battalion was suddenly roused and on the move, leaving only supply and support units, and some guards, in the village of Maiskoe. During the night, we marched some 25 kilometres closer to the front line. Early in the morning we were concentrated in the forest next to the front line. Right there they started to issue us with white snow-camouflage suits and dry tack. Then a task force of combat engineers and a platoon of flame-throwers arrived. By noon we were ready for battle, but we did not know what our mission was. We were soon lined up. It turned out that there was another large group of men, but in a unit four times smaller than ours. They too had snow camouflage suits and even skis. Later, we got to know that this was a ski battalion. Battalions could be different in size. It was only then that I realised how large our penal battalion was for those days.

After a very short time, a 'top brass' group drove up to our formation in Willys jeeps. They were Generals and Colonels. It turned out that the Commander of the 3rd Army, General Lieutenant Gorbatov, had arrived. It meant that we were to be transferred from the 48th Army of General P. L. Romanenko, into the 3rd Army of Gorbatov. A tall and stately General, he briefed us carefully, but not in the way generals usually speak. He spoke softly, almost like a father would speak to his sons. I noticed that the Commander was leaning on a large and strong wooden stick, with many knots, and thought that the General was still recovering from a wound. It was later that I heard a legend, about the 'glorious' General Alexander Vasilievich Gorbatov 'teaching fools' with that stick. In his short, and rather emotional speech, the General said that we had an unusually difficult and important mission. We had to infiltrate through the enemy's lines, and start active harassing of the enemy's communications. He also said that he was hoping that we could complete the mission with honour. The type of the mission, he said, was a proof the trust that the Front and Army Command had in a battalion like ours. He informed us that, from February 17, our Belorussian Front was renamed the 1st Belorussian Front. He also promised that if the mission could be completed with distinction, all *shtrafniks* who proved to be 'stoic' soldiers, regardless of them 'shedding blood', would be freed from further stay in the penal battalion, receive back their officer ranks, and the ones who deserved it would get decorations.

The details of the mission were explained to us by our *kombat* Lieutenant Colonel Arkadi Aleksandrovich Osipov. The mission was to secretly infiltrate through the enemy's defences during the night of February 18 into early February 19. Avoiding contact with the enemy, we would rush to his rear and reach the western outskirts of Rogachev. There, in co-ordination with the ski battalion, we were expected to capture the town, and hold it until the arrival of the main forces of the Army. We were given 72 hours to complete the mission, and for that period we were given ammo and dry tack, i.e. canned meat, dry bread and sugar. The dry tack was not very plentiful, nor was it rich in calories, especially given the fact that we had to travel away from roads and in deep snow. My scout platoon was ordered to take the lead. We thought that the ski battalion would have an easier time than we would! However, I was not too bothered by deep snow. Winter field camps in the Academy in the Far East were still fresh in my memory.

Back then, in early February 1942, the cadets of the Infantry Academy in Komsomolsk-on-Amur, were supposed to spend 18 days in the field camps. At that time, the snow was 'up to your balls', as our teacher of artillery and small arms Major Babkin would say, while temperatures dropped below –35 degrees Celsius. We marched 50–60 kilometres into the *taiga*, in boots with leg-wrappings, carrying felt boots in our knapsacks, in addition to other items. When we arrived in the camp, we built large tents from Siberian pine or fir trees, one tent for each platoon. We were allowed to have a small fire inside the tent, which would allow us to warm up in turns, especially during the night. We put our boots into knapsacks and put on the felt boots. The only problem was that only 5–7 men could warm themselves at the fire, while the rest had to freeze. With the silent agreement of our platoon leader, a fresh graduate of the Khabarovsk Infantry Academy, we gradually added more and more firewood to the fire, until the whole tent suddenly caught fire. Ashes and melted snow were the only things left from our tent. Our platoon leader was severely reprimanded, while we were forbidden from building another tent. We had to make ourselves warm in the tents of other platoons, if we managed to find space there.

We did not have time to freeze during the day. We were either 'repelling enemy assaults', or storming hills, or on long and exhausting ski marches, or walking marches waist deep in snow, etc. When those long 18 days were over, we were ordered to put on boots with leg wrappings again. When we pulled them out of our knapsacks, we saw that they had frozen, as they were wet from our march to the camp. We had to melt them at the fire. I put one of my boots too close to the fire and it shrank. I could do nothing to get it back to its original size. My big toe was so pressed into that boot that it got frost-bitten on the way back, and the skin cracked, although there was no bleeding. The medical department of the Academy provided the necessary medical assistance, and I was freed from wearing any footwear, that meant being freed from all outdoor training, too. But all those things were part of the training at the Academy.

In Belorussia, in 1944, the only things that had skis were sleds for the transportation of the wounded and those killed, if there were any. In case we failed to capture Rogachev, our mission was to attack the enemy's supply lines in his tactical rear that was up to 20 kilometres in distance. We would blow up bridges, destroy staff HQs, and generally harass the enemy. That tactic was to bring chaos and disarray, and to prevent the Germans from bringing up reserves, by destroying and dispersing them. Our main goal was to distract German attention and keep their forces from the front line. There our troops had to go over to an offensive again, hopefully with better success. The goal of the offensive was to destroy the enemy's bridgehead on the Dnepr River and to liberate Rogachev. In accordance with a common practice of those days, liberation of Rogachev was planned for February 23, Red Army Day, as a gift to the Motherland in celebration.

It was forbidden for us to take any papers or documents into the area of the enemy's rear, a rule that was very strict! So we had to quickly hand in all papers, IDs, decorations and other paperwork, to the staff of the political officer at the battalion HQ. They remained on our side of the front line. At that time I did not have any decorations, but I turned in my officer ID and my card as a Communist Party candidate. The procedure took the several remaining hours of the day. After that we had a huge dinner combined with supper, then rest, which we recalled with a special feeling of longing throughout our time in the area of the German rear.

General A. V. Gorbatov described that raid in his memoirs, *Years and Wars*. But he called all of us the 'ski task force', due to the censorship of those times.

> At 18.00 they had an abundant meal and went to rest. Two battalions had only a short rest. At 23.00 they were alerted, and they marched westwards. The ski task force had the important mission of crossing the front line, and storming into the town of Rogachev that same night.

Our brave and experienced battalion commander, Lieutenant Colonel Osipov, led us on that hard and unusual mission. He was a native of Rogachev, and in addition he was an experienced hunter and fisherman, who knew by heart the local forests around the Dnepr River. That was how he knew the best place to approach the German positions, cross their obstacle lines, and cross the front line unnoticed. I was inexperienced in such operations, and I kept being amazed how our *kombat* managed to get almost an entire huge battalion over the Front line, unnoticed, even given the fact that he was native to the area. General Gorbatov used a very good idiom for that operation. He said the battalion went over the German lines 'like a rope through a needle's eye'. Our battalion commander pointed out the exact place for the Army's combat engineers to cut through the German barbed wire. It was perfectly chosen!

A moonless night camouflaged us very well. I believe that the Army's Command especially chose that night before the new moon, for the benefit of our two battalions. The Germans fired 'lamps', i.e. illumination flares. But tough orders before our departure, soldiers' wisdom, and the mere desire to live, forced all of us to 'freeze', and lie motionless on the ground when those lamps were burning in the sky. Our white snow-coveralls also made us almost invisible. German confidence in the unapproachability of their defences also helped us, as they were quite careless. They had a lot of empty tin cans hanging on the barbed wire, along the entire line of obstacles, which would make a noise if someone pulled the barbed wire. But almost our entire battalion made it through one small passage, unnoticed by the Germans!

That mission was my baptism of fire, although I got some experience during static warfare in defence. I guess this is why I can remember so clearly many details of that raid into the German rear. Sometimes, the Germans would fire at the most vulnerable places in their defences with machine-guns, while on duty. I remember that when I was crawling under the barbed wire fence, I sensed that something pushed me. It was later that day that I realised a German bullet had gone through my canteen where it was attached to my bag pack, a *sidor* bag, as they were called then. I could not understand why we always took those canteens with us, if we could not use them anyway. I guess we took them just in case. Later, I understood that a soldier always needs a canteen!

The last in the battalion's column was the company under Captain Matvienko, who arrived in the battalion together with our group of replacements. He already had significant battle experience, which was certified by two Orders of the Red Star on his tunic. One of his men accidentally got entangled in a barbed wire fence, and triggered the German alarm system of empty tins. It alarmed the *Fritzes* and they opened intensive rifle and machine-gun fire on that sector of the barbed wire. By then the Front units of the battalion had already crossed the first German trench, which was almost empty, as most of the German soldiers were warming themselves in dug-outs and bunkers. But those who were in the trench were taken by surprise and were killed by our bayonets. Suddenly we had to make ourselves seen, in order to distract the Germans who were running out of their dug-outs. We also had to help out our friends who were pinned down at the barbed wire. Everyone who was nearby, opened fire on the Germans without orders, while a flame-thrower platoon threw several huge flame streams at concentrations of German infantry in the trenches, and at the entrances to the dug-outs. That was a horrible sight! For the first time in my life, I saw men burning alive and heard them screaming. It was terrible!

Matvienko's company suffered losses, but still managed to break through and join the main forces of the battalion. The companies of the battalion, and the attached platoons that had crossed the front line earlier, had no casualties at all. Then the battalion commander gave me another order, to take the last position in the company. That mission seemed most important to me, as I had to be away from the commander of the battalion, and I had to make my own decisions in an independent and responsible way.

The Germans did not understand at all how large was our task force that crossed their front line. That is probably why in our following battles in the German rear they shouted in panic, "*Russ Partisan!*" As we got to know later, their panic was not ungrounded, there were over 350,000 partisans active in the partisan units and brigades of Belorussia. I did not know where the ski battalion crossed the front line, and we did not meet the ski troops during our raid into the enemy's rear. Apparently, they had a different mission, but they could not join forces with us due to the situation in that area. After our unusual raid into the enemy's rear was over, the Army's newspaper reported that "this unmatched raid was carried out boldly and decisively, by task force Osipov and the ski battalion

of Kamirny". So we learnt that the ski battalion had also successfully completed its mission.

Many years later, I learnt from the Soviet military encyclopaedia, that the ski troops belonged to the 120th Rifle Regiment, 5th Rifle Division and that they crossed the front line twenty-four hours after us, in another place to the north, from Novy Byhov. Twenty-four hours after that, as the encyclopaedia said, "as a result of a brave manoeuvre, one detached regiment of this division captured that area. After joining with the ski battalion, they cut the railway between Rogachev – Mogilev, and the highway between Rogachev – Novy Byhov. The enemy's forces were cut off from the north". Our battalion was fighting a little to the south, and after destroying some large German HQs in the village of Madory, and blowing up several rails on the same railway, started approaching Rogachev from the north-west, cutting the highway fork to Bobruisk and Zhlobin.

Back then, in 1944, even after this "unmatched raid", we only knew about the ski battalion from the short note in the Army's newspaper. Incidentally, that was the one and only case when a penal battalion was mentioned in the press, even disguised as a 'task force', although a 'partisan' task force, maybe? Our penal battalion was never mentioned in any publications during the whole war. Cinema operators, photographers, representatives of newspapers, at even division level, no one ever visited us. Apparently, the 'top brass' made penal battalions and their actions a 'taboo'.

As soon as our battalion reached the area next to the north-western suburbs of Rogachev, our *kombat* established a radio contact with the Army HQ. General Gorbatov again referred to our Penal Battalion as "a task force". "We have received news from our ski task force. They reached Rogachev, but the scouts ran into the enemy dug-in right in front of the city. The commander of the task force made a good decision. He realised that the element of surprise was lost, did not start the assault on the city, but withdrew his task force to the forests, and started harassing the enemy's communications." All that was true. If we had tried to capture the town and hold it, we would have failed. The bulk of the German forces were not destroyed, because we had no artillery or armour with us, not even mortars! Our mortar company under Major Pekura, in which my friend Michael Goldstein fought, was acting as a rifle company in that raid. Meanwhile, the anti-tank rifle company and a flame-thrower platoon were definitely not sufficient in that situation. The Germans had a lot of troops with heavy weapons, both in and around Rogachev.

We soon received an order to act as had been provided in the plan, i.e. disrupt and destroy the enemy's communications. That's what we did, all the time we stayed behind the enemy's lines. We managed to cause great panic in the German rear. Our battalion delivered strikes both in small groups, and together as one quite strong task force. Small groups were destroying the enemy's equipment. The German artillery crews were killed and captured. Cannons were used for firing at prominent concentrations of the enemy's troops and warehouses etc. Artillery and tank officers were among the *shtrafniks*, even pilots, so it was not hard for them to fire several rounds from captured artillery pieces. After that, such artillery pieces or mortars were blown up, or damaged in some other way. We also set food and ammo stores on fire, controlled important road junctions, and cut communication lines. When first captured, the Germans told us that their command believed that there was an entire infantry division or two in their rear, and many partisans. Of course, after interrogation, the Germans were shot, not set free. That was the beginning of our harassing actions in the enemy's rear.

One of the episodes of those battles was the liberation of enslaved Belorussians. I think it was on the second day, around noon, when our forward group-point noticed a large column of civilians moving westwards, escorted by armed Germans. We already knew about Germans taking Soviet populations to Germany, for slave labour. The *kombat*, as I have already mentioned, was from that area, and he made the decision to liberate his enslaved countrymen The German convoy was small, guarded by about fifteen men, who were disposed of in a matter of minutes. We liberated about three hundred Soviet civilians, who were forced by Germans to dig trenches, in frozen soil, under the barrels of their guns. All the civilians dispersed on our command, to go to hide in the forest, and later go back to their villages.

However, as a leader of a platoon that was at the back of the column, I noticed that a group of six young women was following us through the forest. Of course, the group was dressed very differently to us, and could give away our location to the enemy at the worst possible time. I had to explain it to them time and again, but all my explanations were in vain. They followed us until twilight, as they were afraid of being recaptured by the Germans. When it grew dark, I again explained to them that now they could leave us, and go back to their villages unnoticed. It seemed to me that my 'clarification' finally worked. When we stopped for some reason, the young women were nowhere to be seen. But as soon as it grew light, and our column resumed its march, my scouts reported that a strange group was following us. I wondered if it could be Germans following us. But when we took a closer look at them, we recognised our 'old friends', the young women, dressed in some sort of snow camouflage suits. It turned out that, in the darkness, they undressed, took off their white underwear, then dressed again, putting their white underwear on top of their simple peasant clothes. Their sheepskin coats, that had white or light fur on the inside, they merely turned inside out. We felt sorry for them, but we stood there laughing when we saw how they looked! But we had to accept their resourcefulness, and allowed them to follow us for some time, until the situation dictated a wiser decision! A large German truck column was spotted on the highway, moving toward Rogachev. We attacked the column. As soon as the battle started, this female 'squad' had gone in the twinkle of an eye!

I should mention that our battalion column was arranged in such a way that there were machine-guns, anti-tank rifle crews and flame-throwers in the vanguard, in the main section, and also in the rear-guard of the column. The flame-thrower crews were armed with ROKS, i.e. a backpack flame-thrower, with KS liquid. KS liquid starts burning when making contact with air, and is called a 'Molotov cocktail'. However, in those days we knew nothing about that nickname. When the German truck column was spotted, the battalion froze, and as soon as the first trucks drove past our last units, we opened devastating fire from all weapons at the entire length of the column. In the rear of our column, there was an anti-tank rifle platoon under our twenty-year old, but experienced, Senior Lieutenant Petr Zagumennikov. He had previously been wounded, and I had since become friends with him. His men managed to knock out the first two vehicles in the German column. Meanwhile, the last two vehicles were destroyed by anti-tank rifle crews in the battalion's vanguard. The entire German column ended up blocked on the narrow highway, surrounded by deep and soft snow. The Germans jumped out of the trucks, under heavy fire, and fled in all directions, in panic. Some of them lost their senses, and ran straight towards us, towards the hail of lead from the machine-guns and submachine-guns of our men. The bulk of the Germans ran to the other side of the road, shouting, "*Russ Partisan!*" and were almost all killed by the *shtrafniks* who chased them into the forest. Of course, some of the Germans managed to escape, as we could not chase them far into the forest, but we killed many of them with our fire.

I could not bring down one of them by firing my submachine-gun. He was running skilfully from one tree to another, hiding behind them, while I was so excited about the hunt that I fired my submachine-gun without aiming. Then I pulled my Nagant revolver out of its holster, took careful aim, and killed him with my very first shot, at about a hundred metres distance. It was my first individual kill. My faith in the effectiveness of my faithful revolver not only in close range combat, but also at long distances, was confirmed. That first 'trophy' of mine caused some feelings of inexplicable satisfaction. I had killed a man, for the first time in my life, in full consciousness. I killed him, deliberately.

I recalled an incident that happened during my time in the reserve regiment in Ufa. We were training the so-called replacement companies for the Front. Replacements for those companies were coming from Bashkiria, Tatarstan and even Kazakhstan. There were sometimes deserters. On one occasion I was a witness at an execution of one such deserter. He had been sentenced to death, and was to be executed in front of the entire regiment. The sentenced deserter was on his knees, on the edge of our tactical-exercises field, at a freshly dug hole. His back was towards the regiment. I can very well remember his clean-shaven head and unusually large ears, which were red as the sun was setting and the light shone through them. An officer, probably a member of the court martial, read the sentence, and called for volunteers to execute the man. The answer was a scary silence. There were no volunteers in the regiment. Then two men walked from a group that was standing a little bit to one side, pistols in their hands. They walked up to the sentenced man who started to shiver convulsively. As if on command, those two men fired at the deserter simultaneously. He fell into the grave.

The regiment stood, dumbfounded. I could hear either quiet weeping, or groaning, in the ranks. The regiment continued to stand dumbfounded, until the soldiers filled the grave, and covered it with turf that had been prepared in advance. At that moment, I guess many thought that it would be better to die on a battle-field, than die like that, like a mad dog. I noticed another small hillock nearby, already covered with new grass. Apparently, it was not the first execution on that spot. I had a very scary and disgusted feeling in my soul. They had just killed a man who was simply a coward, but one of our people, a Soviet man.

There, in the war, I myself had killed a human being. But he was the enemy, and I had completely different feelings. *Shtrafniks* did not take prisoners, even though some Germans tried to surrender, and shouted, "*Hitler kaput!*" The *shtrafniks* shot them too, saying, "We have bullets for you too, damn you!" What could we do with them if we did display humanity, and took them prisoners in those very extraordinary conditions, behind enemy lines? However, I ordered my men not to kill one man who wore a German uniform. He threw his arms in the air and shouted in Russian, "Don't shoot! I am Russian; I am one of your people, from Kaluga!" I was curious to hear his story, even more so since I did not need a translator. I wanted to know, what made him turn his weapons against his own people? But as soon as he said that he was a Red Army man, and had been captured by the Germans a year earlier, one of the *shtrafniks* shouted a curse, put his submachinegun against the neck of the prisoner and fired a burst. So, my conversation with the man from Kaluga did not succeed, but I was not too sorry about that. In battle, the best enemy is a dead enemy.

Instead of the planned 2–3 days, our raid lasted 5 days. During that time we destroyed several more columns that were moving to the front. In the village of Madory, we destroyed the HQ of some large German unit, and blew up several bridges on the road to Rogachev, from the west. Two guarded ammo stores were set on fire by our flame-throwers, and we could hear explosions of detonating ammo for a long time. In general, our battalion was so active that, by the beginning of the fourth day, we had spent almost all the ammo for our machine-guns and submachine-guns. We received an order to keep the last supply of 10–20 rounds for each SMG, but in many cases we did not even have that amount! The *kombat* was reporting our operations to the Army HQ over the radio. He reported that we had already spent almost all ammo for small arms.

Apparently, the Army decided to send us some ammo by airlift. Two small 'corn planes' appeared over us in the afternoon, but all of a sudden they came under the fire of German AA guns. To our amazement we realised that, during the night, we had arrived at the positions of a German AA battery, but had not spotted it! Meanwhile, the Germans did not spot us! The planes realised what was happening, turned around and, thank God, flew away safe and sound. Our flame-thrower teams managed to crawl towards the AA guns, and literally burnt to ashes both the guns and the crews. It was really great to have a flame-thrower platoon with us! They helped us out at the end of the fourth day, when we spotted a large German infantry column. The flame-throwers destroyed almost the entire column. There was almost no machine-gun fire from our side, but the heart-rending screaming and yelling of burning Nazis rang in our ears for a long time. I guess it is no wonder that the screams of those burning enemy soldiers cheered up our extremely exhausted men, so strong was our hatred of the enemy. I recalled a saying, that 'the enemy's dead body smells well'. Apparently it works even if a corpse burns.

Of course, we could not take with us the equipment that the Germans abandoned. But we took their SMGs, light MGs and, of course, their pistols, mostly Walters and Parabellums. Soon many of us had two SMGs, the Russian and the German one, although with very little ammo for either. We tried to damage or destroy all other equipment that we captured, and took German food to supplement our poor dry tack, which was also finished. We were especially amazed by the German bread. It was sealed in transparent plastic and had the year of baking as early as 1937 or 1938! That was a very long shelf life. We could cut and eat it even when it was frozen. It was much better than our dried bread. We were also amazed by some large bars made from a mixture of *Ersatz* honey with butter, that was probably also *Ersatz*. Sandwiches from this bread and honey butter were just what we needed, and were quite filling. We were also somewhat amazed that, apparently, both men and officers in the German Army received chocolate in their rations, as we came across a lot of chocolate in the captured food stores. It was also welcome, as it supplied us well with calories.

There were a lot of unexpected and unforeseen incidents, but our losses were very low. We transported the immobilised wounded in sleds, as well as a few dead comrades, among whom was our Party secretary Major Zheltov. He was killed while chasing a group of Germans from that large truck column. He was an excellent officer, a former village schoolteacher, and an extremely hard-working political worker. Unfortunately, I rarely met such good political workers during my service in the army, either during or after the war. I cannot remember all the details now, but I can say that during those five days we did not have a chance to warm ourselves, except for warming ourselves at the fires of burning food stores and destroyed German staff quarters, which we had blown up and set on fire. However, we could not stay at that fire for long, as we could not afford to wait for *Fritz* to counterattack. It is also clear that we could not start campfires during the night and could not stay in peasants' huts.

We got very little time to sleep, only when the battalion stopped for a while during the night. Many of us managed to sleep on the move, which was familiar to me from my time in the Academy. I myself managed it. We could not even dream of hot food. On the fifth day, the *kombat* ordered us not to engage the enemy, unless absolutely necessary, in order to save our ammo. We had made so much noise in the German rear, demoralised and crippled their supply lines to such an extent, that the troops of our 3rd Army finally went over to the offensive, and started to move forward.

In those conditions, we had to camouflage ourselves, so that although almost unarmed and without ammo, we would not be spotted by the mass of retreating German troops. In one such instance, we heard an intensive firefight next to us. MGs were rattling, and soon we heard a cannon firing. A *shtrafnik* from our battalion, an ex-artillery officer, apparently shouted to our deputy battalion commander Kudryashov, who was nearby, "Comrade Lieutenant Colonel! That is our 45mm AT-gun firing! I guess those are our troops attacking!" At first no one believed him. The Lieutenant Colonel decided to check the idea of the *shtrafnik*, sending him, along with other soldiers, as scouts or envoys. They started to move towards the firefight very carefully. It seemed that time stood still! We already knew about Vlasov's men and the *bulba's* men, i.e. those Belorussians fighting against the Red Army. We certainly feared that we could come across them, while we were out of ammo! But soon, we saw our two men being escorted back towards us, not by those traitors, but by several Soviet Red Army officers and men. We were overjoyed! Everyone jumped up and ran towards our people, like in the movies! It turned out that they also suspected us of being associated with the same traitor units. When the hugging and greeting was over, our battalion's officers spoke to the officers of the infantry units that we came across. We were also briefed on the situation shortly after that. It turned out that our 3rd Army, and the neighbouring 50th Army, had managed to break through the German defences, but two days later than planned.

They had already captured Rogachev. The 3rd Army mopped up the bridge-head on the left bank of the Dnepr, where it was 45 kilometres in breadth and 12 kilometres depth. As General Gorbatov wrote in his book about this episode, the Army lost only several men to German landmines. Moscow saluted the troops of the Army on February 24, to celebrate the liberation of Rogachev from the yoke of occupation. But we did not yet know about that, as our radio batteries were flat. We did not have any communication with the Army during the last days of the raid. We also did not know that the 2nd Belorussian Front had been formed. Some units of the 1st Belorussian Front were transferred to the new Front, but we were all very happy that our battalion remained in the 1st Belorussian Front under the great General Rokossovski, who soon became a Marshal. Many of our men still spoke about the visit to the Front by Rokossovski. He came to the trenches of our battalion right after the heavy fighting at Zhlobin, when the battalion suffered high losses. Those who had the privilege of talking to him were so impressed! Everyone admired his manner of talking calmly and kindly to both *shtrafniks* and their commanders. I could only be sorry that I did not get to meet him.

That truly unmatched raid into the enemy's rear was over. There were no blocking detachments in our way, as some unfair historians now write. There was trust that those ex-officers, although guilty of some crimes, remained honest Soviet people, and were ready to redeem their guilt with their bravery, stamina and heroism. I should say that the bulk of *shtrafniks* realised that they had been guilty and were now ready to redeem it. We were immediately transferred to the rear, to a nearby village.

Exhausted almost to death, many men were falling asleep right there in the street, without waiting for field kitchens with hot porridge. That was when we needed our canteens! Men were falling asleep, even in front of huts with warmth inside. It did not snow. We had all got tired of that during those hard five days. To our great dismay, we lost several men there. Three *shtrafniks* fell asleep on a stove in a hut, without even taking off their belts and weapons. Apparently, one of them had an F–1 *Limonka* hand grenade on his belt. When he turned in his sleep, it went off. Only one of those three survived and was taken to a dressing station. The other two were killed. We were so shocked! To go through such a test, and get killed when everything was over, on the eve of liberation from the Penal Battalion, was tragic.

As the Army Commander had promised, all the temporary personnel, the *shtrafniks* of the Penal Battalion, were rehabilitated and many of them received decorations, Orders of Glory 3rd Class, Medals for Bravery and for Battle Merit. They were heroes! Previously, their heroic deeds were blotted out by their wrongdoings. But there was then enough heroism to give them well-earned decorations. I should mention that *shtrafniks* were not so happy to get Orders of Glory 3rd Class. According to regulations, the problem was that the Order was for enlisted men and NCOs. Officers were not supposed to get that Order at all[1]. Of course, many of them did not want others to know that they had spent time in a

---

1   The Order of Glory was established in 1943 and all three classes of this order were only awarded to enlisted men, NCOs and Sergeant Majors (in Air Force – up to Junior Lieutenant). The Order of Glory was a direct "descendant" of the pre-revolution "Sign of distinction of Military Order" (i.e. Order of St. George, which was also awarded to

penal battalion, at the rank of a simple *shtrafnik*, and that Order would give it away immediately. Officers of the battalion were mostly awarded Orders. My friend Pete Zagumennikov received the Order of the Great Patriotic War 2nd Class. Philip Kiselev was then a military police platoon leader, a Guards Battalion commander, and his staff received the second Medal for Bravery. By the end of the war he was promoted to Lieutenant Colonel, and was the battalion's Chief of Staff. I should mention that officers highly appreciated that Medal for Bravery. It was approximately of the same prestige as the soldiers' Order of Glory. Company Commanders Matvienko and Pekur received Orders of the Red Banner. Those were considered some of the most prestigious and high decorations. I do not remember all those who were decorated. Along with several other officers, I did not receive any decorations. Apparently we had not yet distinguished ourselves in battle. Maybe there were other reasons, too? However, very soon the Front Commander, General Rokossovski promoted me to Senior Lieutenant, and I took it as a decoration for that raid.

We platoon leaders immediately wrote recommendations and character references for all *shtrafniks*. Based on those papers the *shtrafniks* were liberated and decorated. Our battalion commander, Osipov, personally recommended officers of the battalion for decorations based on their merits, regardless of how high his own personal decoration would be. In the matter of distributing decorations, a lot, if not all, depended on the commanders. For example, General Gorbatov released all *shtrafniks* who had taken part in that raid and had honestly and bravely fought, regardless of their receiving wounds or not. I mention it here, because our Penal Battalion was attached to different armies, and other Army commanders had different attitudes towards our battalion. For example, 65th Army Commander General, Pavel Ivanovich Batov, only rehabilitated those *shtrafniks* who were killed, or wounded in battle. Meanwhile, the rest he used to the end. Lieutenant Colonel Baturin, who replaced our *kombat* Osipov in Poland, was very greedy for decorations, and very unwillingly decorated company commanders and platoon leaders. He was always first, in waiting for his own decoration. He did not want to recommend anyone for a decoration higher than his!

Coming back to writing references for *shtrafniks*, I should mention that those documents were signed by commanders, and then sent to the battalion's staff. There they made lists of those who would be released. After that, all those papers were sent to the Army's HQ and then into the Army's or the Front's court-martial. Orders on return of officer titles were signed personally by the Front Commander. The recommendations for decorations were processed separately by the battalion's HQ. While this bureaucracy was going on, and I guess there was no way to speed it up, our battalion returned to the village of Maiskoe, in the Buda-Koshelev district, from which we left for the raid into the enemy's rear. The local population welcomed us very warmly and with hospitality that they could ill afford. The main food given to us by Belorussians was potatoes, with all sorts of pickles, and moonshine extracted from potatoes again. We had long since spent the 100 grams of *vodka* that we received after the end of the raid!

men and NCOs) and was highly prestigious. Men who had all three classes of Order of Glory enjoyed the same privileges as Heroes of the Soviet Union.

Local girls were joyfully greeting the returning *shtrafniks* and officers, who they were already dating. Our temporary personnel, as they were officially called, were temporarily demoted officers, mostly educated and with a rather high level of culture. Incidentally, our heads were not shaved and we all had normal officers' haircuts. We had all left good memories of ourselves among the locals. One should also take into consideration that kindly people would always pity those who were punished by authorities, and this is exactly who we were in the eyes of local women and girls. The permanent officers of the battalion, mostly young officers 20–25 years old, were also quite popular with the local village girls. Our supply and support units, weapons and ammo depots, were all located in that village. We could not have taken all that with us into the enemy's rear. All our documents were also there. Several *shtrafniks* remained in the village to guard all that. Many more new men, sentenced to serve in our battalion, arrived in the village. As we were fighting for the liberation of Belorussia, the portion of 'encircled ones' grew. The situation at the front, and several failures of our troops, also increased the number of *frontoviks* who were sentenced to a term in our battalion, for their failure to complete a mission.

In any case, we had enough temporary personnel to replace those who were supposed to be released. Even before our *shtrafniks* were rehabilitated, in a procedure that lasted several days, we managed to form two new companies. The procedure of rehabilitation was as follows. Several representatives of the Front and the Army's court-martial arrived in our battalion, and they considered the references in the presence of the platoon leaders. They officially cancelled sentences, gave back officer titles to the *shtrafniks*, some senior officers even received their shoulder-boards insignia on the spot. At the same time, they made decisions about the return of state decorations and provided the necessary papers. After that, the former *shtrafniks* now fully-fledged officers were sent back to their units.

However, the 'encircled ones' were sent to officer reserve regiments, like the one from which I had just arrived with my battle friends. Some of the 'encircled ones' still had old military titles, for example, 'military engineers' or 'technician officers', of all ranks. They were given new officer ranks, one or two grades lower than their original. The same rule was also applied in the army when men were receiving new ranks. Unfortunately, I did not take part in that procedure of 'purification' from guilt to the Motherland as I was sent to lead a platoon in one of the two newly formed companies. Apparently, I was sent there as I had had only one real baptism of fire, and did not have enough battle experience.

Our companies were given a mission, to capture a bridgehead from the Germans on the Drut' River. In order to complete the mission, we had to approach the German-controlled bank of the river, secretly at night, without an artillery barrage. There would be no "Hurrah!" taking the enemy by absolute surprise. Our advance towards the village, whose name I forget, would drive the Germans out of the first trench, and provide for the engagement of other units of the Army from the captured bridgehead.

Once again, the night was almost moonless and cloudy. However, the Germans either did not expect our assault at all, or they had some other reason to be calm, as they did not use their 'lamps' at all. Unlike the ice on the Dnepr River, the ice on the Drut' was quite badly damaged by artillery fire. We had to try it first with our feet, in order not to fall into the breaks in the ice. Maybe that unstable ice was the reason for the Germans being so calm that they did not even illuminate the approaches to their trenches. The only thing they did was fire harassing mortar fire on the ice of the river. As ill luck would have it, I fell through the ice there. The ice had been broken but had frozen a little. I went through the ice immediately and all my attempts to reach thicker ice were in vain, as the ice around me was very thin and crushed in my hands. The current of the river was dragging me under the surface. My padded jacket and pants were getting heavier with every second. If I add that I did not know how to swim, and still cannot, you can understand how close to death I was at that moment.

That serious shortcoming in my training was often pointed out in my post-war physical tests, although I could ski, make long and high jumps, and shoot very well. However, I was rescued by my orderly *shtrafnik*, who was always nearby. Our platoon had been formed at short notice, so I did not have a chance to learn the name of that soldier, although I should have! When he saw, or I should say heard, my floundering in the water and my vain attempts to get out of that icy porridge, he remained on the thick ice and lay down at the edge of the hole. He stretched his submachine-gun towards me and I grabbed its barrel. The soldier slowly pulled his submachine-gun to the edge of the hole that had seemed a door to death for me. Finally, I managed to make it on to the thick ice, breaking the thin ice at the edges. For the rest of our journey on the ice we had to crawl, and it was not we alone who crawled.

In the meantime, as we were approaching the bank, where it was quite steep, a firefight broke out. Our men, who took the Germans completely by surprise, started the firefight there. The German defences on the Drut' river were very strong. They had concrete bunkers with armoured towers, dense minefields, barbed wire fences of three rows, and so on. But in the sector of our attack there were no minefields, while the barbed wire fence was weak. This was yet another proof that the Army Commander tried to avoid unnecessary losses in any situations, even among *shtrafniks*. His scouts also did a great job, finding a weak spot in the German defences. There was no further need to remain silent. We could hear the desperate screams of the Germans, who could not stand hand-to-hand fighting at night. There were the most awful curses of *shtrafniks*, a rallying and victory cry, instead of "Hurrah!" I reached the first trench, together with my orderly and other men who had fallen through the ice. It was already captured by our men and mopped up from the Germans. There were many dead Germans, lying both in the trench and behind it. In some places *shtrafniks* continued their assault and even made it into the second trench.

I was wet and frozen to the bone, and tried to warm myself up by energetic movements, but in vain. My pipe helped me a little bit. I was a chain smoker even before I came to the front. The pipe was massive, with good capacity, classic shape and it kept the heat for a long time. My tobacco was wet and my neighbours in the trench willingly shared their tobacco with me. The pipe kept my fingers warm, but the rest of my body started to lose mobility from the frost. My uniform, saturated with water, was gradually becoming an ice shell, not like a knight's armour, but rather a turtle shell. I could no longer move my arms and legs, it was only my head that I could still turn, like a turtle. My long boots turned into ice cases and I was afraid that my feet would get frost-bitten, much worse than my big toe during the winter camps in the Academy. Company commander Major Syrovatski saw that I was of no use as a platoon leader, and ordered two lightly wounded *shtrafniks* to take me to the dressing station of the battalion. They pulled me, on a big lump of ice, back across the Drut' River later that evening.

Our doctor, Captain Stepan Petrovich Buzun, stocky and with a typical doctor's beard, was taking care of the wounded at the battalion's dressing station, which was in a tent with a stove. I think no one, not even the *shtrafniks*, ever addressed him with his military title. Doctor Buzun and his assistant, Lieutenant Ivan Demenkov, cut my icy uniform with sheers used for cutting barbed wire. They pulled it all off me, and immediately gave me a whole-body massage with spirits. Of course, they also gave me a fair portion of alcohol and then dressed me in dry uniform. Apparently, they had a supply of dry clothes for such occasions, and our uniforms depot was nearby. They even gave me dry and warm felt boots. As the tent was crowded with wounded, they dug a hole for me in deep snow next to the tent, covered the bottom of this snow-hole with fir tree branches, and one part of a *plash-palatka*. Then they put me in there, covered me with the second part of the *plash-palatka*, put more fir tree branches on top, and covered it all with a thick layer of snow, only leaving a small hole for ventilation. I could no longer soberly appreciate all the advantages of that bed. Of course, I was very warm from the spirit massage, and the alcohol in my stomach, and immediately fell fast asleep.

In the morning I got out of my 'lair' feeling a well-rested person, full of energy again. I did not even have a runny nose, which would be typical for such over-exposure, not to mention pneumonia or bronchitis. One week later I had several small boils on my neck. That was the only consequence of my unplanned ice-hole swimming. As our wise doctor, Stepan Petrovich, later explained to me, that was the result of the mobilisation of all the inner resources of my organism, in conditions of deprivation and over-stretching. In those days we did not yet use the word 'stress'. That was the crucial difference between battle and all other types of human activity. As I got to know later, people fell sick much more rarely and in a less serious form. Also, as a matter of fact, there were no epidemics at all. I think that some role, in my case, was played by the fact that I was used to low temperatures from my childhood, and was trained for that in the Academy in the Far East. Incidentally, I was told later that our doctor, Stepan Petrovich, was a former *shtrafnik* who decided to stay on as a permanent officer in the battalion, after rehabilitation. No one spoke about that in the battalion, but I knew several such cases, and had a great respect for the officers who made such a decision.

While I was sleeping in my snow lair, our units completed their mission and even managed to approach the village, where a rifle regiment followed into the breakthrough. Unfortunately, my participation in that battle was over with my ice-hole swimming and sleeping in a snow-lair. I was very disappointed that my battle experience increased by so small a degree. The only thing that remained forever in my memory was the name of the Belorussian river Drut'. I was not there when the rifle regiment entered the gap in the German defences that was torn by our *shtrafniks*. They told me that it was preceded by a powerful salvo of missile launchers, which were dubbed *Katyusha*. Either a *shtrafnik* unit made it too far into the German defences, or they merely failed to report it on time. Perhaps someone at the *Katyusha* battery made a mistake, but several missiles went off next to the *shtrafniks*. There were losses among our men. As eyewitnesses said, it became obvious to everyone why the Germans went into such a panic of fear under *Katyusha* salvos.

After the rifle regiment went into battle in that sector, our companies were withdrawn to the rear, to join the main forces of the battalion. Unfortunately, that offensive stopped due to tough resistance put up by the Germans. We heard news of crossing the Drut' River only in late June, when Operation Bagration started, and the long-suffering land of Belorussia was totally liberated from German occupation.

In the meantime, the new replacements that came back from the other bank of the Drut' River, were quickly loaded on trucks and were taken to the area east of Byhov. Apparently the Army was planning to use the Penal Battalion in that area, too. That was our guess, as we did not have any official information about it. Despite the fact that it was early March, nature surprised us with a heavy fall of snow. Snow fell, like an avalanche, for several days. As soon as we arrived in the area, all the roads became impassable for any traffic. For a whole week we were cut off from even our battalion supply units. Our humorous men would say it was 'diet weather'. As it was impossible to bring more food, our catering consisted of soup of melted snow, the only thing we had in abundance! We had American canned beef, one can for a whole company! We called this canned beef 'the second front'. There was very little fat and some minor bits and pieces of meat. The extremely thin soup only had a smell of beef. In addition to that soup we had one piece of dry bread. There was no way of getting any more food from the locals, to add to this 'diet'. It was a striking contrast to the village of Maiskoe.

After that massive snowfall was over and the roads were opened, having used tanks to open them, the offensive was cancelled. We were taken by trucks to the village of Gorodets, close to Maiskoe. We knew the village from our stay in Maiskoe, so it was easy to find old contacts among the locals. Our term of service with the 3rd Army under General Gorbatov was over. I guess we all had the warmest memories of the kindness of Gorbatov, to the end of the war. There were rumours that both Gorbatov and Rokossovski were once arrested and unjustly sentenced, which explained their humane treatment of *shtrafniks*. I think that here is a good place to tell a legend, or a true story, about that general. The story goes that, after the liberation of Rogachev, engineers built a temporary wooden bridge, for troops and light vehicles, over the broken and unstable ice on the Dnepr. The bridge was narrow and could only take one-way traffic. The commandant of the crossing received an order from Gorbatov to let only vehicles and artillery pass towards the Front. A lot of vehicles gathered on the western bank of the Dnepr, including several Willys jeeps.

The Commandant of the crossing, a tall strong major, followed his orders and did not let them on to the bridge, as he would have had to stop the flow of vehicles going to the Front. General Gorbatov got out of one of the Willys jeeps and demanded that his vehicle pass through urgently. The Major cited his orders and refused to do so. The General got angry at the Major's disobedience and all of a sudden hit him with his famous stick. The Major reacted in an unexpected and unusual manner. He turned quickly and hit the General so hard that the latter lost his balance and fell over the low railing of the bridge, into the snow. It was a shock! Several officers jumped out of the commander's jeep. Some ran to help the General, some, with pistols in their hands, grabbed the Major and held his arms. It seemed that the Major's days were numbered. The General wiped away snow from his uniform, walked up to the Major, and ordered his release. Then he sent for his flask.

The whole Army knew that the Commander did not drink, smoke or even curse. He quit drinking in his youth and, even during the war, if his friends rebuked him for being sober, he would say that he would only drink on Victory Day. So this order to bring his flask caused even greater shock among the officers. Gorbatov personally took a small glass from the flask, filled it with *vodka* and served it to the astonished Major, saying, "Great job, Major! Drink it, and take it as my apology and personal award. I have taught so many idiots with this stick, you are the first smart one I have met. Continue your service, I will send you a real decoration soon". That legend about General Gorbatov sounds unusual, but we all wanted to believe it. Probably it was actually true! It was a pity we never fought under his command later.

After our arrival in Gorodets, we spent a lot of time taking in replacements, arming men and knitting the units together. Battle training was also set up. Its main goal was to train former pilots, supply officers and other specialists, to fight as infantry. It meant forced marches, crawling, digging in, negotiating obstacles, the precise firing of submachine-guns, machine-guns, anti-tank rifles, and even captured a German *panzerfaust*. However, the hardest thing in the training was overcoming the fear that some *shtrafniks* had, of throwing hand-grenades, especially F–1. Its fragments were deadly at even 200 metres distance, while even a well-trained soldier could throw it only as far as 50–60 metres. We trained the men to throw live grenades, which actually exploded. The men had to throw them out of a trench, but still not every man had enough courage to throw them instantly.

This period of formation and training lasted to approximately mid-May. Of course, during this period we established close contacts with the local population. There were some love stories too. Those love stories were not only between our men and the local girls. It turned out that there was an airfield not far from us, with a battalion of an airfield service, the BAS, stationed next to it. Most of the soldiers in that battalion were young girls.

One warm spring day, I remember that an explosion sounded on the road, almost in the centre of the village. As it turned out, the soil had softened and a German anti-tank mine appeared on the surface. A horse that was pulling a carriage of artillery shells stepped on it and the mine went off. It was amazing that the shells did not detonate, otherwise the driver of the carriage would have been killed. The wounded soldier was taken to the dressing station, while a well-fed horse was killed on the spot. Of course, that explosion almost caused panic, but as a result, our field kitchens had a chance to make our rations richer with calories. My orderly Zhenya (I cannot remember his last name) also managed to get a large piece of fat horsemeat. He was a good cook and managed to make a whole pot of extremely tasty meat with potatoes, garlic and some spices that he borrowed from the owners of the house. We invited them to our improvised dinner, while Zhenya also invited the young soldier girls from the BAS that he knew. Of course, the hosts brought some moonshine for the dinner. Everyone was happy and praised the cook, especially the girls from the airfield team. Apparently, their rations were not as generous as those of pilots. However, they all threw up when they heard that it was that very horse! Poor things, they were not yet used to such an 'exotic' dish.

During such a prolonged period of stay in Gorodets there was a lot of dating and dancing in the evenings. When twilight set in and we did not have battle training, we would set up chorus singing in a large hut on someone's initiative. A song at the front line, if there was time and place for it, and if it was initiated by soldiers, was especially moving, and even cleansing in some way. How eagerly everyone sang then! We did not have conductors or chorus leaders, but we had both basses and tenors, both leading and secondary voices. Our singing sounded almost professional, so that the local villagers would gather in and around the hut, and listen to our improvised concerts with tears in their eyes. We did not sing Belorussian songs, as we only knew two Belorussian dancing songs. However, we sang a lot of Ukrainian songs about Zaporozhie Cossacks and others. Mostly, we loved to sing slow and sad Russian songs, including a song about Yermak. In it, we especially stressed the verses, "and his army, furious in battles, fell without drawing their swords". We often sang our favourite song, "Don't circle over me, black raven".

Apparently, those songs fitted the *shtrafniks* and their mood the best. It took us a long time to form the battalion in Gorodets. So we sang many songs, while the local girls decorated our singing with their high and clear voices. All those things made us so close to each other that both dances and dates almost ended with weddings. The weddings never materialised, but what was done, was done! Women had not seen men for a long time, and pitied us, as God only knew how long we had left to live. That was why, when we received an order to load the train immediately, we could imagine how many tears would be shed by the locals. Not only young girls, but also older women were weeping, as they had got used to our help in their households, and felt sorry for the good hearty relations that had been established with our 'complicated' soldiers. Despite all that, loading the train went without any problems, and in the evening our train rolled out of the station on a newly repaired railway. It turned out that we had to be relocated from almost the furthest right flank of the Front, to the left flank, i.e. the south-west of the liberated part of Belorussia.

Our train was moving quickly, as fast as the newly repaired railway allowed. We paid attention to how the Germans destroyed the railway during the retreat. I noticed two unusual approaches. The first was to have a huge plough fitted to the last wagon of the train, which broke cross ties like matches. The second approach was to have some device fitted to the rails that would lift the whole railway vertically in the air, so that it looked like a huge fence several kilometres long.

First, we proceeded via Gomel, Rechitsa, and Kalinkovichi. Then our train went through the Ukraine, via Ovruch, Sarny and to Manevichi. After that station the railway was not yet restored and we had to continue our march on foot. Only the battalion HQ and support units had trucks. In three days we marched over 100 kilometres towards the Ukrainian town of Ratno, which was still in German hands. It turned out that the 1st Belorussian Front occupied the north-western part of Ukraine, on its left flank. There we took up our defences on the Vyzhevka River, replacing a Guards Rifle Regiment.

The river itself was narrow, but its low swampy banks formed a boggy no-man's land, almost one kilometre wide. The trenches that we were supposed to defend, must have been dug by our predecessors during the previous winter. They were on a high spot, at the edge of a young evergreen forest. That was how we ended up in the 38th Guards Lozov Rifle Division of the 70th Army. Then our Army Commander was General V. S. Popov, not Gorbatov.

CHAPTER 3

'Rokossovski's Gang'

So, in late May 1944 our battalion was relocated to the area next to the Ukrainian town of Ratno, which was still under German occupation. The town lay to the north from the Ukrainian town of Kovel'. It too was still held by the Germans. We arrived at the Vyzhevka River and replaced a unit that was sent to another sector of the Front. Our 1st Company was on the battalion's right flank. The company commander was Captain Ivan Vladimirovich Matvienko, while his deputy was an energetic, and very young, Senior Lieutenant Ivan Georgievich Yanin. All we platoon leaders were about 20 years old. My platoon was the third and so took up our defences on the left flank of the company. The second platoon, under Lieutenant Fuad Bakirovich Usmanov, a 'Bashkirian', as he stubbornly called himself, was on my right flank. We called him by a Russian name Fedya or Todd. The first platoon was led by Lieutenant Dmitri Bulgakov. But I do not remember his *patronymic*. Both of them were two or three years older Ivan Yanin and me.

Despite a rather long period of formation, our platoons and companies lacked temporary personnel. Apparently, that was explained by the absence of large-scale operations in the sector, and the corresponding idleness of courts martial. There were fewer 'encircled ones', too. Our battalion was given a rather wide sector of defence. A *shtrafnik* joked about this, with a distinct Caucasian accent. "One Soviet citizen for each kilometre of the front!" Of course, that was an exaggeration. But instead of 8–10 strides between men in the trench, as the field manual would put it, men were standing 50–60 metres from each other. As we got reinforcements, that distance became smaller. The time that we had for formation and battle training was also used for getting to know our soldiers better. Maybe that was why I remember more names of those men, although I do not remember their first names in many cases. I hope they forgive me if I only call them by their last names in my memoirs. According to our TOE, platoon leaders were supposed to have two deputies. They were appointed by the order of the battalion commander, based on the recommendations of platoon leaders and the company commander.

One of my deputies was an experienced rifle regiment commander, who had over two years of battle experience but who had made a mistake in some battle. He was ex-Lieutenant Colonel Sergey Ivanovich Petrov. My second deputy was a 'punished' supply officer of a division, also an ex-Lieutenant Colonel, Shul'ga. I do not remember his name. In my platoon he was responsible for the platoon's supply of ammo, food and all other items necessary for waging a war. He did his job smartly, displaying initiative, and expertise in logistics and supply. To be honest, it was flattering for me, an inexperienced, 20 years old Lieutenant, a mere platoon leader, to have two experienced Lieutenant Colonels as my deputies, although they were temporarily deprived of their ranks. On the other hand, I was hoping to use the battle and life experience of these two men, who seemed quite old to me. That was probably the main thing. My first squad leader was an ex-Major of artillery, a tall, handsome and strong man with an unusual, easy to remember name, Puzyrei. An ex-Captain of border guards was leading the second squad. He had a slim face, with the fine features of a classic intellectual, but his eyes were sharp and there was always an ironic look in them. The third squad leader was ex-Captain of armour Lugovoi. He had the moustache of a grenadier from the nineteenth century. He was quite short, but fast and always ready to act.

My orderly and runner, who was also supposed to take care of me, was an ex-Lieutenant, so young compared to the other *shtrafniks* that everyone called him by his first name, Zhenya. He was a fast soldier, who was on time everywhere. He ended up in the battalion, due to riding a German motorcycle too fast. He knocked down and seriously injured a seven years old girl, in the village where his repair workshop was stationed. His sentence was two months of service in a penal battalion. My informal 'chief of staff', or rather clerk, was ex-Captain Lieutenant of the Northern Fleet, Vinogradov. He knew the German language very well, but as strange as it might seem, that expert knowledge of the enemy's language led him to the penal battalion. The only thing I do not understand, was why he was transferred so far, to the Belorussian Front from the Northern Fleet. He was a chief of some repair workshop of naval radio sets. When checking yet another repaired radio receiver, he came across a speech by Goebbels, the German propaganda minister. Vinogradov did not think about possible consequences, but just started to translate it aloud into Russian in the presence of his subordinates. Someone informed the prosecutor's office, or the Special department of the Navy, and as a result Vinogradov received a sentence of two months in a penal battalion for "assisting the enemy's propaganda".

Of course, the military laws were very strict and their strictness was justified. But in this case it was not strictness of the law that played its role, but rather an atmosphere of informing and suspicion among superior officers. Many people suffered from those two circumstances. They simply made some mistakes, or did the wrong thing. However, there is no serious undertaking without some mistakes. Unfortunately, the rule was to find a scapegoat, despite the fact that it could be the circumstances and not a specific person to blame. Vinogradov's story was just one example. I used him as a clerk, because he had almost perfect handwriting, and could also serve as an interpreter, although I also knew German quite well from my school days.

We were stationed in the sector that was previously held by some Guards unit. They left us well-built trenches, with walls strengthened with wooden poles and boards. The sector for my platoon also had a spacious dug-out, with three layers of logs on the roof. It withstood several direct hits by shells and mines during my time there. Pine trees there had been felled by explosions. I was accommodated in the dug-out together with my deputies, clerk and orderly. The company's CP was in the sector of the second platoon, in a similar dug-out.

As we were immediately briefed, there were no minefields in front of us. But directly behind our trench, there was a booby-trapped forest blockage created by fallen trees. We immediately marked that blockage on our maps. It was a partially cut down young forest, dotted with camouflaged anti-personnel mines. As it turned out later, some of the mines were PMD–6 with 200 gram TNT charges. Others had 74-gram charges. One sector of the blockage was booby-trapped during the winter. The mines were painted white and they were easy to spot during the summer. The second part of the blockage was separated from the first by a path, and was booby-trapped after the snow melted. Those mines were painted khaki. It was much harder to spot them in grass. I had an adventurous idea of relocating the mines from that blockage to no-man's land in front of our company, even more so since our defences looked quite weak to me. I did not have any ex-combat engineers in my platoon, while I had learnt about both Russian and German landmines in our Academy, from A to Z. So I decided to do it myself. I did not want to expose any *shtrafniks* to this danger. As the saying goes, "a battle engineer makes only one mistake in his life". Strictly speaking, I did not have any right to do such a thing.

It somehow did not occur to me then that this booby-trapped blockage was not only on our maps, but also on the maps of our battalion commander, division commander and Army commander maps, as an important element of the defence. Of course, the booby-trapped blockage behind our positions was not built on purpose as a blockage for *shtrafniks*. I should mention that under no circumstances did we have a blocking detachment behind our battalion, as some unfair historians are now writing. There was no need for that at all. I dare to state that Officer Penal Battalions were an example of stoicism in any battle situation.

Of course, I started my 'battle engineer' activity from the sector with white mines. I extracted and defused them during the day. At night I would set them some 30–50 metres in front of our trench, thoroughly camouflaging them with turf. When I was doing this, I recalled the golden rule that our company commander, Senior Lieutenant Litvinov, taught us in the Academy. "If you are scared – don't do it! If you do it – don't be scared!" Some of the mines were unfamiliar to me. They were standard wooden boxes that contained flat glass bottles with TNT powder inside. Fuses were inserted directly into the necks of those glass bottles. The bottles were wrapped in very good waxed paper. That paper was an extremely valuable find, I could write letters home when the situation allowed for it. At that time I was going through a romantic period of writing teenage poems. I was writing poems especially to the girl that I loved. The paper from the mines was very useful for me.

The problem of waiting for husbands from the Front was quite complicated in those years. Unfortunately, there were cases that made Simonov write "an open letter to a woman from Vichuga town". It was an answer to a woman who wrote a shameless letter to her Lieutenant husband at the Front. Officers were sending their wages from the Front, via banks, to their families. She wrote that she no longer needed his wage as she had found another, richer and nicer officer. That shocking letter did not reach the poor Lieutenant. He had been killed in action some time earlier. It is well known that war intensifies and reveals feelings, and views, sometimes degrading them to the level of instincts. Many unpleasant things surfaced in those years. There were also robbers and marauders, including 'spiritual' marauders. Those dissipated people had one justifying slogan, "war will write off all my sins", or "I don't care – it's war!" Those things happened and one cannot avoid writing about them. We had a case similar to that case of Simonov's woman from Vichuga. An officer was on his way to the Front after recovering from a wound. He decided to visit his wife on the way, and caught her with a lover. He shot both his wife and her lover, and was sent to our penal battalion.

The paper from those mines gave me a possibility to write my poems, while their second peculiarity, glass TNT containers, became understandable for me later. My squad leader, Omelchenko, who I ordered to assist me, quickly learnt the science of setting and defusing the mines, and we soon had a certain division of labour. I searched and defused the mines on the blockage, while he set them in front of our trenches! A bit later, when we looked around our sector of defence, we found a forgotten supply of several dozens of POMZ–2 wire-triggered, anti-personnel mines in a small barn. I think the acronym POMZ meant "anti-personnel fragmentation mine, for barricades". Those mines looked like our F–1 hand grenades. They were set on small rods, at about 20–30 centimetres above the surface, and wire triggers were stretched from the fuses. If someone touched the wire, the mine would go off. Setting those mines required even more attention, thoroughness and accuracy. They were of much greater danger than regular anti-personnel mines. Nevertheless, I decided, "why waste the mines", and started to plant them as well! I planted those mines myself, not even trusting this to Omelchenko although he had gained a lot of experience. If I got killed by a mine, it would be me alone!

As time passed, our company commander, an older and more experienced officer, tactfully made me understand that I did not have any right to defuse a minefield that was planted by the orders of our superiors. So I talked our company commander into reporting to the battalion that we were only placing POMZ mines in front of our trenches. The company commander agreed, unexpectedly for me. However, he decided to make a detailed map of the minefield in front of our trenches, with all the types of mines marked on it, just in case. Everything was going well, while I was working with the 'white' mines. We managed to relocate and camouflage around two hundred white mines without any incidents. I also set out about half of the newly found POMS mines, so we had a rather dense minefield in front of our positions.

It had already been about a month since we arrived in that sector of defence. We got used to it and managed to study the terrain well. We found thick blueberry bushes with ripe berries not far from our trenches. They were right behind the booby-trapped blockage, and many of us ran there when we had free time, compensating for lack of vitamins after the hard winter. Our supply units found mushrooms in the forest, so mushroom soups were quite common food for us. It was a very good menu given the war! I think it was then, in that static defence, that our supply units showed their best.

Both the Division's and the Army's supply units worked as never before, and we were receiving our food on time. Officers were getting their additional rations, sometimes even with American canned cheese and canned fish, not to mention tobacco. Officers were issued *Belomorkanal* cigarettes, while I was issued packs of 'light' pipe tobacco. *Shtrafniks*, as enlisted personnel, were issued *mahorka*, while non-smokers received additional sugar. I even tried to smoke *mahorka* in my pipe. The results were very impressive. I almost lost my voice after those experiments. All that relaxation made me recall the shortage of tobacco in the Academy, in the Far East. But there, in the trenches in static defence, we were doing well. Our supply units even arranged a field steam bath for us, two or three times, with changes of our uniforms. We were also quite lucky with the weather. The days were dry and hot, heavy with the fragrance of pine trees.

Without the daily German artillery strikes, and other daily battle activities, one could compare our stay in defence as an unexpected vacation, although the heat was sometimes unbearable. One of my *shtrafniks* had sunstroke. We quickly brought him back to his senses, while I recalled a case that happened to me during drill exercises in August 1941, in the scout platoon in the Far East. That was also a hot summer day. As I was trying to lift my leg higher while marching in ceremonial step, I suddenly noticed that everything started to double in my vision. I lost my balance and fell out of the formation. Other soldiers grabbed me, took me to a shady place, poured cold water on my head and chest, and made me drink extremely salty water. I immediately recalled that, on that morning, I had not eaten the salt that our platoon leader made us swallow before drinking tea. To do it, we would blow tobacco out of a cigarette and stuff it with salt. It was a sort of salt pill, and we learnt to swallow it without tasting the salt itself. It turned out that it was a simple but working method of preventing sunstroke. There, on the Belorussian Front, that personal experience of mine came back to me, and I ordered all squad leaders to strictly follow this ritual of salt injection at breakfast. After that we never had cases of sunstroke while in defence, or during exhausting offensives. The trick worked!

For many years after the war, evergreen forests and the aroma of pine trees would revive all my unpleasant memories of that forest blockage. Back then, in June 1944, I started to shift the green mines. It was much harder to spot them, and after two or three dozen my luck ended, and I detonated one of them. It happened on June 26. I remember very precisely that, around noon, I inspected the positions of my platoon and saw that everything was all right. I ate some tasty blueberries and went to do my regular work on the blockage. That time I managed to defuse several mines and put them on a tree-stump. Then I took a step to the side. It seemed to me that I flew high into the air from an explosion that sounded from under me. My flight was short, and almost immediately I was lying flat on the ground, face down. My first sensation was that my left leg was burning like hell! Then, I thought, I have no leg! I decided to turn around and see what was left of it. But when I lifted my head I froze! There was a mine just a few, perhaps 10–15, centimetres from my eyes! It was a miracle that I did not detonate it with my head. That must have been the exact moment when I had my first grey hair! I regained control of myself and almost automatically defused it. I carefully took out the fuse and bent the pin wire. Experience is a great thing! By that time I had defused over two hundred mines. Then I started looking around very attentively and noticed another mine by my side. Only after defusing it did I turn and saw that my leg and foot were still there. It was just my foot that was turned inside by 90 degrees. I tried to move my toes and they worked. That meant that my foot and leg were still attached to my body!

I realised that my leg was not torn off only because, by chance, I did not step on the mine itself. Apparently, I put my boot on a thick twig lying on the ground, and the twig detonated the mine that was some thirty centimetres from me. Squad leader Puzyrei heard the explosion and threw himself towards me, not looking under his feet, and shouting, "Lieutenant, are you alive?" I realised that he could hit a mine any time and not be as lucky as me. I yelled as loud as I could! "Stop! Don't move! I will get out of here by myself!" I somehow managed to stand up, and started walking to the path, dragging my damaged foot and feeling no pain. The pain only came later. I sensed some liquid squelching in my boot. I realised that it was blood. That was my first wound!

It took me a lot of effort to make it to the path. Puzyrei, and my orderly Zhenya, grabbed me, pulled me to the dug-out, cut open and took off the long boot. They bandaged my foot with a first aid kit, and took me to the battalion dressing station on a cart. God knows where they got it! The dressing station was located close to us, next to the battalion HQ in a village with a strange and easily remembered name, Vydranitsa. On the evening of the same day, after professional bandaging, I was taken to the medical battalion by a horse-drawn carriage. There they gave me two injections, a pain-killer and tetanus, and set my twisted foot. That was when I really felt the pain! They disinfected my wound and thoroughly bandaged it with a splint, as if my foot was broken. I only realised later the trick of those glass bottles in the mines. The doctors took out the large glass splinters from the wound, but those that were smaller, remained in my foot. Those splinters could not be seen, even on an x-ray, and came out of my foot through fistulas that did not heal for a long time.

Several days after my wound I started walking, leaning on a crutch. At first they were unsure, painful steps, but with every day I walked with greater strength and assurance. Soon I gave up crutches and started using a stick. I stopped using it in my unit a couple of weeks later. After one week of treatment in the medic battalion, I managed to talk the doctors into letting me go back to my battalion. I was keen to get back as the clouds were gathering over my head! Our *osobist*, NKVD officer Senior Lieutenant Gluhov, had already visited me and thoroughly interrogated me. He wanted to know who had made a decision to take mines off the forest blockage? I was responsible for the 'liquidation' of that element of our defences and did it without the permission of superior officers. The medical battalion discharged me, writing in my discharge certificate, "discharged, due to insistent requests of the patient for ambulatory treatment in his unit".

While I was away, one more unforeseen incident took place. My assistant in battle engineer affairs, Omelchenko, having gained experience, decided to continue setting POMZ mines without me. He was killed when he accidentally triggered the mine that he had just set in the darkness. Unfortunately, the mine worked very effectively, indeed, a battle engineer makes 'only one mistake' in his life. Omelchenko's mistake was the last one for him in his life. My friends in the battalion HQ told me that they seriously discussed how to rescue me from a court-martial. They wanted to prevent my transfer, from being a permanent officer of a penal battalion, to being a simple *shtrafnik*.

Vasily Afanasievich Lozovoi, our chief of staff, told me later that our *kombat*, then already Colonel Osipov, personally went to talk to the Commander of the 70th Army General, V. S. Popov. Citing my youth, he asked him not to punish me. He said, "this young Lieutenant had gained much experience, and would never again make any hasty, immature decisions!"

One more factor that helped me was that a German scout party ran into our minefield one night. Apparently they were trying to get into our trenches and take a prisoner, in order to find out the new unit responsible for that sector of the Front.

It seemed that our minefield came as a total surprise for them. As a proof their 'visit' the Germans left a blood-covered German boot and some other German field gear!

My 'lucky' wound matched a lull at the Front. During the free time that we sometimes had in defence, the officers spoke to *shtrafniks* about their battle experience. It was an exchange of experience, a kind of military education upgrade, and was also a way to get to know each other. I also remember that time due to all sorts of jokes and anecdotes, which were sometimes vulgar, and even 'dirty'. Sometimes we would sing popular songs of that time, changing the lyrics and stressing the negative aspects of life. For example, for the popular romantic song, "Dark night", we would sing, "and you secretly take sulphidine at baby's cradle" instead of "and you secretly wipe away tears at baby's cradle". Sulphidine was an essential drug against gonorrhoea. The times were tough.

I remember Misha Goldstein, whose real name was written down in his *Komsomol* ID as Musya. He was a veteran of the Moscow and Stalingrad battles, proud owner of several decorations and a severe wound in his head. He liked to tell jokes about Jews. Those were jokes about the front line at Tashkent, about a sniper with a bent rifle, and about two men who replied to the order of their platoon leader, "Forward, my eagles!" that "we are lions, not eagles". Those jokes did not have any 'negative' feeling in them. We appreciated them, even more so that Misha was an excellent story-teller, and had a great sense of humour. In general he was a very cheerful person, good dancer and harmonica player. Our battalion's supply column had a separate carriage for our company. It transported some belongings of the company's officers. That was the place where we stored Misha's harmonica, my gramophone with a collection of records, and other personal belongings that did not fit in our *sidor* bags. The gramophone would often entertain us in free time. In quiet hours in the evenings we would even arrange a 'concert' over the phone, for the Division's female phone operators.

From the stories of experienced officers, I learnt that my lucky detonation of the mine was not all that exceptional, and that other such 'lucky' cases had happened. A story of the company commander, Captain Matvienko, struck me and stayed in my memory. He was once ambushed by a huge German soldier who grabbed him and pulled him over the front line. Ivan somehow managed to stick his foot between the German's legs. The German scout did not expect this, fell down and for a second let his 'prey' go. In that moment Ivan jumped up, punched the German between the eyes and ran away.

One of our *shtrafniks*, ex-Major Avdeev, turned out to be an ex-commander of an Army's independent penal company. An independent penal company consisted not of ex-officers, as in our penal battalion, but of convicted enlisted men and former criminals who had been given a chance to redeem their guilt at the Front. Avdeev told us his story of how he himself ended up in our penal battalion. His company was carrying out an offensive in very hard conditions, and after three days of fighting for a large village, Avdeev, lost over half of his company of five hundred men. The Sergeant-major and the clerk of the company 'forgot' to report those losses when the company disengaged and was sent to the rear. Thus, they received food and alcohol for the whole company and had a great supply of it. Of course, no one wanted to send back all those riches. Avdeev, the company commander, decided to make a memorial dinner for the killed heroes and celebrate the decorations that they received. Avdeev himself received the Third Order of the Red Banner; other surviving officers of the company were also awarded. He invited some officers from the Army HQ, including officers from the Army's G2. He even invited several officers from the court-martial and prosecutor's office. The only ones that he forgot to invite were the political officers and the NKVD officer of his company. Soon after, Avdeev was charged with deception that caused overspending on food and ended up sentenced to five years in jail, replaced by two months of service in a penal battalion. The high decoration that he had just received, and the presence of cour- martial and prosecutor's officers at the party, did not help him at all. There were many things to learn from those stories.

In the meantime, the Germans intensified their propaganda war against us. They were constantly dropping leaflets from planes, and fired special leaflet shells. Those were leaflets encouraging us to surrender, known as 'pass over the front line leaflets', as well as the so-called BIG, 'bayonet into the ground'. There was a huge mass of leaflets about the sons of Stalin and Molotov who had already surrendered to the Germans, and dozens of other stories that we did not believe at all. There were also leaflets with recommendations about how to cause, or imitate, diseases that would put you in a hospital for a long time. First, I should mention that our NKVD officer Gluhov, and some of the political officers looked after us closely, so that *shtrafniks* would not pick up and hide the leaflets, especially the BIG passes. Apparently, they had an order to do so. They soon realised that *shtrafniks* would not use the leaflets, even for rolling cigarettes, but used them only as toilet paper. After that our 'morale police' calmed down, and stopped watching over us.

I noticed in particular one of the leaflets that informed us of a secret order of Stalin not to decorate men and officers who did not have wounds. That was a total nonsense! We had many officers in our battalion who had two or three decorations, but who had never been wounded. However, I should note an interesting coincidence. I was not awarded for the Rogachev raid. I had assumed that I was not awarded for it due to the fact that my father had been arrested in 1942 for negative words about the country's leadership, and failures of the Army during the initial period of the war. I thought that another reason could be that one of my two older brothers went missing in action, in late 1942, at Stalingrad. Could he have surrendered to the Germans? I had all sorts of thoughts on my mind. Such was the time and the way of thinking in those days.

However, after I was wounded detonating that mine, instead of the expected punishment for defusing mines without permission, in early July I received the Order of the Red Star, by order of 70th Army commander, General V. S. Popov. As our 'Dad', *kombat* Osipov told me during the award ceremony, it was for "decisiveness, initiative and bravery in the battles for Rogachev". So, I received the decoration for "overall performance". That was the most common practice in our battalion. Decorations were awarded not for a specific battle but for overall performance in several. Even after that case, however, I did not believe the German leaflets. Apparently, after the raid the *kombat* did not yet have sufficient facts to recommend me for a decoration, especially given the fact that we knew how just and demanding our *kombat* was. His personality was a rare combination of features, such as silence, and stern strictness on one side, and kindness and real fatherly care on the other. That was why we all called him 'Dad', or 'Father', when we spoke of him between ourselves. That was the happy end of my landmine story!

I have already mentioned that the Germans were trying time and again to find out which was the new unit that was opposing them in the sector. Somehow they found out that we were a penal battalion, as a little later the Germans would turn on our famous *Katyusha* song, or the German version "*Wolga-Wolga, Mutti Wolga*" before a propaganda speech over the loudspeaker. Then they would urge *shtrafniks* to turn their weapons against their "tyrant-commanders". They also called our penal battalion "Rokossovski's gang". We had known that this nickname was given to our battalion as early as 1943. That was when the battalion was formed and took part in its first battles at the Kursk salient, as part of the Central Front under General Konstantin Konstantinovich Rokossovski. That period of defence on the flank of the 1st Belorussian Front was full of individual skirmishes. Some skirmishes passed by without staying in my memory. The human memory only picks up what was important later on, but everything that happened during the defence, and the offensive that followed, stayed clearly in my memory.

The impression of 'unexpected vacation' was, of course, far from the real state of affairs. Frequent artillery strikes and intensive artillery barrages sometimes caused serious losses. For example, a heavy mine hit a lightly built dug-out where my friend from the Rogachev adventure, AT-rifle platoon leader Petr Zagumennikov, was together with his platoon. The result was three killed, and two wounded. My friend almost got killed, surviving with shell-shock. He was partially deaf for a long time after that incident. Apparently he could read from my lips the question that I asked him, "Why aren't you in the medic battalion?" He answered, "It will heal itself!" And so it happened!

As I have already mentioned, the Germans tried to uncover and smash our defences. A 'frame', i.e. an FW 189 twin-boom German scout and artillery observer plane, got into the habit of circling low over our positions. One machine-gunner *shtrafnik* made an improvised AA stand, from an old carriage wheel, for his DP machine-gun. During one of the visits of the 'frame' he hit it with such a good burst of tracer and armour-piercing bullets that the 'frame' started to fall. It barely made it across the river, crashed to the ground and exploded. The pilot did not even have time to bail out. We were so happy! Not only because 'we were leading!' but mainly because all the *shtrafniks* were happy for their friend! We knew that for personally knocking out a tank, or shooting down an aircraft, a *shtrafnik* was decorated with the Order of the Patriotic War! That meant an unconditional release from the Penal Battalion, without being wounded. It was great news, especially in defence, when time passed slowly for *shtrafniks*.

Unfortunately, there were other sorts of 'heroic deeds' among some *shtrafniks*. As I have mentioned, the Germans were bombarding our positions with artillery on a daily basis. Our artillery, as a rule, did not respond. There was a strict order to save ammo, both in the artillery and in the infantry. We noticed that famous German punctuality which seemed strange to us. They bombarded our positions during certain times, almost always after nine o'clock in the evening. Although we all tried to be in the trenches after nine, all of a sudden we started having a lot of *shtrafniks* with light muscle wounds, mostly wounded in their buttocks. If a *shtrafnik* was wounded it meant that he had paid for his guilt with his blood, and was released from the Penal Battalion. The number of such wounded grew suspiciously large. So then our *osobist* officers, I think with the assistance of other *shtrafniks*, found out the method and technology of receiving such wounds.

It turned out that cheating *shtrafniks* would throw a hand-grenade into some wooden barn, during a German bombardment, and then take the splinters out of its walls. They would find an SMG cartridge, take out and throw away bullet, put away half of gunpowder from the cartridge and insert a splinter of proper size into it instead of the bullet. After that it was simple. During another bombardment someone would shoot this bullet into their own muscle, and this 'lightly wounded' *shtrafnik* would receive the desired release from the battalion. After that trick was uncovered, most of the 'wounded' were again court-martialled for intentional self-mutilation, and deserting from the penal battalion. Not all those 'smart guys' came back to the battalions. Some of them were sentenced to death, given also their previous crimes. They were executed, many publicly, in the presence of other *shtrafniks*. Most of the witnesses to those executions approved both the sentences and the public executions. There was a very negative attitude, to put it mildly, towards cowards and such 'cheaters' in our penal battalion.

I cannot help writing about another cowardly *shtrafnik* who arrived in my platoon when we were in defence. I am slightly twisting his last name in this story, although it sounds almost the same, Geft. I do this on purpose. If the descendants of this person ever read this book, they would be extremely embarrassed about their ancestor, who they believed to be a hero of the war against the *Nazis*. He arrived in our battalion some time in early June. When my deputies and I read of his sentence, we all had a feeling of disgust. Speaking in modern terms, he was sentenced for sexual harassment, and rape in a perverted form. He had the rank of Engineer-Major and was heading some supply unit in a large HQ. He arranged to eat alone, and forced female military personnel who served as waitresses, not only to serve him food but also have sex with him during his breakfasts and dinners. We knew what that meant, although we did not know much about sex in those days. Geft threatened the poor female soldiers that if they refused to do what he asked, or complained about it, he would send them to a penal company. The poor girls did not know that women could not be sent to penal companies, by definition. His sentence was severe, ten years in jail, replaced with three months of service in a penal battalion. That seemed a very just sentence to us.

When he reported to me, and saw from my small stars on the shoulder-boards that I was only a Lieutenant, he stressed his own rank, arrogantly calling himself "Engineer-Major Geft". I had to remind him that he had been stripped of that rank, although temporarily, God willing. I also mentioned to him that he had to try hard in order to get his rank back. There, in the penal battalion, his rank was the same as all the others, he was a 'temporary soldier'. I held a small military council with my deputies, and we decided to send Geft away to Puzyrei's squad, in a remote sector of our defence. We strictly warned him that he must always, especially during German artillery bombardments, observe the no-man's land. That was in order to prevent Germans from secretly approaching our defences, and entering the trenches under cover of artillery fire. I especially stressed that the Germans had been on the hunt for a prisoner for a long time in our sector.

On the very first night, Puzyrei reported to me that Geft would lie down on the bottom of the trench and cover his head with *plash-palatka* during a German bombardment. For that he was beaten up by another *shtrafnik*. I ordered the squad leader to teach that 'engineer-sexual' in a different, more convincing manner. Soon after, the pervert was dragged into my dug-out by his squad leader and other *shtrafniks*. He was again beaten up for cowardice. Geft realised how serious consequences of repeated cowardice for him could be. He fell to the floor of the dug-out and screamed like an animal. It was a disgusting sight. That desperate scream of Geft was proof that he understood the full seriousness of the situation. He could well be executed if we reported his behaviour to our *osobist*.

He very rarely visited the trenches. To be honest, I had no idea what his job was like, as he was always sitting in the HQ. Sometimes he would send a runner to call for a *shtrafnik*, who would return to the trenches half an hour later. In that situation, however, I understood that my order "to teach in a more convincing manner" was properly fulfilled, and I only ordered that Geft's weapon be taken from him so that he did not do anything stupid. Then I had him put in a separate foxhole under guard. It became a sort of improvised man-watch. He was shivering with fear in that hole till the next morning, when I had a long conversation with him. To be honest, it was not a pleasant conversation. Although his arrogance was gone completely, I had never before dealt with such a pathological case of cowardice. I ordered the squad leader to give the weapon back to Geft, but kept an eye on him during his entire term in the battalion. I received reports that Geft stopped hiding during the artillery bombardments, and I thought that he had overcome his cowardice. I hoped that after that incident he would serve the full three months in the penal battalion, but that hope did not come true.

During that rather long defensive period, both supply and field post worked well. We even received, although in small numbers, national newspapers such as *Pravda* Red Star or, as we called it, Little Star, *Komsomol Pravda*. Meanwhile, I received letters from my mother and sister in the Far East. Their letters always arrived, although with some delays. It was during that defensive period that I received the grievous letter about my older brother. Ivan was killed at the front the year before, in 1943. That news saddened my heart for a long time.

Our political officers were working very intensively too, informing us about the course of events at the home front, and other sectors of the front. We received the news of the Second Front opening with mixed feelings. We felt satisfaction and joy, but with a certain amount of annoyance. We had been waiting for that event for three years. We even saluted our Western Allies with rifle and SMG fire at the Germans, although we had strict orders to save ammo. If there had not been two years of talking and postponing, the lives of numberless soldiers, POWs and civilians in the occupied territories could have been preserved! In 1944 we all knew that our push west was unstoppable and irreversible. The Soviet Union did not need the Second Front as urgently as two years earlier. But one should not look a gift horse in the mouth. We gave thanks for the landing, too! As is known, the Allied landing in Normandy took place on June 6, 1944.

At the Front we also remembered that it was the birthday of our great poet Pushkin. That day too was the birthday of my beloved girl Rita, who was then at the 1st Belorussian Front, serving as a nurse in a field hospital. Her letters came quickly, which meant that she was somewhere close. I made an agreement with Rita to cheat on the military censorship, and we informed each other of the places where we were. We used a very simple code for that. In our letters we would write of who we met, and to whom we would send greetings, making the name of the locality coded in the names of the people that we met. For example, if I received greetings from "Sonya, Lena, Ukhov, Tsarev and Kolya", it would mean that the hospital was stationed in Slutsk. Military censorship never learnt about that trick.

We read newspapers and the latest handwritten news broadcasts "from the Soviet Information Bureau" with great interest. After much delay we received news of the death of General Vatutin, who was mortally wounded at Sarny. According to the official news, he was wounded by a group of Bendera's men, who were active on our side of the Front. There were many gangs and *Nazi* mobs in the forests. The news about a great number of captured German generals, officers and men being marched through Moscow was unexpected, but nevertheless impressive. It was about the same time that we learnt about the heroic death of Guards private Yuri Smirnov from the 3rd Belorussian Front. He was tortured by the *Nazis*, and cruci- fied on the door of a dug-out. But they failed to get any information from him. That made our hatred of the *Nazis* even stronger, and caused a lot of spontaneous meetings with promises of revenge for 'our Yuri'. The national newspapers reported the beginning of the offensive operations of three Belorussian Fronts. They had one codename, Bagration. Especially pleasant was the news of the libera- tion of Zhlobin, where our battalion fought in December 1943, especially given the fact that it was liberated on June 26. That too was the cursed day when I detonated the mine!

Our 1st Belorussian Front stretched over 900 kilometres from the south to the north. As we got to know later, there were 63 German divisions opposing the Front. From the intelligence reports, we learnt that Field Marshal Busch, the unsuccessful commander of the German Army Group "Centre", was replaced by Model. Officers of the battalion joked, "You say Model? OK, give us Model!" Apparently, some officer modified the phrase of Chapaev from the famous pre-war movie: "You say psychological assault! OK, give us a psychological one!" We could see that our time in defence was about over and that we were supposed to join the offensive soon. Judging by the repeated orders to spot the enemy's weapons emplacements, and to take prisoners, the offensive in our sector of the Front was near.

We had all sorts of tricks for getting intelligence information about the enemy. For example, in our company we had 20 years old Senior Lieutenant Ivan Yanin. He had been awarded three orders without being wounded. I always recalled a line from Maxim Gorky's poem, "we are singing a song about the madness of the brave", when I saw him in combat. In order to draw the enemy's fire, and thus spot his weapons emplacements, our little Ivan would put on his shining decorations and his spare golden shoulder-boards. Where on earth did he get them? We only had field green shoulder-boards. He would then stand up on the breastwork of the trench, and slowly walk along it, on a bright sunny day, in full sight of the Germans. The *Fritzes* thought that he was a high-ranking officer, as his shoulder- boards shone like a General's. They would open fire, often even with artillery or mortars, while our observers would spot the places where the fire was coming from, thus preparing a map of all the German defences. Strangely enough, that crazy, brave officer was not even wounded during his promenades under German fire. It was as if a protecting spell was on him! He was killed much later, without once having been wounded. But I will tell that story later. Sometimes we managed to provoke the Germans and make them fire by teasing their machine-gunners on purpose. Our virtuoso machine-gunners were playing special melodies firing MGs, like "ta … ta … ta-ta-ta!" and after the fifth or sixth burst a *Fritz* would lose his nerve and fire a long burst in our direction. That was just what we needed!

Our *kombat* Osipov, his chief of staff Lozovoi, and even some political workers started to visit our trenches more often. I am not trying to say "all political officers are useless", that is not true! During my life at the front and my long post-war service in the Army, I met a lot of brave, smart, responsible and necessary political officers. Major Olenin, our political officer, spent almost all his time in our trenches during the defensive period that I described. He replaced Zheltov who was killed in the Rogachev raid. I should say that he was a good replacement. Olenin was a good, upright and brave person. He did not keep his distance from us, and even when he led us, it was by his personal example. I don't want to hide or disguise my feelings of that time. The fact that his last name sounded almost like Lenin also had an impact on us. In general, well-organised and skilfully implemented political work among the troops had a great significance and raised morale. We officers, as communists, also carried out political work with our own methods, both with personal conversations and personal example. I think that every *frontovik* communist officer considered himself to be a little bit of a commissar, in the best meaning of that word. We did not often use the slogan "For Motherland, for Stalin". In a good many instances the circumstances were inappropriate for that. But I used that slogan quite a lot, although I was not a political officer. We were like that in the 1940s.

The Division's scouts tried to take a prisoner several times, but failed. Then a special mission was given to our Penal Battalion. First, the commander of the 38th Rifle Division, General G. M. Soloviev, wanted to carry out a reconnaissance, in force, with our entire battalion, or at least one company. But our *kombat* found a better solution. We knew almost everything about the German MG nests, and their other weapons emplacements, and he decided to take prisoners in another way. A reconnaissance in force would have led to unnecessary losses, especially unwanted before a major offensive. Our 'Dad' cared for the lives of *shtrafniks*! According to the idea of our *kombat*, our 1st Company and the AT-rifle company's men were supposed to imitate the construction of a crossing, on the river in our sector. Vasily Tsigichko, a tough, stocky officer, with amazingly puffy lips, and a quiet, but juicy bass voice, was especially active in that undertaking. Apparently, the Germans had an inkling of our coming offensive. Meanwhile, the swampy and boggy terrain that our troops were supposed to cross, in a dashing non-stopping offensive, needed the construction of at least some road or bridge across it. That was necessary even for light cannons and vehicles, so our entire fake operation would look quite logical and realistic. Captain Pavel Tavlui's second company was ordered to cover our so-called action.

We brought several logs to the river during the night, as the booby-trapped forest blockage was no longer dangerous. Then we began to chop the logs with small entrenching tools instead of axes, imitating cutting logs, and nailed them together. A strong ambush was laid on the opposite bank of the river, right across from the 'bridge'. There was no 'catch' on the first night. But on the next night, which was light due to a clear sky and full moon, our observers noticed a group of Germans who were crawling towards the swampy bank of the river. They were assaulted by our ambushers without making a single sound. The Germans who tried to resist, or made a noise, were killed with SVT bayonets, while three were gagged, bound and transported alive to our bank of the river. After a brief interrogation by my clerk-translator Vinogradov, they were sent further on to the battalion HQ. We took three prisoners, including one officer! As a result, eight *shtrafniks* who took part in that ambush, were released from the battalion before completion of their term, and were recommended for decorations, although only with medals.

After the successful capturing of the prisoners, I felt some sort of unusual feeling growing up in my heart, and being excited about the looming offensive, I wrote an application, and I was not the only one, for membership of the Communist party. Only those who distinguished themselves in battles were accepted into the Communist party, hence the huge growth of influence of the party in our battle life at the front. To be a communist was not only an honour, but also rather a responsibility. Communists were not only responsible for themselves, they were also responsible for the mission given to them and to their subordinates. The only privilege, for those who really valued their title of communist, was to stand up first in the assault, and go first under the enemy's fire. The applications were short. "I would like to be in the first rows of the defenders of the Motherland". The rallying cry, "Communists, forward!" was not popular in the penal battalion, but it was still in the souls of officers who were joining the party. It was much later that I started to distinguish between real, genuine communists and others. There were those who joined the VKP (b) and then the KPSS in order to make a career, or to get some small but still governing-party office, e.g. a battalion or regimental party secretary, or regional party secretary in civil life. It was much later that they became 'flippant'. But back then, at the front, some of them could be easily discerned, by their insincerity and hypocrisy. We could already see such people in our environment during the war. Those people were absolutely alien among officers, they were mocked or avoided.

Speaking for myself, I had been a candidate for VKP (b) since the autumn of 1943. But it was only in the summer of 1944, when I was promoted to Senior Lieutenant, and received an Order for Combat, that I decided I was worthy of becoming a member of the Bolshevik party. Even now, so many years after those days and nights of war, I am proud that I received my brand new party ID in the political section of the 38th Guards Lozov Rifle Division, one day before the beginning of the offensive. It was equivalent to the highest governmental award, but issued to me in advance.

My initial period of life at the Front was over. By then my life was governed by other, higher values and standards. From that moment I was a Communist. I had a much greater responsibility for success, and an even greater one for failures or mistakes. From that time on, I had to lead even more by example, both in battle and all other aspects of life. I was proud of the role and increased responsibility. I had to prove that I was fit for the role both during the looming offensive and for the rest of my life.

Operation Bagration was designed and led by our Front Commander, at that time General of the Army Rokossovski. The battle is known in history as the battle for Belorussia. It started on June 24, 1944, almost exactly three years after the outbreak of the war.

CHAPTER 4

Operation 'Bagration'

Finally, our turn came to join Operation Bagration which was already in full swing. We were well stocked with ammo during the two weeks prior to the offensive. We received 200–250 cartridges for each PPSh submachine-gun. The cartridges were packed in 'zincs' as we called the boxes of thin zinc covered iron, and their impregnated carton packages Many submachine-guns had two round ammo drums, each one for 71 cartridges. Soldiers armed with rifles received two additional canvas ammo pouches to be worn on the waist belt. MG crews were also supplied with a great amount of ammo. Apparently, there had been good reason for that order to save ammo in defence. We also received dry tack, which was not much different from the dry tack that we received before the Rogachev raid. The only difference was that this time we received small cans with American cheese with an unusually strong smell. We still called all US and UK equipment 'from the Second Front'. The yellowish Ukrainian lard I guess we received because we were stationed in the Ukraine. Both ammo and dry tack were issued for 3–5 days of active offensive operations. We were supposed to receive hot food at least once per day. We all got used to a regular supply of hot food from our field kitchens while in defence. Of course, we could only receive hot food in the offensive when the situation allowed for it.

Our supply units took good care of even the repair and exchange of worn out footwear. We had long marches and battles on the sandy and swampy soil of Belorussia. We had to march more than 100 kilometres to the border with Poland. 'Encircled ones' wore low boots with leg wrappings. Most personnel in our battalion wore long boots, i.e. all officers, although deprived of their ranks, so we received replacements in long boots as well. Many officers had to exchange their nice, but worn out, long leather boots for *kirsa* long boots. We received replacements of footwear in the form of brand new, English-made, low boots, also known as 'the Second Front'! Those boots shone, and looked more fit for parades. To us they looked quite thick and non-elastic, with an unusually thick and non-bending sole. As it turned out later, the soles were made of pressed and glued cardboard that would swell after two or three days of marching in the swamps of Belorussia. Meanwhile, the boots themselves would immediately lose both their shine and hardness. I must praise the leg wrappings that were supplied with the boots. They were tough and long-lasting. They could be used for different things, even making stockings, as they were double. We used to give them as gifts to the girls that we knew.

Repair of footgear, especially in front line conditions, always required a certain economy and a soldier's knowledge of repair materials. One pair of boots would be cannibalised for repairing several pairs. But there was one significant incident. Our supply unit brought us several pairs of brand new, war-booty German long boots. They offered all of us an exchange of our worn out *kirsa* boots, for well-made footgear, as we had a long journey in front of us! The famous propaganda poster, depicting a Red Army soldier putting on a new long boot, with a sign, "We will make it to Berlin!" appeared just around that time. There was not a single person who wanted to take the German boots. Apparently, other propaganda posters depicted those German boots with nails tramping over our Motherland. Those were still fresh in our memories.

Skilled craftsmen from among the *shtrafniks* somehow managed to make fashionable 'Jimmy' long boots with narrow points, especially for dandy young platoon leaders. A good many of us tried to follow the young fashion of that time. They made the long boots from soldiers' *plash-palatkas*! In order to make them look like leather boots, owners often abundantly anointed them with some unimaginable mixture of lard, sugar, and something else! The long boots shone very well, but it did not make the boots any stronger. Just like the English-made boots, they fell apart in the very first days of the offensive. We did not march on asphalt roads, but on swampy and sandy soil. *Voentorg* also 'took part' in preparing us for the offensive, and visited us sometimes. As they said then, whatever you could imagine, *Voentorg* did not have. It did not have cigarettes, *eau-de-cologne*, razor blades, not even toothpaste. They did not have a thing! The only things that they brought to us for sale were small pieces of paper, cut to size for rolling cigarettes, the army's tin buttons, and green collar-tabs for overcoats. There were rumours that all the more practical things were sold off before they made it to the front line trenches.

Preparation for the offensive was about over. I received an order to clear several passages in the minefield that we set during the night of July 18, 1944, as we were ready to storm the German positions. I think it was the first time that I heard the idiom "initiative is punishable". Although I had planted those mines myself, it was much harder to defuse them. It was again new moon, and the night was already dark but not for too long. I could not use a flashlight, so I had to do everything by touch. I did not want to employ anyone from the platoon. I did not want Omelchenko's tragedy to repeat itself. I made the passages safely, and marked them with small twigs with white pieces of cloth attached. I made it before dawn, but my *gimnastyorka* tunic was soaking wet with sweat. It was quite a stressful job!

As soon as it started to grow light, we heard thunderous artillery fire. That was the long-expected artillery bombardment. While the artillery was pounding the German positions, our units successfully crossed the minefield and almost reached the riverbank. The final salvo of *Katyushas* was the signal for the assault. It was already growing light and, just like in the movies, one could see all our men standing up and rushing towards the German trenches. Everyone was extremely excited. The most amazing thing was that the Germans did not return fire at all. We thought that our artillery did a really great job and must have destroyed absolutely all the German MGs! With difficulty we swarmed down the swampy banks of the river, and across the Vyzhevka River itself. It turned out to be very shallow. When we jumped into the German trenches with our thunderous "Hurrah!" we were even more amazed. They were empty! We knew that, along with Hungarian troops who we dubbed Magyars, there were also elite *Nazis* from the *Totenkopf* Division. Where on earth did they all go? Apparently, they got to know both about the date and time of our offensive. So our "Hurrah!" faded away with disappointment when we saw that the trenches were empty. On the one hand, it was good, that the Germans had withdrawn themselves, but we were ready for a hand-to-hand fight! The offensive, as we understood from the order, started on the entire left flank of our Front.

The direction of the offensive of our Battalion, or rather the 38th Division to which we were attached, was towards the town of Malorita, and then further on to Domachevo, south from Brest, in order to seal the encirclement of Brest. Soon we got to know from the situation, and from the messages of our HQ, that the Germans were retreating in many places. They were setting up delaying parties, blowing up bridges and planting mines on the roads. But how far did they retreat and where were their delaying parties? If I remember correctly, the regimental commander of the 110th Guards Rifle Regiment had our company on his flank. After we reached the second trench, a runner from the commander passed on the order to sharply change the direction of the offensive, in order to capture part of the town of Ratno. There the enemy was still putting up stubborn resistance. We had to capture it, and prevent the Germans from blowing up the bridge over the Pripyat' River. Before we marched the 200–300 metres on the dry land towards the bank of the Pripyat', our marching columns came under several long and heavy MG bursts. Our 1st Company, and the following 2nd Company under Captain Pavlui, ducked for cover and immediately started to prepare both small arms and hand-grenades for battle.

Shortly after that we saw a signal for the assault. During that period of the offensive, such a signal was a series of green flares. The company rushed along the bank of the river, covering itself with intensive fire from SMGs and MGs, and ran into Ratno. The Germans had several concrete and wooden bunkers in the town. Throwing hand-grenades into any places where German fire was coming from, and literally following Germans, a rather large group of men from our company, mostly from Usmanov's platoon and mine, ran on to the bridge. We managed quickly to kill the sentries and the combat engineers who had tried to blow up the bridge. We captured the bridge and consolidated our positions on the western bank of the river. Of course, we had losses. It also turned out that there were several wounded *shtrafniks* on the western banks of the river. They refused to leave the battlefield. They had a right to do so, as they had already redeemed their guilt 'with their blood'. But they were capable of fighting and so continued to fight! There were many such cases. They demonstrated that *shtrafniks* valued the common battle interests higher than their personal ones. Of course, there were *shtrafniks* who declared every scratch to be 'abundantly shed blood' and who tried to leave the battlefield as quickly as possible. But that was a matter for their own consciences. And some had no feeling of battle solidarity.

As soon we reached western outskirts of Rutno, we saw tanks rushing across the bridge behind us. I could not understand why the tanks could not capture the bridge before us. It was intact! However, at that moment I did not have time to analyse the situation. I needed to put my platoon together and use the moment of respite for counting losses and finding out about the further mission. Both troops and armour were moving up on the Brest highway, while we still had a long way to go to Malorita. Then, unfortunately, I saw that we had significant losses. I had three killed and three wounded in my platoon. But Geft was not among them. No one saw him among the killed or wounded. Squad leader Puzyrei just shrugged his shoulders with bewilderment. We included Geft in the list of missing in action, but we found out the real reason for his disappearance much later.

It took us about thirty minutes to gather together our platoons that had dispersed and mixed with each other during the assault on the Ratno suburb and the bridge. We also sent away the released wounded into the rear. Then we received an order to rejoin the regiment that had crossed the Pripyat' river to the south from us and to continue the assault towards the village of Zhirichi, and further on towards Turskoe Lake. At the approaches to Zhirichi the regiment and we too, again came against strong German resistance. Our small units were urgently sent to the spearhead of the assault, to the most dangerous spot, in order to reinforce the regiment. When we mixed with the riflemen, we saw that their morale immediately grew. They understood very well that there were former officers, of all ranks, alongside them and we would all assault together. It seemed that the riflemen received some injection of a morale boost. It was indeed a wise decision to make a task force from different branches of the service.

A machine-gunner *shtrafnik* from my platoon, unfortunately I cannot remember his name, noticed that several *Fritzes'* MGs were inflicting intensive fire on us from the attic of a large farmhouse. They were firing through the holes that they had made in the roof hay. The Regiment's riflemen returned fire, but it was ineffectual. As we were lying out in the open, and had only dug shallow skirmishers' trenches, we could expect high losses from that MG fire, even before the assault, while during the assault they would have mown down a great many. So this *shtrafnik* said, "I will smoke them out of there". He picked up a clip with incendiary bullets and loaded his MG. I realised that he wanted to set that unfortunate farm on fire. It was a good farm and it was a pity to burn it, but we were at war. In the evening twilight I could clearly see tracer bullets from my brave machine-gunner's MG hitting the roof the farm! Hot summer weather had lasted over a month and had dried the hay to the uttermost. So it caught fire several minutes later. The German MG fire ceased, and we saw green signal flares in the sky. Was it a coincidence?

The *shtrafniks* and then the riflemen of the regiment, at first only a few at a time, got up from the ground, and ran towards the village, cheering themselves on with SMG and rifle fire. The battle was short. Some 15–20 minutes later the village was completely in our hands. The brightly burning hut illuminated the village in the twilight. There were many dead Germans around, but there were also many Germans who fled. They retreated altogether, as if they had received an order. Using darkness and the thick forest west of Zhirichi, they disappeared from our sight. We received an order to stop for a brief rest. Again I counted losses and gathered my platoon. I was extremely upset to hear that the machine-gunner who had just smoked the Germans out of the hut was also killed. There were many paradoxes in battles. He made sure that our losses would be minimal in the battle for the village, but he was himself killed in that action, giving his life for the sake of the others. Of course, there was no law of war. But there was some fatal logic in battles, and I came across it time and again.

It was completely dark when our field kitchens and ammo carriage found us. It was a surprise for us. They came at the right moment, as during the whole day we did not even have a chance to take a bite of dry tack. We were low on ammo, too. And we received half a canteen of some thick soup, and a large portion of buckwheat porridge with meat. We even had the battlefield 100 grams of *vodka!* The deputy battalion commander, supply, was Major Izmailov. He fitted our *kombat* well. He was tall, big, and somewhat slow in speech and movement, but quick in decision-making. He knew how to keep men supplied with food and ammo in the hardest possible situations. I will always remember our catering supply officer Moses Zeltszer, and our ammo supply officer Boris Tachaev, with strong feelings of gratitude.

Before we could finish our meal, the only meal of the whole day, and pick up our ammo and hand grenades, the runner from the regimental commander brought a new order. We must catch up with the Germans, and deprive them of the opportunity of consolidating their positions at some good natural obstacle. Our companies were again sent to the right flank of the regiment, for independent action. It was obvious that the Germans would not merely retreat, but also set up delaying parties and lay ambushes, in order to slow down our offensive. That would consolidate their positions on good defensive grounds. Of course, we assumed that one such good natural obstacle would be the Bug River, or as we called it, the Western Bug, in order to distinguish it from the Southern Bug that flowed through Vinnitsa, Nikolaev, and then on into the Black Sea.

The night was dark but full of stars. It was the night of July 19. It was the time of the new moon. We started to slowly move towards Turskoe Lake, almost completely by touch, finding our way by the stars, and the compass that we cautiously illuminated with a flashlight. We maintained sound contact with each other by whispers. During that night we moved in darkness so carefully and secretly that we lost communication not only with the regiment, that was now on our left flank, but also for some time even with our battalion's HQ. After a short delay, our company commander decided to bypass the lake from the left, independently, and advance towards the village of Tur, where one could expect another delaying party of Germans. On our right flank there was another Rifle Division. We did not have any contact with them at all, so both our flanks were exposed. That was considered a very dangerous situation. What if the Germans hit us on our flanks? That time we were lucky!

When we approached the village of Tur, in the dawn of July 20, we again established fire contact with the enemy. Our forward 'point' came under quite intensive MG fire. The main forces of our two companies, the mortar platoon of Misha Goldstein and the AT-rifle platoon of Petr Smirnov, engaged the enemy. Smirnov had replaced Peter Zagumennikov and been appointed AT-rifle company commander shortly before the offensive. We did not know where the third company and the other units of the battalion were. But all of a sudden we heard a firefight breaking out on the opposite edge of the village. It turned out that it was the second part of the battalion with whom we lost contact. They bypassed the lake from the right and arrived just in time. The entire penal battalion, although suffering losses, kicked the Germans out of the village and started to chase the retreating *Nazis*. Our morale was high, but fatigue was obvious, as the men could no longer keep up with the pace of the retreating Germans. Of course, that was the result of our exhausting attempts to catch up with the fleeing enemy and to deprive him of the possibility of respite and consolidation. We realised that if we stopped for time and delayed our pursuit, it could result in higher losses against well-built enemy's defences.

After the Germans were kicked out of the village of Tur, our units marched through a rather wide patch of thick forest and arrived at a completely dry field that stretched several kilometres in all directions. As the Germans were again out of sight and their ambush had no place to hide, our platoons again formed marching columns. However, the Germans left a nasty surprise for us. Of course it was easier for columns to march on the roads. The first platoon formed the spearhead of our company and started to march along a road south from Malorita to Hotislav, in the new direction of our advance. All of a sudden an explosion sounded in the middle of that platoon. One man had stepped on a mine. The company commander called me to the spot. I already had a reputation of 'mine expert' in the company. We found several more mines that were not so well camouflaged. Apparently, the Germans were planting them in great haste. Men of Dmitri Bulgakov's platoon were most likely looking for a possible German ambush and did not look at the road itself, which caused that tragic incident. We urgently reported the mines to the battalion HQ, made improvised probes from rifle ramrods, and resumed our advance. From that time on, men stopped and looked around and under their feet. We did not come across any more mines, but we had learnt the lesson. Of course, the pace of our advance slowed down even more. The mines were not the only surprise in that open field.

All of a sudden, a large formation of German *Messerschmitt* fighters, with black crosses on their wings and fuselages, appeared in the sky, and started strafing our column. We quickly dispersed and managed to avoid serious losses. Soldiers were firing on the *Messers* chaotically, but unfortunately, it was all in vain. Before that group of German 'carrion-crows' flew away, we heard the roar of engines, and a second wave came of larger German planes, apparently bombers. As an ex-Air Force officer *shtrafnik* told us, those were *Heinkels* or *Junkers* bombers, I do not remember exactly. Soon we clearly saw that some objects started to drop out of the planes and with a frightening speed flew towards the ground. It was my first time under an air raid. But experienced officers and *shtrafniks* immediately knew from the sound that the Germans were dropping bombs along with some other objects that were spinning in the air and producing terrifying sounds. It turned out that the Germans threw all sorts of scrap metal from their planes in order to scare and terrify our troops. The German planes themselves dived with a nasty noise. All that scrap metal that was flying through the air produced unimaginable noises and whistles, which were even scarier than the bombs themselves. The exploding bombs were both fragmentation bombs and high-explosive ones that lifted tall pillars of dirt and smoke into the air. There were also 'frog bombs' among those that fell on us.

As the officers then explained to me, those were cassette bombs that contained multitudes of small bombs that looked like hand grenades. They covered a vast area and then exploded. I don't know why they were dubbed so, probably because their explosion sounded like a duck quacking or a frog croaking. My first impressions from the air raid were that the sky was torn and there was an endless series of some-thing squeezing, screaming and falling through that hole in the sky. All the sounds were mixed up, the noise of diving planes, sirens screaming, some ringing and thunder of explosions. I had only one thought. The bomb that would kill me would be there in a second! There would be one moment of sharp pain my entire body, and that would be it. I felt a disgusting weakness, and it took me a lot of effort to overcome it.

Those air raids delayed us, but nevertheless, we were approaching the village of Hotislav, which was on the Maloryta River. The town of Malorita was on our right and was probably already captured by the armour of the division that was attacking to the right of us. We had to cross two rivers, Ryta and Maloryta, on the way to Hotislav. Those rivers were shallow, as it had been dry weather for over a month. The Germans apparently did not stop to build any defences on those rivers. They only left weak delaying parties behind that opened fire at us and forced us to unfold the marching columns into attacking lines. After a short firefight they withdrew. The German *Messers* again tried to strafe us, but were chased away by our 'falcons' with red stars on their wings. They flew out of the sun and were greeted with a loud "Hurrah!" from our soldiers. The AT-rifle crews fired at the enemy's aircraft more actively. But also in vain, though, as they were probably afraid of hitting our fighters. That was the first time I saw a dogfight in the sky, so close up! The battle was short, as the German pilots immediately flew away after one of their planes was shot down, caught fire, fell to the ground and exploded some distance from us.

It was easy to cross those rivers. One interesting detail was that the river was called MalorYta while the town on its bank was MalorIta! We simply forded them and passed through the village of Hotislav without encountering German resistance. Many villages and farms looked incredibly alike, but they all had one fate. They were either bombed to the ground or burnt down, together with their inhabitants, by German punishment units that took revenge for partisan raids, or just as part of the forced retreat. Some villages only had stoves and chimneys left standing on fireplaces. Hotislav was no exception.

Building on its success, the entire battalion continued to advance. Our company received an order to advance towards the highway, to the north, from the village of Oltush. During the night our company approached the highway between Malorita and Kobrin. There we encountered strong German resistance. Apparently, they left a 'stringer' delaying party on the high embankment above the highway, allowing for setting up stronger defences. In any case, as I remember, in the early morning before the assault, our mortar crews had a chance to demonstrate the preciseness of their fire. Their bombs were landing exactly on the German positions, behind the embankment above the road. It looked like an artillery bombardment before an assault, although it was not so intensive for our taste. The order to assault, and a quick rush to the highway, did not leave the majority of the Germans any time to flee. So we finished them off in a hand-to-hand fight. I will not describe the details of that fight. It was tough, harsh and cruel. The *Nazis* seemed to be shocked by the fury with which our men attacked. I would not be able to describe all the details of hand-to-hand battles, each one of them was different. However, they all had something in common. A *frontovik* female poet, Julia Drunina, who died very young after the war, wrote the following poem about it:

> The one who says that war is not that frightening,
> Knows nothing of the war or fight.
> I saw a hand-to-hand fight one time in waking.
> And a hundred times it haunted me at night!

During the war we were in hand-to-hand fighting many times. That haunted us in our dreams long years after the war.

At that time the German delaying party was destroyed. But immediately after the battle was over, we clearly heard the sound of engines in the silent morning air. We thought that the German armour was about to emerge from the forest, on to the highway, we would then be in a tough situation. However, the noise of engines gradually faded away. Then, we realised how their delaying parties had slipped away from us so easily. They had trucks! I wished we had tanks! But the tanks, of course, had to avoid swampy terrain and were advancing in other areas. Everyone had his own mission and destiny. Our pace of advance was slowing down with every hour, and every kilometre. We went without sleep for three nights. There had been no time for sleep on the last night before the offensive, either. So we were all completely exhausted. We were not merely marching forward, we were assaulting, and often engaging in heavy battles. Our men did not have wings, and there were so many bypasses that they had to make! The kilometres that soldiers walked on foot were sometimes extremely long!

Our *kombat*, all-understanding and all-sensing 'Dad', Arkadi Aleksandrovich, although he himself was mostly driving around in his Willys jeep, realised that our battalion had reached its limit. Men were about to fall asleep and would fail any mission! I do not know if he co-ordinated his decision with the Division commander, but in any case he ordered us to stop the offensive. He gave the battalion at least three hours' rest, while there was no danger of an encounter with the enemy. By that time, and it was already around noon, our companies had walked through a rather wide area of forest. We entered a dry elevated field, from which we had a good view towards our next goal, the village of Radezh. The *kombat* chose that place for the battalion to rest. A German delaying party had found no place to hide, so nothing could prevent us from having such a necessary rest.

You had to see the men in order to appreciate the decision of our caring commander. Everyone was exhausted by the non-stop advance, often under the enemy's fire. We had progressed over the swampy wetlands of the Ukrainian and Belorussian Polessie area. All the men were pinched-looking, with eyes red from sleepless nights. Everyone had just one longing, to drop down, fall asleep for at least a minute, at best an hour. During the previous seventy-two hours, we had not had a single second when we could stop and have a nap, to recover just a bit. Even more so that only sweet memories were left of the dinner that our field kitchens brought up, after capturing the village of Zhirichi. It was obvious that our enlisted *shtrafniks*, and officers too, immediately dropped to the ground and fell asleep when they took in the meaning of the order "rest". The mighty snoring of hundreds of exhausted men sounded in the air. It was extremely difficult to make some of them sleep in shifts, in order to set up guards.

My deputy, who I would prefer to address by his former military rank, Lieutenant Colonel Sergey Ivanovich Petrov, understood very well how hard it was for me to keep up the pace with the men. My leg had not yet fully healed. He understood it well and cared for me, and offered to set up guards himself, while I had a nap. It was a huge relief to have someone else take the responsibilities of a platoon leader off my shoulders, even for a short period. I immediately fell fast asleep, just like all the other men. Petrov barely managed to wake me one and a half hours later. It probably took several minutes for me to wake up. I must have looked pretty shocked! But when I finally woke up, I realised that I had to change guards, as they also needed rest! I was extremely happy to know that my deputy had already taken care of that, too. I was thankful to him for relieving me from the hard task of waking up men for them to take up guard duty. Our supply units had arrived with their kitchen and the ammo carriage. Despite empty stomachs, many men first ran to get more ammo, and only then went to the kitchen. All the officers received the *kombat's* order to explain why 100 grams of *vodka* were not issued at that time. Even those 100 grams of alcohol could aggravate the state of extreme fatigue if taken on an empty stomach. That was why we only received *vodka* immediately before a "forward march!" order.

Our further advance was through Radezh, which turned out to be a small but very attractive village. For some reason it was almost completely intact. Every house in the village had a thick orchard with fruit trees and bushes in full blossom, although it was already well pass mid-summer. A few villagers emerged from the cellars, and treated us to aromatic fruits as we marched through the village. Apparently, something stopped the *Fritzes* from burning down that beautiful village. However, we could not stop there. But of course we wanted to thank the villagers for such a welcome. It seemed that the name of the village, Radezh, came from a word *radost*, i.e. joy or *raduga*, i.e. rainbow. We were again a hurry, in order to deprive the Germans of the possibility of fortifying the western bank of the great Bug River. All the Soviet troops in that sector rushed to the river. It was a much wider, deeper and faster river than the Pripyat' Ryta, Maloryta and the other small rivers and irrigation channels, with their swampy banks, that we had already crossed. In the late afternoon of July 21, we again came under fire of the enemy, between the highway and the railway, in some 3–5 kilometres before the Bug River. We managed to cup those communications later that night, south from Domachevo. Quite soon after that we finally came close to the Bug River. The Brest Fortress, as yet unknown to us, was located there.

In contrast to our expectations the Bug was a rather narrow river, with a slow current. We had to cross it too. An unexpected and, as it seemed to us, sinister silence hung over the river. The enemy was not on our bank of the river. As we were supposed to cross the river at dawn, we had some time for the men to rest. However, some time was spent finding crossing points, and preparing for battle. Our company was mostly armed with PPSh submachine-guns, dubbed *papashas* or 'daddies'. Loading additional cartridges into PPSh ammo drums was quite difficult, especially at night. In order to do so, one had to disassemble the drum, i.e. take off the lid, tighten the ejector spring, without dropping the cartridges out of the drum, and upload additional cartridges by touch. It was not an easy thing to do. As experienced men said, it was the same with soldiers receiving boots with leg wrappings for the first time. The inexperienced men time and again had the roll of leg wrappings slipping out of their hands and unrolling at the worst possible moment. Then the soldier had to start from the very beginning!

During the night we also had to silently find and mark fords across the river. We had to upload our weapons and prepare them for crossing such a large river. It would be hard, especially given the fact that we did not have any means of crossing it. There was no time to make rafts or anything similar. We were amazed, and pleasantly surprised, when an officer from the neighbouring regiment arrived with two men. He told us that he was ordered to fell several trees on the riverbank with TNT, in order to make it easier for us to ford the river. The officer added that he would try to blow up the trees in such a way that the roots of the trees would remain on the bank, while the trees' crowns would fall into the water. In order to keep it secret, he would blow up the trees during an artillery barrage. I do not know if it was our *kombat* who proposed such a plan to the commander of that division, or vice versa, but we doubted that the officer could fell the trees so precisely!

The artillery opened fire at dawn. Our mortar crews also joined the barrage. We had long since forgotten the offensive nickname of 'miss-mortar' that we once had for them. We could clearly see dry wheat fields, and a mud road going into a small forest beyond the river. It seemed to be a familiar native Russian landscape. However, it was already 'abroad' there, beyond the Bug, and that thought did not leave our minds. The visiting combat engineers blew up the trees, but only managed to fulfil their plan in the sector of my platoon. The tree indeed fell as they had promised, its roots on the bank, its crown in the water. We were happy to see that the crown was not taken away by the current. I thought that fortune was again on my side! My swimming skills had not improved at all, after my ice-hole swimming on the Drut' River in Belorussia. When we started crossing the river, the tree made it much easier for us. As it turned out, it covered the deepest part of the river's course with its trunk, and the rest was simple. For those who could not swim it was almost like a bridge. We then gathered all the leg wrappings that we had in our platoon and made one long rope out of them. All the men from our platoon held on to it even those who could swim.

That was the second time the Germans gave up their positions, almost without a fight, despite such a good obstacle as the river. They returned fire quite weakly, mostly from small arms, and again retreated. They were alarmed at the vigour and speed of advance by our infantry, who managed to keep up with the German motorised delaying parties. We concentrated on the western bank of the Bug, and started to prepare our units in the order necessary for battle on solid ground. We again received an order to form company columns on the road, and to advance by parallel routes. We then continued the pursuit of the enemy on roads and in forest clearings. We received an order to pay special attention to scouting and reconnaissance, including the spotting of mines, on the route of our advance.

We were already on Polish territory. The long-expected historic event had come. The western border of the USSR was already behind us! It had been exactly three years since the thirty days of the defence of the Brest fortress. We had had an honourable, but hard mission, to regain the western border of the Soviet Union and liberate long-suffering Belorussia and glorious Brest. The heroism of the defenders of the Brest fortress was only appreciated many years after the war. We spoke a lot about all that while sitting in the trenches on Soviet territory. A clear majority of us had not even thought of ever going abroad. Some *shtrafniks* were participants of the liberation march into Western Belorussia and Western Ukraine in 1939. They were living witnesses of those events and told us a lot of stories, including stories of the hostile attitude of the Polish population. For example, they told us a story of Poles greeting the Red Army with flowers, while some bunch of flowers that they threw at the Red Army soldiers had hand-grenades hidden in them! We did not want to believe such stories but they kept us alert.

As we marched into Poland, our company column was formed in such a way that we could quickly unfold an attacking line. We had a strong 'point' marching in front of us, including several soldiers with probes to detect mines. We had only marched one kilometre when we met an elderly Pole who could speak quite good Russian. He was well disposed towards us, as he smiled and spoke happily. He told us that the Germans had left on trucks immediately the artillery barrage started on the river. It must have been two hours previously. There were no signs of a delaying party or an ambush. Our company commander had briefed us even before we crossed the river. After marching some 3–4 kilometres from the Bug River, we were supposed to turn due north, to reach the Brest – Warsaw highway east from the Polish town of Byala Podlyaska. We had to build a strong blockage on the highway. It was the one and only route of retreat for the four German divisions encircled in Brest. Our battalion and the regiments of the 38th Guards Rifle Division, were given a mission to seal the encirclement of that German force, and to cut their routes of retreat to the west.

We were determined to reach the highway as quickly as possible. So we marched, without respite, on a rather good wooded road through a forest, that grew thicker all the time. All of a sudden a loud explosion sounded in the middle of the second platoon! It sounded like a large-calibre shell. We immediately thought that the Germans had placed a strong delaying party in front of us. Right before my eyes, I saw men from my friend Fedya Usmanov's platoon dropping dead and wounded on the ground. Several men from my platoon also fell in that explosion. I also felt a strong blow to my chest and remained barely standing. Almost immediately weaker explosions started to sound on both sides of the road, where men ran for cover. It looked as if the Germans were firing with small-calibre mortars on a pre-sighted spot. Men were falling on the sides of the road too. Those who ran to help, were also falling down, something unimaginable was happening. It was strange that there was no typical sound of incoming mines, and the shell exploded without a typical 'whisper'. As it turned out, we were all deceived. It was not artillery or mortar barrage, but it seemed that the platoon ran into a minefield of so-called *Spring-Minen*, i.e. jumping mines. I knew of them from my classes in the Academy. I knew them by the name SMI–35. Such a mine was planted into the ground with two almost unnoticeable trigger wires sticking out of the ground. When the mine detonated, it first flew to 1–2 metres height and only then exploded. The mine was stuffed with many hundreds of metallic balls and hit men like shrapnel. So, one such mine planted on the road mowed down almost the entire second platoon. As well as that, on both sides of the road the Germans had planted over two dozen regular anti-personnel mines. Those bastards anticipated the reaction of survivors. They would dive for cover in the forest, where it was all booby-trapped. We mistook the explosions of regular mines for mortar fire.

The strangest thing was that the 'point' had walked on the road with probes, followed by the company commander with his small staff of 5–6 men, then the entire first platoon. None of them stepped on that mine! But the second platoon was not so lucky. If they had not detonated it, then someone from my platoon would have definitely done so. I do not know which supernatural power protected me that time. I did not have any talismans, I did not know any prayers or spells, and was a strong atheist from my childhood, even when I was part of the UMA, the Union of Militant Atheists. I survived, because several minutes before the explosion, I felt discomfort from my SMG. It was hanging on my chest and always hit the same spot on my stomach as I walked. My orderly, Zhenya, noticed several times that I was trying to adjust my SMG, and recommended me to tighten its belt, so I did. The explosion shook the air almost immediately after that. One of the prefabricated metallic balls from the mine struck my SMG so hard, that it left a very large cavity. That was why I was almost knocked down! The entire hitting power of that piece of metal was distributed over the mass of my PPSh. It was clear that if the SMG had remained on the previous spot, I would not have a cavity in the SMG but rather a hole in my chest. I got off with a huge bruise right across my breast. I was lucky in the same way as almost a month previously, when defusing the mine in the forest blockage. I had similar luck on my side when it came to mines and bullets during the entire war. Many were not that lucky. Almost the entire second platoon was dead. Two men from my platoon were killed, while I survived.

What could you do, it was war! Luck is an important factor in any war. It was luck that was not planned or provided by anyone. It had nothing to do with the level of training, experience or skills. It was rather what we called fate or destiny. Fedya Usmanov was severely wounded by that mine. His thorax was pierced right through. Was he lucky or not? He could have been killed just like the others. It took him a long time to recover, but after his recovery in hospital he came back to the battalion. Quite a number of officers who did not want to share the fate of *shtrafniks* did not return to the battalion after recovery from a wound. One could understand their choice. None of us condemned them.

We lost many men at that spot. Most were killed, or died of wounds. The treachery of those *Spring-Minen* was that they exploded at such a height that they mostly hit stomachs. Stomach wounds were lethal in most cases, of course, unless surgery was performed immediately. That was impossible in battle conditions. I saw many sights in the war, just as many others did. That incident was the first time that I saw so many killed and wounded by one mine. It was not even a big bomb. Bodies lay on the ground, some already motionless, others convulsing in agony. The screams and groans of the wounded, and the grunts of the dying, rang out around us. It was fearful. One could not get used to such sights, even for the rest of the war. For me, that was the first huge shock. Perhaps it made my heart less sensitive to the following deaths in the war. We did not believe in paradise after death. If we went into battle, risking our lives, it was not for paradise after death, but for the sake of our country, our Motherland, and its people.

We left a small group of men, mostly lightly wounded, to guard the rest of the wounded. Our company commander reported the losses to battalion HQ over the radio, and informed the HQ where to send medics and vehicles to evacuate the wounded. We hastily buried the dead and also made a small sign with the names of those buried in that mass grave. We had to move on. Our company, which fielded no more than two platoons, moved on, to complete the mission. We came under German fire at sunset.

The firing came from the birch grove that we dubbed 'square grove' for its shape on the map. We were on the western edge of some village. The grove was quite far away and we hoped that we were out of range of German small arms. So we did not care about taking cover, or camouflaging ourselves. However, a heavy German MG opened fire from the grove. A tall *shtrafnik*, who stood next to me beside a barn, slowly fell to the ground. He was mown down by the burst that almost hit me and the others. The bullets went right through his breast. Of course, we did not have any female medical personnel in the penal battalion. Medics were *shtrafniks* appointed in each squad. That meant they had more bandaging material than the others. We bandaged the wounded man, pulled him behind the barn, and then sent him to the gathering station for the wounded. In those days, based on experiences of veteran soldiers, we were for some reason sure that a bullet going right through one's breast was not that dangerous if a person did not die right away or if blood did not spurt from the wound. However, the only case that we had to prove our theory was Fedya Usmanov.

It turned out that the square grove was the place where the Germans had stopped and put up stubborn resistance. Their defensive lines were no longer small delaying parties. Each was a pocket of resistance, be that a small village or a name-less hill, and had to be stormed and destroyed. We also had to repel counterattacks, sometimes three or four times a day. But despite serious losses, our morale was high and vigour was great. It was not due to the large number of political officers in the battalion. I did not see any political officer in our company during those hard days, except for the formidable Major Olenin. Perhaps they visited other companies. Our offensive became much harder and slower. Sufficient to say that we only covered 10–12 kilometres in one day, in hard, exhausting battles. Both our *kombat* and the commander of the neighbouring 110th Regiment would stop night assaults. At least that gave some time for men to rest and eat. Sometimes they even treated us to *vodka*, of which we received more, due to losses. *Vodka* was a real medicine against stress in those extreme physical and psychological situations. Men did not get drunk from such small amounts of alcohol, but it gave us strength, and lifted our spirits a bit.

It was noon on July 25 when we threw the Germans out from their last defensive position between the railway line and the Brest – Warsaw highway. We were ordered to stop and hold ground till the last man. We had to deprive the Germans of the opportunity to escape from the trap in Brest. The highway, blocked by us, looked like the blade of a knife trying to penetrate our defences. The enemy tried their best to break through on that narrow highway blade. They pressed towards our positions with extreme strength, killing, crippling and torturing our men. On the very first day of holding the defences, we felt how desperate were the Germans to get out of that encirclement. Their assaults came, one after another, and the battles intensified immediately.

We had to dig in, utilising all the defensive features of the terrain. That above all was what we needed to do. The special feature of that terrain was that we were in a rather dense forest and visibility was low. The situation was quite tough and dangerous for us. The Germans kept us under constant fire. They fired explosive bullets at us, which we were not used to. The bullets exploded when hitting the trees and one got the impression that someone was firing nearby, even from above, in the crowns of the trees. It was a scary thing when you did not know where the fire was coming from. It could be from the flanks, from the rear or from above you! I immediately recalled stories of Finnish snipers in trees. We had been told a lot about them during our classes in the Academy. I had to do a lot of running from one man to another in my platoon, giving them instructions about digging in. Ex-air force officers, supply officers and even tank officers needed such supervision, as they did not have any experience of the 'queen of the battlefields,' i.e. the infantry.

The enemy attacked, regardless of obstacles and losses. Before night set in, which to us seemed ages, our small task force had to repel as many as five German assaults! That meant that almost every thirty minutes a shower of bullets fell on us. There were uncountable outbursts of shouting and firing. Sometimes drunk *Fritzes* ran at us, and it seemed that there was no end to them! They all ran at our positions. It was a frightening situation, when it seemed impossible to lift one's head from the ground under such heavy automatic fire. We had to fire back in all that hell, aiming carefully, in order to kill the enemy and not let them through. Here and there our men dropped dead on the ground. Many *shtrafniks*, even being seriously wounded and having the right to leave the battlefield, stayed and fought on.

While repelling the third or fourth German attack, I was making a rush from one place to another, when I was knocked down by a hard blow to my left leg that had not yet fully recovered. Well, I thought, that leg got hit again! But when I fell I did not feel any pain. When I looked, I saw a hole in the upper part of my long boot. It seemed strange, a bullet hole was there but my leg was intact. I put my hand into the long boot, to check if there was any blood in it, and pulled out my stainless steel spoon. It was bent and twisted! It turned out that the German bullet had either lost its hitting power, or had perhaps gone through a thin tree, but could only hit and twist my spoon. It was similar to the fragment from the jumping mine that had knocked me down. I was again lucky! Truly, that spoon, just like my SMG, was my talisman. It was a pity that I did not keep the spoon till the end of my war. But souvenirs were the last things on my mind then.

By evening our supply units brought us plenty of ammo, and we all stocked up with it. Most men even stuffed their gas mask bags with ammo and hand grenades, throwing away their gas masks. The night was hectic. Some German armoured cars tried to slip through our defences on the highway, under cover of darkness. But our AT-rifle crews and 45 mm AT-guns of the regiment knocked them out, even in the darkness. I must mention the lucky find of Misha Goldstein's mortar platoon. During their retreat, the Germans left an entire ammo depot with 81mm mines. Their calibre and size fitted our 82mm mortars very well. One just had to adjust the sight due to the different calibre. Goldstein fired those rounds on the highway all night long, putting up strong defensive fire. He assisted our AT-crews very well. In the early morning we saw a large group of mounted men, horse-drawn carriages and artillery on the highway, coming from the German side. They came under strong fire from our artillery and mortars, and the surviving ones turned back.

On the morning of July 26, the German assaults were renewed with the same intensity. In one of those assaults, the Germans threw at us up to two battalions of infantry, supported by 24 tanks and aircraft. Soil was flying through the air, there were explosions of all sorts of bombs and shells, and all merged into one long thunderous rumbling. That time, only two or three German tanks broke through, but that was it. The remainder of the armoured vehicles were stopped by the determination of our *shtrafniks* and the Guards of the Division. They fought with complete selflessness, and their morale remained high. A special feeling happens in a battle, especially if it is hard and intensive. There is some sort of euphoria in the midst of it, when you no longer have fear or fright, and just the joy of battle is left! Yes, however strange it might sound, it was joy, unconscious but quite tangible joy! In such ecstasy a soldier often does not even notice wounds and does not feel the pain from them. I know this from my own experience and the experience of my brothers-in-arms. Everyone fought with bravery and determination, and no one left their positions. I remember that I had an idea of comparing our mission, of not letting the enemy through, with other examples of stoicism of the Red Army in the battles of Moscow and Stalingrad. "Let your foxhole be your personal battle of Moscow and Stalingrad!" I told my subordinate *shtrafniks*. Maybe those words sounded high-flown but I saw that they had their effect. The enemy suffered severe losses, but our losses were also exceptionally high. It was as if the Germans made us suffer for their relatively weak resistance in the previous battles and their relatively low losses.

... In 1985, for the 40th anniversary of Victory, I managed to find brothers-in-arms from our Penal Battalion, and organised a meeting. Among the few attending *shtrafniks* and officers, was General Major Philip Kiselev, who was a Captain that battle on the highway, and the first deputy of the battalion's chief of staff. During his trips in the General's rank he visited the battlefield at Byala Podlyaska. In those days, as he told us, there was a large mass grave of Soviet warriors. I don't know if it still exists today, as there were so many acts of vandalism on the graves of Soviet soldiers in Eastern Europe. He said that he had never seen a grave that had so many names of officers on it. They were mostly names of *shtrafniks* from our battalion. Judging from that grave, one could judge the high price of Victory in general, and of the liberation of Brest in particular ...

The Germans desperately tried to break out from the encirclement for two more days, and only after that did they start to surrender. But both the Guards riflemen and our *shtrafniks* fought to the death. It is only now, that I start to realise how stretched were our physical and psychological strengths in those days. At dusk on the second day we no longer had any fear of being killed. On that day, July 26, the Germans again assaulted from early morning, and closed with us in tight formation. On that day, they no longer marched arrogantly, but kept close to the ground, either being afraid of execution by their own officers, whose threatening voices we could hear, or in the worst degree of desperation. Nevertheless, they managed to close in for a hand-grenade fight. Despite their intensive fire, we were the first to throw grenades at them.

When I emerged from my trench and threw yet another hand-grenade into this creeping mass of Germans, a machine-gunner was killed next to me. I threw myself to the light DP machine-gun that went silent and at the same moment I felt a strong hit on the side of my body. It seemed like an electric shock. As I fell to the ground, I completely lost the feel of my right leg. It was written in my hospital wound certificate that a "penetrating bullet entered the upper third part of the hip, with nerve damage". In simple words, I was hit in the right part of my groin, while one nerve was completely cut. I could no longer control my right leg and no longer sensed it at all.

The German assault was repelled and the surviving Germans crept back. My faithful Zhenya pulled me into a depression in the ground, probably a shell crater. There I found that the bullet had also damaged a large vein, as all my clothes around the wound were soaked in blood, and I could not stop the bleeding. I could not press on that vein as the wound was in a very uncomfortable spot. I could stand on the wounded leg and use it as a point of balance. I did not feel any pain at all, but I could not move it at all, no matter how hard I tried. My orderly pulled me back some 50–60 metres into the rear. I am still very sorry that I cannot remember his last name, as I only called him by first name. He very quickly found a female medic from the Guards regiment. I pressed the wound as hard as I could and managed to stop the bleeding to a certain extent before her arrival.

The medic was pretty young and completely inexperienced. I could see that this battle was her baptism of fire. She grabbed a rubber tourniquet for stopping bleeding, but when she saw that there was no place to apply it, she became completely confused. It was a very difficult place to bandage. The girl was extremely embarrassed when she accidentally touched my genitals, which was completely unavoidable, given the spot in which I was wounded. I even had to shout at her in order to speed up the process, which was equally unpleasant for both of us. My personal bandage package and the bandage that she had were not enough for putting a tight pressing bandage on the spot. I refused to take Zhenya's bandage as he was then not 'insured' against being wounded himself. We had to use my sweaty and salty undershirt for a bandage. When they completed the bandaging, the medic and Zhenya dragged me to the regiment's dressing station which was some 200 metres behind the line of fire. I took a last look at the battlefield, and all of a sudden a thought struck my mind. It was not a battlefield, but rather a forest, completely broken down by that awful battle. Bullets and splinters, like a hurricane of lead, had shattered the trees. The crowns and branches of the trees were hanging limply.

I immediately sent Zhenya to my deputy, Sergey Petrov, who, as I hoped, was still alive, and sent him an order to take over the command. About an hour later, a carriage arrived and I was loaded on to it together with 15 more wounded. There were both *shtrafniks* and the Guards riflemen among the wounded. Next to me sat a *shtrafnik* from my platoon with a terrifying face wound. An explosive bullet hit his nose from the side, making his left eye one huge bloody hole. His courage and patience could be seen in his fists, clenched so tightly that they were as white as snow. His silence also seemed unnatural. Apparently, he concentrated solely on overcoming the unimaginable pain, afraid of opening his mouth in case he let out a scream, or a groan.

The horse was German, a huge artillery horse, which could pull two such carriages. This monster of a horse took us to the regiment's first-aid station and there we received our first-wound certificates, so called front-line cards. They certified that we were wounded in battle. We were taken to the nearest medic battalion, on a truck stuffed full with lying and sitting wounded men. There they put us all in a very full, long barn, on a thick layer of fresh aromatic hay, with a strict warning against smoking. We could all burn! I touched my pockets and realised that I had lost my pipe in that battle. It was a pity, as it had served me faithfully for a long time.

How sweet was the almost forgotten peaceful fragrance that came from our common bed of hay! It was so different from the smell of sweat, gunpowder and blood that saturated us! Before I could see any doctor, in order to show my wound certificate that requested immediate surgery, I fell fast asleep, without feeling pain. But apparently I did not sleep long. Then I was wakened by a nurse. When I saw her, I realised that I had ended up in the same medic battalion that I had been in, after the ill-fated detonation of the mine exactly one month earlier, on June 26. It was Tanya, a nurse from Kalinin, with whom we played guitar and sang Russian romantic songs, to entertain the wounded.

I was happy to realise that I was in the hands of doctors whom I already knew. I immediately hoped that they would also be successful in treating this wound. I hoped I would go back to the Front quickly. They took me for surgery on a stretcher to a small school or something like that. I could hear screaming and groaning coming from the next room. It turned out that it was the surgery room. Loud Russian curses from that room drowned out all the screams. I heard the voice of the doctor saying, "Anaesthetic! Give me more anaesthetic!" Soon the voice went quiet and the stretcher-bearers took away a deceased patient from the room. As Tanya explained to me, the patient had a very serious wound, but for some reason the anaesthetic did not work. The patient died right there on the surgery table either from his wound or from an anaesthetic overdose. As I found out later, he was Petukhov, my *shtrafnik*, and a former pilot from the division that was led by Stalin's son Vasily. Sometimes this Petukhov told a lot of exciting stories about his division commander, and I did not imagine that I would ever meet him.

I was the next one to be taken to the surgery table. I remember that some sticky feeling of fear overwhelmed me. I really did not want to die during surgery, as did my predecessor. I did not want to die there, and not on the battlefield! It was one thing if they wrote, "fell like a hero in battle" on the death certificate, but "died from wounds" was a completely different story. It was similar to the fear that I experienced during my first days at the Front, in defence at Zhlobin, when I suddenly came under German artillery fire on an open spot in the forest. Then it seemed to me that the whistle of each incoming shell was 'my' shell, and that it was going straight for me! After several minutes that seemed an eternity to me, my only wish was for 'my' shell to fly in as quickly as possible, and then everything would be over. I confess that the fear was strong. But the trick in war is not absence of fear, but the ability to overcome it, which I managed to do quite well. I learnt to distinguish the sounds of incoming shells and bullets, and realised that I did not always have to duck for cover. There, in the surgery room, I had a completely different fear, which later vanished by itself. That was to be another page of my front line story, my hospital life page!

CHAPTER 5

Wounded

After the deceased soldier, *shtrafnik* Petukhov, was taken out of the surgery room, my turn came. I hobbled to the surgery table with the help of the nurse. I had to gather all my courage to lie down on the table where a man had just died. It was not a very comfortable feeling, but I tried my best. I was ashamed of showing that I was afraid. It was a bright day; the sun was shining through the windows. The surgeon was female, but I could only see her eyes and high eyebrows, the rest was covered by a mask. Apparently, she was a new person in the battalion. I had not seen her during my previous stay. Several medics in sparkling white dresses, or so it seemed to me after many days of dirt and smoke on the faces of men and officers in combat, undressed me and tied my legs and arms to the table. It was obvious that they did it so that I did not kick during surgery. I did not resist.

One of the nurses in a mask, apparently an elderly one, stood at the head of the table and threw a gauze mask on my face. The other nurses took off the blood-saturated, massive bandage, made out of my undershirt. Quietly, almost whispering, in a good-natured way, they cursed the person who did it. I recalled the young and inexperienced female medic with a feeling of gratitude, as she had managed to stop the bleeding! The nurse started to pour ether on my mask, while the surgeon told me with a nice calm voice, "we are giving you anaesthetic. You will fall asleep and will not feel the pain. So be calm, relax, and start counting one, two, three and so on". As if some demon possessed me at that moment, I answered, "I am not counting. Just do it!" Gradually, with every breath that I took, the voices of the nurses grew distant. The nurse at the head of the table asked me something, but I was too lazy to answer and I felt the surgeon start to cut my flesh. There was no pain at all, as if she was cutting my trousers, not my skin. That was it. Almost immediately I fell into deep black water. The world around me vanished.

I woke up in the post-surgery room from someone slapping my face and the familiar voice of Tanya saying, "Wake up! wake up! It's all over". The very first thing that I asked about was my behaviour during the surgery. How did I behave and did I curse? I would have been extremely ashamed if I unconsciously did the same as my predecessor, and I was glad to hear Tanya's answer, "Everything went well. You were absolutely calm and did not distract the surgeon at all". I heaved a sigh of relief that I had not embarrassed myself in front of all those women. Due to the continuing effect of the anaesthetic, or from the extreme fatigue of several days of continuous fighting, I fell deeply asleep again. I slept for the rest of the day, all through the night, and finally woke up only for lunch the next day. I was so soundly asleep that I did not notice the changes of bandages and inspections of my wound.

The unusual feeling of an uncontrollable leg still bothered me, but all my worries were dispelled by my doctor, who had treated my leg before. "Come on, it is just one small nerve that is damaged! It will grow together, you will be alright." The doctor added that I should thank my lucky stars that the bullet missed a large artery by several millimetres. If that artery had been hit, I would not have lived to get to the regiment's first-aid station, losing all my blood. If the bullet had hit me several millimetres in the opposite direction, then the nerve, that was only partially damaged, would have been completely cut, and I would have never again been able to control my leg. That would have been the end, I would have been crippled for life! However, fate decided to spare me. "So you are lucky again, Senior!" That was their nickname for Senior Lieutenants, the surgeon told me. That was the third time of my great good luck, not counting the spoon twisted by the bullet. My lucky cases seemed to support the theory that a thing that happens once is a mere chance, the thing that happens twice is a coincidence, but if it happens three times, it is a regularity. Many things seemed to be a regularity in the war, but even more things seemed to be absolutely random.

It turned out that they did not extract the bullet during surgery. It travelled around my pelvic bones in a tricky way and they failed to find it. Also, they did not have an x-ray machine. The bullet let me know about its existence one year later. I felt it under the skin of my buttock. It made it uncomfortable to sit and to lie on my back. It was cut out soon after the end of war, in a completely different hospital.

I was not allowed to stand up during the first two days after surgery. On the third day we, a large group of heavily wounded men, were evacuated to the rear, into an evacuation hospital. The medical battalion needed more space for the new wounded coming in. Then they would move closer to the front line of the division that had now advanced further west. Judging from the large numbers of wounded coming into the battalion, the battles were hard. From stories told by wounded soldiers, we had some idea of the course of the battle against the breaking out German forces. The 38th Guards Rifle Division, together with our Penal Battalion, securely sealed and held the encirclement perimeter. By noon of July 27, our troops established contact with the Soviet troops who had bypassed Brest from the north. The enemy was straining its remaining strength in order to break out of the trap. By dawn of July 28, parts of the German forces were taken prisoner in Brest. But some German units still tried to break out. Eventually, by the morning of July 29, our troops caught those demoralised and defeated units in difficult forest terrain and completely destroyed them. They reached the area of Byala Podlyaska. So the battle of our Penal Battalion, attached to the 38th Lozov Guards Rifle Division, was finished during the days I spent in the medic battalion. Moscow saluted the glorious troops of the 1st Belorussian Front who liberated Brest, with twenty salvos from 224 guns! It was good to realise that our blood had not been shed in vain.

As we learnt later, all the participants of those battles received written thanks from the Commander-in-Chief, Stalin. We, the personnel of a Penal Battalion, received those gratitude certificates for the first time. One can only guess how important were those standard printed letters with the portrait of our Commander-in-Chief, for boosting the morale of our men, and for the positive feelings that they generated!

The change of bandages became my daily routine in the hospital. Two days later I was strongly recommended, not only to stand up, but also to move as much as possible. However, I had to use a special breech-band made of bandage that was set under the foot of my uncontrollable leg. After some time, I replaced the bandage with some canvas belt and the entire structure became more secure. I did not feel any pain. My leg remained nerveless and uncontrollable, but with the help of the 'belt drive' that I invented, I learnt to walk quite securely, although not as quickly as I wanted to. The part of the hospital reserved for us, as recovering officers, was located in a large room with bunk-beds on two levels. Of course, I, 'a man without a leg', was put into the first level, while above me there was a handsome Senior Lieutenant Nikolai. He was the same age as me. His arm was covered with *gyps* as a bullet crushed his bones. We got acquainted by chance, but became friends very quickly. We had a lot in common in our experiences and views. That was how it happened in the war. A short meeting, a strong friendship, and you had memories of it for the rest of your life. Our nurse was a Tartar girl Aza, a well-educated and knowledgeable person. It was interesting to talk to her, and soon relations between her and Nikolai grew into something more than friendship. I asked Aza to find me some books to read, as I had plenty of time, and I was missing the enjoyment of good reading. I was extremely glad to find out that the hospital had a decent library. So my good relations with Aza were also quite useful for me.

Two weeks later the hospital was supposed to move closer to the front line as our troops had advanced. But many of us had to be evacuated to the far rear for long-term treatment. That would have meant that we would never return to our own units and perhaps be sent to other Fronts. I have already mentioned that my romantic attitude and the ambition of a young person made me proud of leading senior officers, although they were temporarily deprived of their ranks. I did not want to lose that unusual status at all. Nikolai also wanted to go back to his unit after leaving the hospital. We even had a conversation with an elderly Major, a chief of staff from a Guards Rifle Regiment. He advised both of us to go to his unit as company commanders, or staff officers. But we did not give in. His offer did not look attractive to me, because the office of platoon leader in a penal battalion was anyway equivalent to the office of company commander in a regular rifle unit. Even my officer rank was Captain. In addition to that, our monthly wage was, just as in Guards units, 100 roubles higher than in regular units. That was why we jokingly called our penal battalion 'almost a Guards unit'. If in a regular and even a Guards unit, one day at the front was counted as three days of regular service, one day at the front, in a penal battalion, was equivalent to six!

Therefore, in order to avoid evacuation, we decided to escape from the hospital and go into some hospital closer to the front line, to complete our recovery. We knew very well that without wound certificates, i.e. the front line wound cards, it would be quite hard to explain our arrival at another hospital, so we decided to steal them. We did not want to frame Aza in the affair, and asked her just to leave the room with the documents in it, for a while. Then we would commit our 'crime' and flee from the hospital. With all the noise and mess of evacuation of the hospital to another place, we took our wound cards, packed our small belongings and left. It was probably funny to see two young Lieutenants, one with his arm in *gyps*, and the other moving his leg with a strange belt gear made of a canvas waist-belt. We slowly sneaked away from the hospital as it was being loaded on trucks. We managed to walk about two kilometres unnoticed, and reached a road crossing where there was an extremely cute female traffic controller. We talked her into stopping a truck going to the Front. We quickly but clumsily climbed into the truck, and drove away from our hospital. We had spent more than two weeks there.

After travelling in that way with varied success, sometimes on foot, three days later we ran into a dressing station of an artillery unit close to the Front and asked them to change the bandages, as I felt some itching under it. The medics decided to leave the *gyps* on Nikolai's arm untouched. A relatively young medic Captain with a moustache took us into a tent with a Red Cross on it. When he unfolded the bandage, I was terrified at the sight of fat white worms swarming in my wound, each of them at least two centimetres long. Apparently I looked extremely scared and the doctor immediately started to calm me down. "Don't worry, Lieutenant, it is good that there are worms in your wound, they have been cleaning your wound for three days and removing the puss. There is no danger." He disinfected my wound, bandaged it again, and then let us go, giving us directions to the nearest medic battalion. It was quite close to the front line. I was really amazed to see that it was my old medic battalion! An unbelievable coincidence and luck again! Nikolai passed through some other medic battalion on his way to the hospital, but we were both welcomed. At first they thought that I had received yet another wound, but when we told about our escape from the hospital and our motives for this, the doctors understood us.

All that happened some time around August 15. On August 18, the Day of the Air Force, we were again evacuated to the nearest hospital. Men were issued the 100 grams of *vodka* not only during offensive operations, but also on holidays. As that was a holiday, we had lunch with 100 grams of *vodka* before our departure, although we had nothing to do with the Air Force! Our trip was short. In a strange chain of coincidences, we were brought to the same hospital from which we had escaped! The hospital was in a small Polish town at Byala Podlyaska and was receiving wounded in that new place. Nikolai immediately ran to look for Aza. As it was just lunchtime, we were again offered food and alcohol. Of course, we did not object. Before we managed to catch our breath, we were urgently taken to the chief of the hospital. He was a short and slim Lieutenant Colonel. He looked as if his body was dried, and his narrow medic shoulder-boards looked quite wide on his shoulders. However, he possessed an amazingly loud bass voice, which did not fit his small stature. He yelled at us so much! It seemed that the room was shivering and vibrating, as if during artillery bombardment or an air raid.

The Lieutenant Colonel called us deserters, and threatened to send us to a penal battalion as he had already reported to the Special department about our escape, and a nurse was already severely punished for helping us to escape. In order to make his speech clearer, the Lieutenant Colonel added a fair amount of obscene Russian curses into his speech. But for some reason the whole situation seemed more funny than scary to me, probably because the double ration of *vodka* had something to do with it. I calmly replied to him that I was used to penal battalion life, and deserters normally travelled away from the front line, not towards it! I added that the nurse had nothing to do with our escape, as we simply stole our papers during the muddle and rush of the hospital's evacuation. Apparently, despite his deafening bass, the Lieutenant Colonel had a good heart. He calmed down quite quickly but strictly warned us that if we ever wanted to repeat our 'heroic escape', we should first talk to him and he would arrange the matter legally.

Thank God for that! We felt sorry for Aza. She was not angry with us for getting her into this episode, her joy from meeting Nikolai was so great that I thought that the story had a happy end.

I thought that my new doctor was rather cute. She was a female Captain, about thirty years old and paid too much attention to me. At first I was flattered, and I recalled the female Captain who had served in our regiment in Ufa, in the South Ural military district. Literally all officers of the regiment were in love with her and tried to find any excuse in order to see her. I could understand them. Captain of Medical Corps Rodina, that was her last name, was an amazingly slim, bright brunette of amazing beauty, with large brown eyes and beautiful rich hair under a *pilotka* that fitted her very well. We sang the song about the Motherland which had a line saying, "We love our Motherland like a bride", much more often than the other songs. However, no one had a chance with her. One of the regimental commander's deputies was her husband, Major Rodin. He was a tall and handsome *frontovik* with many decorations. Here, in this hospital, this interest and attention of the medic Captain started to stress me.

Finally, one day she appointed a date for me in the evening "just to have a talk". The offer seemed quite unattractive to me, either because she was ten years my senior, or because my love was so strong for my girlfriend Rita, who I had met in the regiment in Ufa. I seemed to successfully simulate diarrhoea and did not go to that date. I did not condemn her, moral standards were quite different in the war, and the 'call of flesh' was different with every person. Of course, the attitude of the female Captain immediately changed after that, and I was transferred to another doctor, a man. I was quite happy with that. Even more so that I told all my friends in the battalion, as well as Nikolai and Aza, that I was married, showing them a picture of my girlfriend Rita. I treasured this small faded photo a lot, and was sure that our romance would lead us to marriage, unless one of us got killed.

For some reason they again started to pick up officers for sending back to the rear. We were ready to go to discuss it with the chief of the hospital, remembering his words. Our caring Aza found us just before we were ready to go. She informed us that the chief of the hospital had transferred us to the team of recovering officers. That would mean that we were staying at the front line hospital. We knew that the Lieutenant Colonel would prevent us from repeating the same trick of escaping. We were indeed recovering. Those days we were still very young, and wounds, both physical and psychological, heal better when you are young. We had a lot of such wounds in our souls, due to the deaths of our comrades. They finally took the plaster from Nikolai's arm, although he still carried it on a breech-band and he was already attending physical exercises. I gradually started to feel the recovery of the nerve of my leg. Although I could not yet get rid of the breech-band, I also started physical exercises under the supervision of my doctor.

The next day we were loaded on trucks and went to the Polish town of Kalushin, which was liberated as early as August 1. I do not remember how far it was from Warsaw, but some of the forward units of the Front had already crossed the Vistula south of the Polish capital. We were accommodated in a well-preserved building, on the second floor, in small rooms for 5–6 persons. We were not yet used to such luxury! A wounded Captain from our penal battalion soon arrived in our officer room, but he did not return to the battalion after recovering from his wound. He told me great news. The Commander of the 70th Army rewarded the troops who took part in the destruction of German units in Brest and I was awarded the Order of the Patriotic War. I know that you will understand my joy. When a local photographer, a weak-looking guy with spectacles, walked around our rooms, we all took up his invitations to take pictures of ourselves with decorations. The others talked me into taking a picture with two orders, my own Order of the Red Star and someone else's Order of the Patriotic War 2nd Class. I did not think long and agreed to this, and was very excited to receive rather high quality pictures of an officer with two battle orders. I could not hold back, and wrote letters to my mother and sister in the Far East, and to my beloved girlfriend, whom I had passed off as my wife. It seemed that her field kitchen was nearby, as her letters arrived quickly. That photo session with someone else's order put me in a very uncomfortable situation quite soon, and it taught me a good lesson for the future.

In the meantime, my leg was again becoming obedient to my commands. The upper layer of the side muscle of the entire right thigh, I don't know anatomy, and do not know the correct name, remained completely insensitive. The sensation was as if a large patch of tarpaulin was glued over my skin. The sensitivity of my muscle under this insensitive layer was quite high, even a small press on the muscle caused a rather strong pain the lower layers of the muscle. I started to get used to this inconvenience quite quickly. Following the doctor's advice, I massaged the muscle for a long time, quite roughly, every day, taking the pain. I had to continue that massage for ten more years after the war! I like *banya*, a Russian steam bath, and massaged the uncontrollable part of my leg until I had bruises. As a result, the upper layer of the muscles was fully recovered, even though it took ten years.

I was about to be discharged from the hospital. My friendship with Nikolai grew during that time, based on mutual respect. Nikolai was discharged from the hospital a bit earlier than I was, so we exchanged our field post numbers, but we did not manage to keep in correspondence. I am afraid that he was killed quite soon after. A war is always war, and death is common. I am still very sorry that our friendship was so short, although I have remembered it for the rest of my life.

We, a large group of officers, were discharged from the hospital on September 1. In my wound certificate it stated, "discharged to his unit with sanatorium treatment for 17 days". I guess I will never be able to understand why they wrote 17, not 15, and not 20. There are so many things in medical science incomprehensible to simple men, and this was apparently one of them. Also, what did they mean by "sanatorium treatment"? Where and when was I supposed to go to a sanatorium? What sort of sanatorium could be there at the front? I did not understand that at all then. Talking of our arrival at our own unit, I was still amazed how we managed to find our battalion in that huge mass of troops. It would have been easy if we had been given a point on the map! But finding a penal battalion straight from the hospital, while the battalion could have already been transferred to another army or reattached to another division?

Of course, we had maps with us in the hospital, but during the period of my treatment, the battalion, just as in our case, had long left the piece of map that we had. We could only rely on the officers of the road traffic department who were setting up traffic to military units on the large highways. They had information about routes and locations of some units. We were also hoping to find the road signs that were placed on road crossings and forks. Those signs, made from plywood or wood boards, openly showed the direction of movement for "Field Post #07380", or "Osipov's household", that was the nickname for our penal battalion. Incidentally, some humorous *shtrafnik* interpreted the acronym "8 DPB 1 BF" not as "8th Detached Penal Battalion, 1st Belorussian Front" but as "8th Distinguished Piano Band of the 1st Belorussian Philharmonic". Quite nice!

We hitch-hiked on cars and trucks to the front, although the drivers were quite reluctant to take passengers. So slowly, but steadily, we made our way to the front. Three men from our battalion, I and two former *shtrafniks*, although without shoulder-boards, decided to travel to the front together. At around three o'clock in the afternoon we reached a small Polish town with a large church. We called all Catholic churches of Poland just churches. We decided to have a stop and lunch somewhere. We walked into a house that looked quite rich to us. It had a nice fence next to the church, and asked the owner to give us some food, telling him that we would also give him our dry tack that had been issued to us in the hospital. Our hopes were in vain. *"Niec nema! Wsistko German zabrav"!* "I have nothing! The Germans took everything"! That was the standard answer from this Pole, and then from almost all other Poles, for any of our requests. It was a huge contrast from our Soviet Belorussians and Ukrainians, who had been indeed robbed by the Germans. Later we realised that if we offered some money or goods for exchange, they would never say "the Germans took everything". In fact, they had both lard, goose and *bimber*. *Bimber* was the Polish moonshine, brewed on the well-known Carbide Calcium. It was really awful! I guess they used Carbide not in order to neutralise the smell of oils, but rather to replace the missing alcohol percentage with its stinging taste. Our stomachs were still strong in those days, but we had horrible headaches after that moonshine.

However, we got to know all those details much later, but on that day the cunning Pole found a nice way to get rid of us. He sent us to the Polish priest who lived just across the street. The Pole said that the Germans had not taken anything from the priest and, he was rich and would welcome the Soviets. We got curious and decided to go there just to see a real Polish priest. We walked to the gate and pulled the chain with a ring, as there was no bell button. A doorbell rang on the other side of the fence, and a small window opened in the gate. The face of a red-haired, round-faced young Polish girl appeared in the window and she looked at us with curiosity. When she realised that we wanted to see the priest, she rushed from the 'gun-port' as fast as her feet could carry her, forgetting to close it. Thus, we had a chance to see the clean yard of the priest's house, with some houses and barns around the church. We managed to see several other chubby and young Polish girls in the yard, who were also curious to see who was visiting them. Several minutes later the same girl came back, opened the gate and invited us in, *"Proshu, panove Oficery"* i.e. welcome, Officers.

She took us to one of the houses, which was the well-built dwelling of the priest. The latter welcomed us with a wide smile and with a broad gesture invited us into the house. "Please come in, sirs of the Red Army". We were surprised at how well he could speak Russian, and were happy that we would not have to look for words to explain ourselves. The priest looked smart, smiled a lot, his eyes were calm and full of wisdom. The priest took us into a modestly but nicely furnished room, apparently a dining room, and sat us on the sofa. He sat down in an armchair and a conversation began. He was an interesting conversation partner, citing *Matters of Leninism* by Stalin, *Short Course of VKP (b) History* and referring to Marx in many matters. Quite a priest! He seemed much more competent in the works of Lenin and Stalin than we were, although we were also quite trained in those matters. From his words we could understand that the Polish people were thankful to us for liberation. He liked the Soviet State and the Red Army, but he would hate to see *kolkhozes* in Poland! We could never understand why they hated *kolkhozes* so much, as we thought that this was the most rational form of agriculture. We knew very well that we could not have lasted in that war if we had no *kolkhozes* in the USSR. It was much later that we got to know that *Nazi* propaganda slandered the USSR for a long time in the most intricate manner, trying to make Polish people hate both our country, and the Soviet people in general.

While we were discussing matters of politics, the girls came and went in and out of the room, one by one. There were at least ten of them, serving at the table, and when the hospitable priest invited us for dinner, we were simply dumbfounded. We had never in our lives seen so many dishes, snacks and wines, served especially for us. Of course, we feasted as much as we could. Wine was a quite unusual thing for us, and I tried *cognac* for the first time, but I did not like it! We learnt the taste of genuine Polish *vodka* from Wyborowa and Monopolka, and many dishes we also got to taste for the first time. The neighbouring Pole was not mistaken. In that place the Germans really did not take anything, and perhaps added something.

The conversation and the dinner lasted almost till the fall of darkness. As politely as we could, we thanked the priest for his hospitality, excellent dinner and an interesting discussion. We told him that we would remember that night for a long time. Indeed, I still remember the meeting and the dinner very well! We left the house, escorted by the priest and all the girls, who followed us at a distance. We said goodbye, and bowed to the girls, without understanding why there was not a single male servant in the priest's house. We went back to the house of the first Pole who had sent us in the right direction, in order to thank him for his good advice. Also, after all the excellent wine that we had, we wanted to talk to that Pole, too, and to stay in his place overnight as it was already dark. One of the first questions for the Pole was about the dozen girls serving the priest. Our new host asked, "Don't you know why?" and told us an interesting joke.

When God created Earth and human beings, he also created a priest, and as a priest was supposed to be God's representative on the Earth, God forbade him from marrying. God was also merciful. He knew that a priest was just a mortal human being and allowed him to date a woman one day per year. Either God forgot to tell the priest on exactly what day he could date, or the priest forgot it, but in order not to miss that day, the priest would go dating every day. Anyway, we saw that the Pole had been around and was a happy guy. He made us understand that he was not such a pious Catholic, apparently, just like many other Poles. We stayed overnight at his place, ate our dry tack for breakfast and drank *kava*, i.e. coffe, that the Pole gave us. We gave him a can of US-made cheese, which had a strong smell and we did not feel like eating after the party the night before.

After that we continued our journey. Strangely enough, we found our penal battalion rather easily, although we were a bit puzzled by the signs, "Osipov-Baturin household". We thought that there was some other unit under some unknown Baturin next to us. But it turned out that our *kombat* Colonel Osipov had left our battalion, and was promoted to either be directly the commander of a rifle division, or a deputy division commander. Quite a great promotion! From the office of battalion commander, even an independent penal battalion, he went directly to divisional commander! However, we all knew that he was promoted to Colonel while leading our battalion and he had rights of a division commander. We were happy for our commander, and we felt sorry that he had left the battalion. Our battalion chief of staff, Vasily Lozovoi, also got promoted to a chief of staff of a brigade. Fillip Kiselev, officer of the same age as me, and also my good friend, took over his office. In general, as I have already mentioned, our unit commanders had rights, and the possibility, of getting a rank one grade over the regular units. So a platoon leader was a Captain, company commander was a Major, and deputy battalion commander was a Lieutenant Colonel. That was the special feature of a penal battalion and its hierarchy.

I repeat again that we were both happy for our 'Dad' being promoted but were also sorry that this caring, smart and honest commander left us. Lieutenant Colonel Baturin was appointed battalion commander instead of him. He was a political officer himself and served the whole war as a political officer somewhere deep in the rear. When he was transferred to the office of line officers, he only had an anniversary medal, "20 Years of the Red Army". He was a not very attractive man about fifty years old, short and chubby. His belly was so big that it always entered a room first, before its owner. He looked very much like Ivan Ivanovich Byvalov, a character from the *Volga-Volga* movie so excellently played by the famous Soviet comedy actor Igor Il'inski. As it soon turned out, Baturin was not a comedy actor at all, while his qualities of a commander and attitude towards *shtrafniks* only surfaced later. We had more than nine months of war still in front of us.

On the very first day of our arrival at the battalion, when I was turning in papers to the HQ, I learned that I was indeed awarded, but not with an order, but just with a Medal for Bravery. I have already mentioned that for us, officers, it was appreciated as high as an Order of Glory for enlisted men and NCOs. Of course, I was happy and proud, but at the same time I was tortured by my conscience for taking a picture in the hospital with someone else's Order of Patriotic War and then having sent those pictures to all my relatives. What a shame! The new *kombat* Baturin, I do not remember his first name and *patronymic*, handed me the Medal. He did it in a very casual way, not caring for ceremony as Osipov would have done. He asked me about which decorations I already had and somehow grinned when I looked at his only medal which he had received not for merits in battle, but merely on the 20th anniversary of the Red Army. His handshake was cold, weak, and indifferent and left a bad impression. The first impression almost always remains for a long time. It is almost always like that. If your previous superior was good, the new one is always met with some doubt. How would this new boss behave, would he be soft or hard, would he be just or not, would he care for his subordinates, or only for his own ambition and career? We had answers to those questions very soon.

So, together with pride for the "Bravery" medal, worry also came. Would I manage to earn any decoration at all in future battles, and even more so, would it be that very Order that I needed so badly? I decided to be silent about it, even to my friend Fillip Kiselev, with whom I had very good relations. I did not tell anyone about that ill-fated photo of "an officer with two battle orders". I could not hold back, and wrote to my girlfriend and my family about my award with the Medal for Bravery. But I did not write a single word about my embarrassment with the Order.

Our battalion was stationed somewhere in the area of Minsk-Mazovecki. It was close to the Vistula, south of Warsaw, if I am not mistaken. I only have the name of the place in my memory. I can only remember that there was a *Ludowe Woisko Polsko* or Polish Army unit stationed next to us. Of course, as we were neighbours, we got to know the Polish soldiers, the *zolniers*. For all we knew we could go into battle together, and it was always good to know the people with whom you might go into battle. Just as we had expected, most of them were Russians, sometimes even without Polish names. Others had Polish names but had lived in Russia their entire life. They had been formed into the Polish Army in Russia, anyway! Their headgear, traditional four-cornered Polish hats, was quite unusual to us. They were *visor* hats with a square top, not round, as in the Red Army. They saluted each other not with the entire palm of their hand but with index and middle finger together. We were surprised by many things. For example, they had morning prayers and Sunday masses. We heard a lot of rumours and jokes about that. For example, that all priests in the Polish Army were Communists and ex-political officers of the Red Army, and if they refused to participate in the religious services, they were threatened with being sent to our penal battalion. I also recalled the Polish priest who proved God's existence to us, and the Pole who told us the joke about God, the priest, and women.

It was nice to have this 'Polish' unit as our neighbours because they often arranged dancing nights. They also had a lot of female soldiers, so we could always find partners for dances there. They danced mostly polonaise, Cracovienne, mazurka and other traditional genuine Polish dances, among which I heard a name that sounded almost vulgar to a Russian ear, the Kuevyak. It sounded almost like a 'penis' dance in Russian! Quite a lot of men were not so interested in dancing, but were attracted to those evenings by the presence of girls in Polish uniforms. The Polish officers tried strictly to prevent contacts between our officers and girls from their unit, although they often failed to do so.

Our Polish neighbours were receiving a lot of replacements from the newly liberated *gmina* and *voevodstvo* areas of Poland. They were training the newly arrived *zolniers*. We were also forming a company and some independent platoons from new replacements, which were not as numerous as before. We also had training sessions, mostly for the *shtrafniks* who had arrived from the branches of service other than the infantry and had no infantry experience. The good part was that most *shtrafniks* themselves had huge battle experience. So we did not have to train them and they themselves served as instructors. They did this eagerly, with enthusiasm, each one of them had their own methods and sometimes they cursed the new *shtrafniks* or even hit them from time to time.

Having again become used to life in the battalion after the long break, I was bitterly shocked by news of the deaths of many fellow-officers, my deputy *shtrafniks* and several squad leaders. I also felt sorry that many had not yet returned from the hospitals. As I was told, my great squad leader Puzyrei had also been killed. I still clearly see his image in front of me, sixty years after the war. He was slim and tight, with thin lips and a sharp look, always ready to act. Of course, I also wanted to know if there was any news about Geft, who went missing on the very first day of the offensive. I was so annoyed to hear that he reappeared immediately after the battalion disengaged in the area of Kalushin. He appeared with a wound certificate. It turned out that his wound certificate was issued by a hospital from the part of the front where he had served before joining our penal battalion. The certificate, of which I saw a copy in the file, stated that Geft was wounded in his ear-lobe. It was signed by Medical Major Epstein. I remembered the last name very well. I do not know if I am right, but I think that the Medical Major knew Geft and helped him to sneak out of the penal battalion. But what can one do, the certificate about a wound was there, and Geft, just like all wounded *shtrafniks*, was released and rehabilitated. If my guess about him bribing the Medical Major is correct, then let it be a burden for his conscience, just like all the previous things that he had done to those female soldiers.

I was very well received in the battalion. The officers celebrated both my return and my medal. Company Commander Ivan Matvienko, who had recently received the Order of Suvorov 3rd Class from our previous *kombat*, was for some reason again taking care of the formation of the company. Officers who arrived to replace Matvienko were staying in reserve of the battalion. Probably I was biased, but I thought that Baturin was plagued by the presence of the prestigious decoration on the breast of my company commander. Well, maybe I was wrong! Matvienko insisted that I would again join his company, and I gladly agreed.

I was introduced to some of the new officers of the battalion. The MG platoon leader, Senior Lieutenant George Sergeev, was especially noticeable among the new officers, due to his extremely awkward look and silent character. He turned out to be a brave and intelligent officer, who had already seen a lot at the front, judging by a huge scar on his face that covered his entire cheek. At that time, our MG crews received the new heavy Goryunov MGs. They were almost half the weight of the previous Maxim MGs, just 40 kilograms instead of 70 kilograms! But their ammo belt was the same, with 250 rounds. A platoon leader replaced Fyodor Usmanov who was still recovering in hospital, but the company commander was sure that he would soon be back. The new leader was Junior Lieutenant Ivan Karasev, a tall and physically strong officer, with an amazingly calm character. It seemed that Mayakovski wrote about a person of his kind, "I can deal with two enemies with pleasure, and if you get me angry, with three!"

To be brief, our battalion was forming quite energetically under the supervision of our new battalion commander and his staff. As replacements were arriving quite slowly, we formed first of all a single rifle company, but not all rifle companies at the same time, as we had done before. That one company received MG, mortar and AT-rifle platoons, as only one company of the battalion was to go into battle at a time. Of course, the staff of the battalion always had a signals platoon at the ready. That platoon was to provide for stable communications between the battalion staff and the company in battle at any time. All day long, from early morning, we carried out company training. After lunch we received the new replacements, studied their sentences, and found them a place in our platoons. Of course, there was no talk of "17 days of sanatorium treatment"! Our Captain of Medical Corps, Stepan Buzun sent his medic, Lieutenant of Medical Corps Ivan Demenkov, who bandaged my not fully healed wounds. He also massaged my leg, and Buzun showed me the technique of that massage, so that I could recover the sensitivity of my leg for myself.

We got to know that the Warsaw uprising had started. Even we inexperienced commanders felt sorry for the bad timing of the uprising. Neither our troops could help them, nor could they help us. Troops of our 1st Belorussian Front had fought their way through 250 kilometres of German defences in complicated terrain, with many natural obstacles, and our supply units fell hopelessly behind. Even we, who were not in battle, felt the shortages of supply. Of course, the artillery had almost entirely spent all the ammo allotted before the beginning of Operation Bagration, while the men spent both their ammo and their physical strength. The bulk of the tanks and other equipment required repairs. As we got to know, the uprising started as early as August 1, on the signal of the émigré Polish government in London. That was when we were still mopping up the area of Brest in the 70th Army. Meanwhile, the main forces of the Army captured Byala Podlyaska, and fought in the area of Sedlec, which was almost 100 kilometres from Warsaw. Although the forward forces of the Front had already captured the Magnushev bridgehead at the Vistula, south of Warsaw we had not enough forces to continue the assaults. Meanwhile, the enemy's resistance stiffened, and they managed to deliver strong flanking blows at other approaches to the Vistula. However, a lot of effort was later spent in condemning the Soviet leadership, and personally the Commander-in-Chief Stalin, for his 'deliberate' unwillingness to assist the Polish fighters.

From our village we could clearly see on September 10 or 11, a huge task force of US bombers, 'Flying Fortresses', appeared over Warsaw. There were 80 bombers with fighter escort. It was a strange sight to see how they started to drop supplies to the Poles fighting in Warsaw. In order to avoid the German flak fire, they were flying at over 4.5 kilometres altitude! Of course, when the supplies were dropped from such altitude, they spread out over a wide area and fell outside the areas controlled by the Poles. Most of the cargo fell into the waters of the Vistula, or on the German side. Nevertheless, German flak fire managed to shoot down two aeroplanes from the task force and the 'Fortresses' never reappeared in the sky over Warsaw. Then, from September 13, following a late request from the leaders of the Polish resistance who finally established communications with the staff of Marshal Rokossovski, our army started to supply the Poles. They dropped supplies from low altitudes. Those missions were flown mostly by *kukuruznik* planes, as we dubbed Po–2 light night-bombers.

Completing the description of events that happened in our experience at that complicated time, I should say that our formation and training were very intensive. The Company commander took another officer, Senior Lieutenant Davletov, into our company. He assisted me in knitting the platoon together, and set up training sessions on necessary elements of battle training. After some time, the company commander transferred me to reserve, apparently taking into consideration my recent wound and the necessity of "sanatorium treatment". So Davletov took over the platoon completely. He was a nice guy, with a good personality, and he replaced the absent Fedor Usmanov. They were much alike and they were both from the Urals. One from Bashkiria, the other was from Tatarstan. They both had a good sense of humour, and good but tough personalities. Davletov was a dark-complexioned person with high cheeks, a little bit stooping, and thus always looked like a person ready for immediate action. Fedor Usmanov came back to the battalion soon after that, and we then had the 'two Tatars' in our company, as they called themselves.

Nevertheless, we had several days of relaxation during that period, when a mobile movie theatre came and we watched humorous comedies, such as *Volga-Volga*, *Circus*, *Happy Guys*, as well as movies about the famous Red generals of the Civil War. And we had brief movies about our favourite heroes in the evenings. In those brief movies Komdiv Chapaev[1], for example, with phrases like, "You can't get me", was shown swimming over the river and leading his division into battle during the Second World War. Nikolai Schors[2] with his Bogun regiment, was also shown, destroying *Nazis*. While the famous character from the three-part movie about Maxim, who was played by Boris Chirkov, also exhibited 'miracles of hero-ism' in battles against *Fritzes*. Even *The Good Soldier Schweik*, played by Boris Tenin, was skilfully cheating German generals! Those movie evenings boosted morale and cheered up our men. The only thing that we missed was that they never sent us the front line concert brigades that had the stars of the stage. Probably, the political officers were afraid of them coming in contact with *shtrafniks*, but that was a mistake. Only once were we invited to a concert by the Poles, when nurses from the amateur dancing group of the neighbouring military hospital performed there. That was a great joy for all, both *shtrafniks* and officers. We had time for jokes and good humour, too. Chief of communications of the battalion, Senior Lieutenant Pavel Zorin, would sometimes make the following joke. He would sit his radio operator next to a group of chatting officers and would make him search for music on air. At the same time, he would transmit at the same frequency the voice of Levitan, a well-known narrator from the central radio station of the USSR, "an urgent message" which would contain Orders of the Commander-in-Chief about the decoration of several officers with an extremely high military award. Then he would mention one of the officers in the group as having the "Order". You had to see the face of the officer and how they would all laugh at the joke.

I remember that one time we had a conversation about which branch of the service had had the hardest time in the war. Many officers argued, and most of the men agreed, that the infantry had the hardest time. Ex-pilot *shtrafniks*, who had had to fight as infantry, would often say that they would give all their best Air Force rations to the infantry. Then Valery Semykin, signals platoon leader, who had already become one of the most admired officers in the battalion, entered the discussion. His argument was that "the infantry captures the enemy's trenches, or digs in at the new defence line, and that was it. Then the infantry can rest, unless

1   Red commander from the times of the Russian Civil War, who was killed in battle and then became the main character of an extremely popular movie.
2   Another legendary Red commander from the times of the Civil War.

they are digging in, or repelling the enemy's assault. In the meantime, phone operators carry the heaviest possible rolls of wire, phone sets, run around trenches setting the phone line and establishing communications, going at least 500 metres extra to the neighbouring unit or to the rear. If artillery fire tears the line, a phone operator has to run back and forth, loaded like a mule, carrying also his bag pack and personal weapon. He has to go here and there, or march on foot for dozens of kilometres with a heavy radio set, which would weight at least 20 kilograms. When infantry is resting during breaks in a march, a signals soldier has to turn on his radio set and establish communications to his superiors."

Then, when everyone was silent, having nothing to answer to Valerie's arguments, someone, probably Vasily Tsigichko, said in complete silence with a calm and quite low voice "and all your efforts are in vain"! After a second all the officers and men were laughing out loud. Valery was laughing as loudly as the others. I should mention that Valery was, or looked, an extremely calm person. At least his personality had three good features, true sincerity, ability to work very hard, and real modesty. Soon, when the company went into battle, he showed what he could do in real action.

In the meantime, the small units of the battalion were in such good shape that a company was ready to go into battle independently, with not only rifle platoons, but also fire support platoons. Also ready were an MG platoon, AT-rifle platoon, and mortar platoon. Men of those platoons had learnt all systems of weapons. They had learnt not only to load and unload, but also fire PTR AT-rifles, MGs and mortars very accurately. Through my friend, chief of staff Fillip Kiselev, we got to know that we were about to receive a battle mission.

The situation at the Front was not at all favourable for us. As early as September 5, the 65th Army captured a bridgehead in the area of Pultusk-Serotsk north from Warsaw, at the Narev River. But they could barely hold the bridgehead. However, after September 15 the Germans brought up their 'sledgehammers', i.e. armour, and managed to reduce the perimeter of Batov's men and almost collapse the flanks of the bridgehead. The bridgehead still held out. The German military leadership called the Narev bridgehead, "a pistol aiming into the heart of Germany", and continued to do their best to destroy our forces there. As commander of the 65th Army, General Pavel Ivanovich Batov wrote in his memoirs, "In Battles and Campaigns", on October 4, "the Germans delivered a smashing counter-blow. It was a complete surprise for us. The enemy went over to the offensive! German tanks penetrated our defences and almost reached the bank of the river." As it turned out, not all the defences on the bridgehead could stand that blow. "Many battalions were in retreat. Our losses grew with every day. The enemy broke through the two units and reached the Narev River. On the afternoon of October 6, the German tanks managed to penetrate our defences. The enemy attacks lasted till October 10".

In those days I was just a platoon leader and my view was at a really low tactical level, so I could not even judge the reasons of that failure of our troops. The situation on the bridgehead was so critical that the Front Commander, Marshal Rokossovski, transferred his command post directly to the CP of the 65th Army. Rokossovski ordered the Front Reserve, a tank corps, as well as several rifle divisions, to move to the bridgehead to assist Batov. Apparently, the Marshal also recalled the "gang of Rokossovski", as the Germans dubbed our penal battalion. He must have remembered the level of training and the fearlessness of the *shtrafniks*. So, on October 16 we were ordered to load the trucks that would take our entire battalion to the bridgehead. Like a small stream, we entered a huge flow of troops that was moving to the bridgehead, day and night, without any prolonged breaks.

There was a narrow stream of exhausted people who could barely move, with barefooted children with swollen feet, moving in the opposite direction to us. They were people liberated from the German concentration camps. We also bypassed army trucks full of female soldiers, either from hospitals or from medical battalions, or from the steam bath and laundry units. We actually had such units at the front, too. I don't know why, but as soon as we overtook such trucks, our men shouted, "Air alarm! Frame in the air!" I guess that was their way of showing their interest in those girls. During a short stop in the town of Vyshkuv that was captured at the same time with the bridgehead, i.e. in early September, from the road signs we saw that there was a front line sanatorium for officers in that town. "This is what they meant in my hospital certificate", I thought. Apparently, the doctors from the hospital thought that even platoon leaders, Lieutenants, could find a spot in those sanatoriums. I don't know if anyone in the rank of Lieutenant could be sent there. I guessed not.

Soon we reached Narev and after crossing it on a pontoon bridge we stopped in a small village. For some reason those small villages were called *Volwarks*. Our battalion staff stopped in one such *volwark*. Our new *kombat*, who was expected by the Army's liaison officer, soon called on our company commander Matvienko. The latter came out of the building, gathered all the platoon leaders and briefed us. I unconsciously compared Baturin and his works with our previous *kombat* Osipov. I immediately thought that the former *kombat* would always go out and talk not only to the officers, but also to simple *shtrafniks* and cheer them up with words of good luck. However, our new *kombat* did not consider it necessary, or perhaps he thought it was beneath him to come out and talk to men that he was sending into combat. Some of them would never return. As a former political officer he should have known the importance of a greeting from a superior to his men, and known that he was absolutely obliged to say some cheering, morale-boosting words. At that moment, not a single political officer said a single word, with the exception of Olenin, who volunteered to join the company in combat.

As we learnt from the order that our company commander read out to us, the company was to move to the front at the bridgehead. We had to counter-attack jointly with some other regiment, but I don't remember its number, in order to drive the Germans out from their positions and advance as far as we could towards Serotsk. The new battalion commander did not let our party secretary Olenin go with our company. Probably he thought that the Major would frustrate the decisions of our company commander, or for some other reasons. I do not know. We were soon to start battles for recapturing the positions of the troops of the 65th Army.

CHAPTER 6

The Narev Bridgehead

I did not get to go into the battle on the Narev bridgehead right away. First it was Matvienko's company with all its three platoons, under the leadership of Bulgakov, Davletov, and Karasev. Then there was the AT-rifle platoon under platoon leader Smirnov, and the MG platoon under Sergeev. All went to the front line, where they were supposed to start battles for the recovery of lost ground. Yanin remained deputy company commander. On the morning of the next day, I think it was October 18 or 19, the company stood up from the trenches without any preliminary artillery barrage, as it was planned to be a surprise attack. Only in the course of the assault did our ground attack planes start to escort and support the company. The company charged forward with such a rush that *Fritzes* could not avoid the hand-to-hand fight that the *shtrafniks* wanted to impose on them. As the participants of the battle told me, it was a short but cruel fight. Deputy Company Commander, Ivan Yanin, told me the following about the battle. He was always at the 'spearhead of the main assault'. I will try to repeat his story here since Senior Lieutenant Ivan Yanin will never again tell the story to anyone.

When the charging *shtrafniks* were almost at the first German trench, Yanin managed to throw the first grenade into the trench and jump into it immediately after its explosion. He fired bursts from his PPSh left and right at the outlines of the German soldiers who tried to leave the trench. Next to him he saw several *shtrafniks* wielding rifles with bayonets, rifle butts, and entrenching tools. He could only hear German flesh and bone cracking under their strikes! The hand-to-hand fight, a heated, fast-paced battle, continued from the trench into the German rear. It continued as long as his men had enough breath to get at the Germans. The ones close to were killed with bayonets, the ones that were further away were killed with small-arms fire.

As the result of that attack, which was inspired by Ivan Yanin, the best-loved officer of our company, the entire German first trench was in our hands. The company did not stop there and continued to pursue the fleeing German infantry, who were also being strafed by our *Shturmoviks* and fighter planes. The German reserve who were in the second trench opened fire, both on our assaulting *shtrafniks* and their own fleeing troops, as our *shtrafniks* literally did not get off the backs of the fleeing ones. Excited by the battle and the successful hand-to-hand fighting, in which we suffered only insignificant losses, the men threw the Germans out of the second trench. Then they stopped on the order of the company commander in order to get their breath and reload their weapons. The Germans used every second of the respite given to them and set up a counter-attack with the support of tanks and self-propelled guns. Those were similar tanks but without rotating turrets. As the eyewitnesses told me, it was hard to repel that assault. There were many moments when our men and the Germans mixed so much in the hand-to-hand fight that it was impossible to see who controlled the trench. It was only after some time that it became clear that the positions were still in our hands.

Fedor Usmanov and I were both attached to the reserve, and were listening to the sounds of the nearby battle and waiting excitedly for the moment when we would be needed. All of a sudden we saw Deputy Battalion chief of staff–2, Valery Semykin, and the recently arrived political officer Lieutenant Mirny. Almost immediately behind them drove the Willys Jeep of our *kombat*. It turned out that the company commander had sent a radio message in which he urgently requested our presence in the battle. Well, we thought, it must be really 'hot' there because we had to replace some losses already! Just let him be wounded, not killed! All four of us jumped into the Jeep and the driver drove us forward at breakneck speed, without caring much for the road or the potholes. We drove at such a speed that, when we drove at the breastworks of the trenches, the Jeep merely jumped over it all.

It turned out that at the moment of our arrival the company had already repelled the German attack. Two burning tanks were standing behind the positions. There was also a German self-propelled gun that seemed intact, at the same spot. We drove up to the scene at the moment when a huge AT-rifle man was approaching a group of Germans who seemed ready to surrender, and were standing beside the tanks. The AT-rifle man held his rifle by the barrel and furiously waved his weapon, which was almost two metres long and over 20 kilograms in weight. He shouted something and seemed to try to smash the heads of the Germans or drive them somewhere. At that moment he looked pretty much like the Russian warrior Vasily Buslaev, from the movie *Alexander Nevski*, who slashed German crusaders on the ice of Chudskoe Lake with his baton. They showed that movie to us, as well as many others, before our departure to the Narev bridgehead, and our impressions of the movie were still fresh.

There were several of our men running around the German SP-gun. All of a sudden it shook, the engine roared, they turned it and fired several rounds at the Germans. It turned out that our former tank officers managed to start the steel monster, despite one of its tracks being torn. I am sure that if the SP-gun could have been driven, our men would have jumped into it and continued to assault the fleeing Germans. In the meantime, ahead of us, where we were still moving forward, our platoons stubbornly chased the enemy, moving literally right up to the retreating Germans. We had strong air support, from Il–2 *Shturmovik* ground attack planes that we dubbed 'flying tanks' and 'kings of the battlefields'. They were decent partners for the 'queen of the battlefields'. The Germans dubbed them 'Black death'. Those planes fired missiles and large-calibre MGs, encouraging our assaulting infantry, so that the distance between *shtrafniks* and the fleeing Germans grew smaller with every minute.

Literally several minutes later an unpredictable incident took place. Either the platoon leader Davletov was too far in front of his troops, or a *Shturmovik* pilot could not see where our troops and the Germans were. But one burst from a large-calibre MG in a *Shturmovik* killed the Lieutenant on the spot. As soon as I caught up with the company commander and learnt about the tragic incident, I asked his permission, and rushed to the platoon that was left without a leader. The platoon was already consolidating gains in the next German trench. The men of the platoon knew me, as I had trained them together with Davletov. The deputy platoon leader, now my deputy, informed me of the losses, which were luckily quite low. But the death of the platoon leader was a severe loss. Fedor Usmanov replaced another badly wounded platoon leader, Bulgakov.

Quite soon after this we had to repel another German attack that attempted to recapture their lost positions. The Germans must have recovered from the first shock, but failed to gather sufficient forces, so we managed to repel their assault. The day was approaching its completion and the company commander gave us an order to take all necessary measures for the firm consolidation of our gains. We had to prepare our weapons for possible night combat and be ready to repel German night-time counter-attacks. We could see some stone buildings, and some destroyed wooden houses with stone basements and stone first floors. We had to capture them at dawn. That was to be our last mission for that stage of the operations.

We had to get replacements of ammo and eat at least dry tack. I can't help but praise our catering officer, who did not look like a war hero at all, but managed to set up a delivery of food to us in thermoses that evening. He did not supply us with any alcohol, though, as we had consumed our daily ration in the morning, before the first assault. Our new political officer, a Lieutenant with a Guards badge on his tunic, turned out to be a rather brave and open person and everyone liked him immediately.

The night was relatively quiet. Our phone operators quickly laid phone lines between the platoons and the company commander's CP, and from the company's CP to the battalion staff. Apparently, the presence of the Deputy Chief of Staff–2 (Communications and Coding) Valery Semykin, helped the quick establishment of communications. Valery did not want to sit in the battalion staff and thought that his presence was more necessary there, in the company. We all received a handwritten table of codenames. My digital codename was 18. The company commander's codename was 12, his codename sounded very familiar, it was Bug. The battalion staff's codename was Vistula. It was interesting to hear the conversation of the operators, "Vistula, Vistula, I am Bug" as it was a description of our previous places of battles. Even more so that the Narev was one of the tributaries of the Bug that we had just recently crossed. Later, when we had to change our positions and we went over to a long-lasting defence, our codenames changed radically. All of this was on the order of Semykin, who seemed to have an unending fantasy for names. I write about this with such detail because soon after that Valery distinguished himself in a matter that was far removed from staff or coding work.

The night was really quite calm. The Germans did not undertake any counterattacks. They also, apparently, tried to fortify their positions, as they knew that we would renew our attacks at dawn. Of course, they delivered harassing mortar and MG fire at our positions and bothered us a lot. But our sentries were on guard and did not notice any German preparations. During the night the company commander managed to get hold of the division's staff on the phone line and coordinated the time of beginning of the attack, the length of the artillery strike and the signals for the assault the next morning. The buildings that we saw were quite far away, I would guess a couple of kilometres. So our area of deployment was almost 1.5 kilometres from the trenches that we occupied.

The company commander decided to get us to the deployment area during the night. Without any noise, and using the lie of the land and any foliage, we would be ready before the start of the artillery strike, and wait there for the assault signal. For some reason I remember that the night was moonless, as if the moon was again on our side. We advanced to the deployment area in short moves from bush to bush, and by crawling along the ground, mingling with the grey grass of late autumn. We had checked our *sidor* bags that evening so that nothing in them would make any sound or give away our position. Thus we managed to advance to the jump-off area, unnoticed by the enemy, and camouflage our positions well so that the Germans would not realise that we were so close to them. Sweating from excitement and stress, it already felt like late October when rather warm days were followed by cold nights. So we were chilled to the bone in our damp tunics, either from excitement at anticipation of the assault, or from the morning cold.

As soon as it started to get a bit light, the sky seemed to crack open. The artillery strike was opened with a salvo of *Katyushas* that sent their fiery comets into the sky of the early morning. I was a bit afraid that they would fall short again and hit our positions, as happened at the Drut River in Belorussia. But this time everything worked well. Artillery and mortars continued to fire for some ten more minutes more, and red flares shot into the sky before the final salvo of *Katyushas*. Those red flares seemed to throw us all up from the ground. The assault was fast at the entire front of the company. The company followed the creeping barrage and the enemy did not manage to recover from the shock before we were already at their trenches. Even our new 'political worker', as we called good political officers, did not shout "For Motherland, for Stalin!" but was always in the assaulting line and did his soldier's duties well. Just as we hoped, the Germans did not realise that we were so close to them and the short artillery strike from our side deprived them of the opportunity to prepare for repelling our assault. Our AT-rifle and MG crews set up good fire support for our assault, delivering aimed fire at the rather narrow windows of the stone basements that were more like the gun-ports of bunkers. That fire support ensured the fast and unimpeded advance of the penal company.

We captured those buildings at the first attempt, and as it turned out, there was significant war booty of both ammo and food. Incidentally, that was the first place where I saw the illuminated lamp bowls that the Germans used instead of candles. They consisted of a plastic carton, or small round jar, that was filled with paraffin. In the centre of it there was a wick on a special base. It was quite convenient. It would not capsize, and the melting paraffin would not spill like a regular candle, and it was also smelt quite pleasant! We used those lamp pots on many occasions, although we used *Katyushas* more often. They were empty artillery cartridges, flattened at the neck, and would have a wick pressed into it. The wick was most often a piece of cotton fabric. Petrol, with the addition of salt, so that it would not explode, would be poured into the empty cartridge through a specially drilled hole. The *Katyushas* gave a brighter light than the German lamp pots, but produced much more soot.

Now, i.e. many years after the war, people ask me whether the *shtrafniks* took prisoners. During the above episode we captured a lot of prisoners, in contrast with previous battles. The Germans surrendered in those stone buildings. Our men rushed into the houses only after throwing hand-grenades. But when we gathered all the surviving Germans together, there were more of them than our entire company and all its attached platoons. I think that was the first occasion when *shtrafniks* captured so many prisoners at one time. We put them all into one basement, took away their handguns and then, as our war booty, their watches, lighters, cigarette cases and other belongings. Then we set guards at the door. It was only later, during the night, that we sent them away to the battalion staff. Escorting them to the rear were lightly wounded *shtrafniks*. Several men, who could not walk themselves due to heavy wounds, were transported on makeshift stretchers. We made the Germans carry them. I heard later that the Germans carried our wounded very carefully, probably realising that the escorting men would severely punish them for any rough treatment of the wounded.

In the meantime, night was still far off. The company commander had an order to consolidate our gains and not to retreat from the *volwark* or farm that we were in. We had to report the completion of our mission, and the situation, and receive orders for further actions. However, it turned out that our radio set was 'wounded,' i.e. damaged by a bullet or shrapnel that had hit it. Nevertheless, some 10–15 minutes later we had a phone line installed. One could hear, "Vistula, Vistula, I am Bug! Hear you well!" We all felt great relief that we had that connection.

The men started to fortify the windows of the basement with bricks, and some chunks of concrete that were there on the floor. By doing so, they turned our basement into a bunker. It looked as if we had killed or captured all the Germans who were defending those houses, as we did not see anyone fleeing from them. That meant they had a second line of defence at some distance and were preparing all sorts of nasty surprises for us, especially as they had some fresh units there and their artillery must have pre-sighted the area where we were. However, they did not yet fire at us. All of a sudden in that silence we heard the clatter of horses hooves and saw the field kitchens, with smoking chimneys, riding at us at full speed, just like MG-carriages from the Chapaev division in the Civil War! It was our long-expected breakfast, combined with lunch and probably dinner, delivered to us by Sergeant-major Jacob Lazarenko, the right-hand-man of our supply officer. It was already afternoon. By the way, we had an unspoken rule in our battalion, or perhaps in all the units at the front, that said don't eat before the morning assault! We believed firstly, it was much harder to run forward on a full stomach, and secondly and most important, one had much more chance of survival if one suffered a stomach wound. That hope always calmed us down, giving us some illusory confidence and assurance of survival!

We had dinner without stopping our fortification works, each drinking a cup of *vodka*. We filled our glasses from a standard half litre bottle, one bottle for five men. It is amazing how our supply officers managed to deliver *vodka* in glass bottles, without breaking them when riding off-road! The field kitchens and carriages often ended up in explosion craters, and were jolted around the bumpy roads. How could glass bottles remain intact? I mention the catering in battle so often because it had the same importance as the supply of ammo. One should not underestimate either of those supplies. The presence of ammo provides the technical ability of a warrior to fight, while his psychological and physical condition to a great extent depended on catering. The morale of a soldier depends on his psychological condition, while morale is the most important thing for victory.

On that day we somehow managed to get used to the silence! There was no firefight, no artillery, nor any mortar fire. Aircraft did not buzz above us. We completed the works on consolidating and fortifying our positions, both in the basements and first floors of the buildings, and in the trenches between them. We even had time to pull out the bodies of dead Germans from the captured buildings, and bury them in the German trenches. They had dug their own graves! We even had time to relax and started to doze off. But then a firestorm of artillery and mortar fire destroyed our hopes of a peaceful night.

Before the company commander could report to the battalion commander, the phone line was damaged and we had no more connection with the battalion staff. Apparently the wire got damaged during the artillery strike, and we only had one line in the chain of communication of "platoon-company-battalion". The trick was that the line operators would only lay one wire between the phones, while the second wire was the soil! We would put the second contact from the phone into the ground. The quality of sound was quite bad, but we saved 50% of the wire! At that moment, when we had to urgently report the situation that could change any second, we did not have any connection, no radio, no phone! Valery Semykin was sitting at the radio set, trying to bring it to life.

Shtrafnik Kasperovich, a tall blond Belorussian man from my platoon, volunteered to go and find the torn phone wire. I had paid attention to him even before battles as we had very few 'encircled ones', but he was one of them. He even had an old rank, not of the new Red Army. It was either *technik-intendant* or military technician of some low grade. He was always somewhat silent, idle, timid, and, as I thought, was always thinking of his own skin. So I was a bit amazed at him volunteering for that mission, but I was also happy to see him finally overcoming his fears and depression. I was happy for him. However, even ten and twenty minutes later the line was still down. After the first long artillery strike, the enemy fired salvos at our position and at the immediate rear every five to seven minutes, and I thought that my Belorussian *shtrafnik* must have been killed like that MG-gunner who smoked the Germans out of the farm in Belorussia. I again thought about the strange logic of the war. However, I need not have worried, as it will emerge.

Captain Matvienko, our company commander, hurried the signals operators to try to restore the line as quickly as possible. Then Senior Lieutenant Valery Semykin, deputy battalion chief of staff, threw away the radio set that he was trying to mend, rushed out of the shelter with the words, "I will go!" and disappeared into the twilight of the evening. To add a bit more about Valery, he seemed to be an easily impressed and emotional person, but he had a strong will and could always control his emotions. Strong emotions only caused him to control emotions even stronger, because from the outside he looked calm in almost any situation. Some ten minutes later the signals operator, who had been shouting into the receiver, "Vistula, Vistula, I am Bug!" without any result, all of a sudden yelled, "I have a line!" In the meantime, the Germans continued their artillery fire.

The Captain grabbed the receiver and after some time the line became stable. The company commander managed to report the situation, received some orders, and then the line went down again. Suddenly it was up again, and some ten to fifteen minutes later Valery returned. He had not found the *shtrafnik* that went before him. He found the broken end of the line, but could not find the other end for a long time. It turned out that the German shell had exploded right on the wire, which shot the second part of the wire a long way off. Crawling under the enemy's artillery fire, covering a wide area, Valery hoped to find both the second part of the line, and the killed or wounded *shtrafnik*. Soon he found the second part of the line but he could not connect the wires together, although he held both ends of them in his left and right hands. The distance was that of his stretched out arms. Valery realised that every second was precious. Under the next German artillery strike he took off the isolation from both wires, with his teeth, and put the steel wires under the skin of his hands, making his body part of the line!

After the war I read a lot of literature, and many stories of soldiers' sacrifices during the war, and came across a similar case. A line operator put the two parts of the wire into his mouth, but he was killed. There were many similar incidents in the war.

When Valery sensed that the phone conversation was over, he got out the roll of wire that he always carried, just in case, connected the wires and even covered them with tape. A real signals operator always carried some. What a professional! When we asked him, how did he know that the phone conversation was over, Valery answered that he could feel weak impulses of electricity going through his body during the conversation. The strong impulse that went through his body, when the phone operator hung up the receiver, could not have been unnoticed. Valery Semykin was awarded the Medal for Bravery for that deed. We have been friends for almost sixty years now.

Speaking about Kasperovich, it turned out that he fled from the battlefield and deserted. At that time I was still inexperienced and an easily deceived person. I mistook him for an honest person, just as in the similar case with Geft. For a long time we thought that Kasperovich was missing in action. But in January 1945, after the battles for Warsaw, he was caught somewhere in Belorussia and sent back to our battalion.

Short harassing artillery strikes lasted all night long, and all night long we expected a counter-attack. It started only at dawn. The Germans started it with their classic pattern. They repeated a strong artillery strike, which did not hit us as we were well protected by the thick roofs and brick walls of the basements. There were no direct hits in the trenches either. During the artillery strike their armour and infantry approached us at such a distance that they could already deliver well-aimed fire at our positions, which meant that we could return it. However, our company commander ordered us to remain silent, and only open fire on the signal flare of red smoke. We too had such flares. It was a scary thing! To see the approaching enemy, holding a finger on the trigger but without permission to shoot. But then the German infantry who were walking behind some five to six tanks in the attacking line, appeared from behind the steel monsters and ran forward. That was exactly what our company commander was waiting for.

He fired the signal flare and all our MGs, both light and heavy ones from George Sergeev's platoon, opened up. The German attacking line grew thinner before our eyes. MGs and AT-rifles concentrated their fire on the observation slits of the approaching tanks. The driver of the lead tank apparently lost his bearing due to bullets hitting his observation slit and turned to the side, exposing the weak side-armour to our AT-rifles. It was immediately knocked out. The *Panther* caught fire and the German crew started to bail out. Senior Lieutenant Sergeev jumped up from the trench with a pistol in his hand, and ran at the tank crew, shouting "Cover me!" to his deputy. He was the only *shtrafnik* with a beard with a famous last name, Pushkin. I don't know how he could discern our officer in that group of German tank crew, in their black uniforms, but Sergeev fired several rounds at the Germans, ran up to one of them and knocked him down. Then he held him pressed to the ground until some other *shtrafniks* ran up.

That was the turning point of the battle. The rest of the tanks tried to turn round, exposing their side armour to us. One more tank was knocked out, while the rest drove away. Then our company commander gave the signal to "Charge!" The *shtrafniks* ran forward and with some special fury finished off the German infantry who did not flee in time. Meanwhile, George Sergeev and the other men who had run to him, pulled up and disarmed the German tankman. He turned out to be a *Hauptmann*, i.e. Captain, who was the commander of the tank battalion. Sergeev got quite a precious prisoner! The prisoner was sent back to the rear under escort of the AT-rifle crews who had knocked out the German tanks, and who according to our common opinion, deserved early release from the penal battalion and some awards. That was the last serious attempt of the Germans to recapture the lost positions on our flank. They did not dare to counter-attack again. Meanwhile, we built on our success and chased the routed enemy for a couple of kilometres. We managed to capture their second, maybe their third echelon of defence, in a village next to the town of Serotsk that we could clearly see on our left, and stopped there.

The Germans undertook some more attempts to regain positions, but apparently those were just probing assaults to find out the strength of our defences and ability to fight on. We repelled those assaults easily, compared to the previous battles. Two days later, our company was replaced by a rifle battalion. The battalion commander, a Major, seemed to be more interested in the origins of our company and its men, than in the enemy's strength in the sector. It looked like they were not planning to advance any further. We had done that job for them. Our company, just like the entire battalion before, served as a ram that would crush the German defences and then we would give our sector to another regular unit. That was our destiny. Nevertheless, the mission of our company was completed in three days with fairly low losses for such a good result. Not only had the company managed to recapture lost positions, but they also advanced some 2–3 kilometres from the old perimeter of the bridgehead. Of course, the order to disengage was interpreted by the *shtrafniks* of the company as recognition of the bravery, heroism and decisiveness of those former officers by the Army Commander General Batov. *Shtrafniks* thought that they had deserved forgiveness and release from the penal battalion even without getting wounded and maybe even deserved awards. At least that was what another Army Commander, General Gorbatov did, and all the men in the battalion knew about it.

When we passed the familiar stone basements that were already occupied by some CP or supply units of the battalion replacing us, the company commander ordered a small break in our march. I walked to the knocked out tanks with some other officers, in order to have a closer look at them. I was amazed to see that in some places the armour was broken, but only the upper concrete layer of the armour was destroyed. I thought that Hitler was already running out of his praised Krupp's steel armour and that he had to use that *Ersatz* armour on his tanks. I was probably wrong, but that was my first impression about his much-praised tanks[1].

Our Captain again ordered our company to fall in and thanked all the men for an exemplary completion of a battle mission. "Should we sing now?" was the last phrase of his short speech. It turned out that our young *politruk* Lieutenant Mirny had a strong and loud voice. From the very first step of the march, which was considered a good sign among us, he sang the popular song of the artillery corps. "Artillery men, Stalin gave an order, Artillery men, the Fatherland is calling". Apparently, he had served in the artillery before the penal battalion. All *shtrafniks* sang that song with great encouragement and continued to sing other songs all the way till we arrived at the house where the battalion commander was stationed. The company commander stopped the column at the house, ordered "Attention!" and walked into the house to report. The minutes of waiting for *kombat* Baturin seemed an eternity, and then he walked out, calm as usual, while our company commander followed him like a beaten dog. I think everyone of us had a foreboding of something nasty.

Without commanding "at ease" or maybe he just did not notice that the company was standing at attention, Lieutenant Colonel Baturin made a rather long speech, which was full of clichés and formal phrases. The point of his speech was that he, the *kombat*, on behalf of the Motherland, thanked us all for completing our mission. On behalf of the Command of the 65th Army, and in the name of the Motherland, he rallied us to serve faithfully and with full dedication. We were not to spare our lives if it could be for the good of the Fatherland. "We must fulfil the new orders of the Soviet State for the sake of the coming victory", and so on and so on. Some men started to murmur and move, although the "at ease" order did not follow at all. Baturin sensed that the men were agitated and quickly completed his speech, giving us a new mission on behalf of the Army Commander. The mission was to expand the right flank of the bridgehead, which would be as 'easy' as the mission that we had just completed. I thought I heard some discontent in his voice. I wished he knew how 'easy' it was to complete that mission. Probably, he already knew? When with a false patriotism the *kombat* completed his pathetic speech with "The Fatherland is calling you for heroic deeds!" we thought that we had just sung a song with words "Fatherland is calling us" It was if we invited our bad luck, that would be a true mysticism!

Depressed, and deprived of the last hope of receiving appreciation of their great performance, the *shtrafniks* ate dinner without jokes and conversations. Even the 100 grams of *vodka* did not lift our spirits. Right after dinner, without any rest, the company had to carry out a forced march of 15 kilometres. It was necessary in order to take over a sector of the front, before dawn, on the right flank of the bridgehead. We both marched and ran, and long before dawn, sweating like horses after a race, we fell into the trenches of the 108th or 37th Rifle Division. Alas, I don't remember which.

---

1   Apparently the author speaks about *zimmerit*, an anti-magnetic paste applied to the armour of German tanks that was supposed to protect them from mines attached with the use of magnets.

Much later, after the war, in the memoirs of General Batov, "In Campaigns and Battles", I read the words of the commander of the 108th Rifle Division. He wrote, "The battles at the Narev bridgehead were some of the hardest for our divisions during the whole war". They were tough for us too. The 444th, 407th and 539th Rifle Regiments were fighting in our sector, but I don't remember which units gave us the right to assault the Germans first and which units replaced us after our success. I did not know it then either, as our penal company was acting almost completely independently from other units.

Long before dawn, as we entered the trenches, the units that were there immediately departed, so that the Germans would not to notice the change of troops. The only thing that we managed to learn from the men who were leaving the trenches was that the German trenches were just 150 metres from us. They told us that the Germans were delivering powerful artillery strikes both day and night, and that numerous snipers and MG-gunners were hunting for our men during the day. We had not yet been given the mission, but we knew that we were there not just for strengthening the defences. During the day we received replacements of ammo, including many assault RG–42 and RPG–43 hand-grenades. Those had a short killing range in contrast with F–1 defensive grenades. The new grenades were supposed to be used on the move, which meant assaults. Each squad also received one RPG–40 AT-grenade, from which we concluded that we could come across German tanks in the area.

I would like to draw the reader's attention to the fact that our battalion was constantly receiving new weapons in quite sufficient amounts. We had new PPS SMGs instead of PPSh. We also had PTRS anti-tank rifles, with a clip for five rounds. In general, we never sensed the lack of weaponry. I have written this, because there are too many books and articles written today saying that the *shtrafniks* were sent into battle unarmed. It has been said that we were given one rifle for 5 or 6 men, so that ones that were unarmed wanted the armed ones to be killed as quickly as possible. The Army's Detached Penal Companies were sometimes over a thousand men strong. Vladimir Grigorievich Mikhailov, who was then commander of one such company in the 64th Army, told me after the war that sometimes they simply did not manage to bring enough weapons for all the men. If there was no time before the mission, for a company to procure more weapons, then some *shtrafniks* were given rifles and the others just bayonets. I am ready to swear that this had nothing to do with Officer Penal Battalions. Stories about deliberate sending of unarmed *shtrafniks* into battle are a lie. We always had enough weapons, sometimes even the most modern ones.

Gradually our men calmed down and the discontent with our *kombat* started to abate. Apparently, our *kombat* did not want, or did not dare to ask General Batov to disengage the battalion, and release the ones who had distinguished themselves in battles. Above all I felt sorry for our AT-rifle crews, whom Baturin for some reason disliked. Many times he gave me back my recommendations for their release and decoration. Why do I mention this in such great detail? Because I am still angry with Baturin for this, although it has been almost 60 years since those events. Also, because the battles that followed cost the lives of so many experienced battle officers who fought in our battalion due to some 'wrongdoings'. They very well understood their guilt, but by their bravery and readiness to sacrifice their lives, they proved their loyalty to their oath and to the Motherland.

However, events that day unfolded in such a manner that we even managed to get a bit of sleep. Some slept sitting, some could even lie down in the so-called under-breastwork niches. Those were long foxholes dug into the walls of trenches. Their ceilings were also soil. The soil there was sandy and could collapse from nearby explosions, while the foxholes were so low that one could only rest in them lying down. Massive artillery strikes that our predecessors mentioned to us came along quite soon. Apparently, the Germans had a lot of artillery in that sector, including the six-barrelled mortars that some dubbed *Vanyushas*[2]. We dubbed them 'boars', most likely because their sound was something like a pig squealing. The boar rounds fell into the trenches almost vertically and their explosions were especially dangerous for those who were in the trenches. That was the reason for our predecessors to dig foxholes in the walls of trenches.

I have already mentioned that *shtrafniks* often tried their best to preserve the lives of their commanders. I have also already mentioned that our deputy company commander Senior Lieutenant Ivan Yanin, an officer of insane bravery, was admired and loved by the entire company. In order to hide Ivan from the rounds of those six-barrelled boars, *shtrafniks* found one such foxhole for him, and in order to make it even safer, made the foxhole larger so that two more men could lie down in the foxhole on both his sides, covering him from splinters. During one artillery strike the *shtrafniks* insisted that he would lie down in this foxhole and covered him with their bodies. Immediately after they all lay down there, a heavy German shell exploded nearby and the entire foxhole collapsed, burying alive the three men inside. They managed to dig out the first one, the second one was dug out barely alive, but by the time that they had dug out Yanin he was already dead. The bravest officer that I ever knew, Ivan Yanin suffocated under the weight of the ground without receiving a single splinter or bullet wound. He was never afraid of those. And he never spent a single day in a hospital. That was just one more paradox of war.

We were all deeply shocked by his unexpected and, as we all thought, totally unnecessary death. Although death at the front was not uncommon, even so it was paradoxical. We said our last goodbye to our battle friend and sent his body to the rear for a proper funeral. Our chief of staff, Philip Kiselev, came to the trenches in the evening, escorted by the chief of staff of a rifle battalion. To be more precise, he was a senior adjutant, as that office was then called in rifle battalions. Other officers came too, some of them unknown to us. Philip mourned together with us and told us that Ivan was given a proper funeral. I and all our men and officers, will remember him for the rest of our lives.

....Many years later I was chief of the ROTC course of Kharkov Road College. There were many foreigners, including Poles, studying in that College then and I asked those who lived in the area of Pultusk-Serotsk to try to find the grave of Ivan Yanin during their winter break. In those days, Poles still appreciated the memory of Soviet soldiers who fell in the liberation of their country from the *Nazis*. So the Polish students that came back to school after their vacation told me that they found a name on the huge common grave at Pultusk, "Yan Yanin, officer". I had no

2   Also known by their German name of *Nebelwerfer*.

doubt that that was our dear Ivan. The only thing that I don't know is if his grave is preserved to this day, as there were a great many cases of vandalism in the countries of Eastern Europe during the last decade …

Back then, the company commander gathered all the officers and reported to Philip that he was planning to appoint me deputy company commander to replace the dead Yanin. I was at the same time to be kept in the office of a platoon leader. Kiselev agreed and told me that he would ask our *kombat* to approve that decision. Matvienko handed over to me the signal pistol and a bag of flares that had belonged to the late Ivan. I was not too happy about all of that. Then Kiselev introduced the officers who had arrived with him. They told us that in the near future we were supposed to attack the German positions, capture the trenches and hold them until the arrival of reinforcements. Again our company was given the 'honour' of being at the spearhead of the assault, breaking the German defences and recapturing the area lost by the other units. The mission was quite similar to the one that we had at Rogachev, when we were supposed to cross the Drut River. In that case we were also supposed to capture the enemy's trenches and provide for the entry into battle of other troops. However, in the present instance we did not have a river in front of us. The Narev was behind us and we did not have to cross it. We just had to prevent the Germans from doing so.

Officers from the rifle unit promised to us on their departure that combat engineers would arrive before the assault and defuse the minefield in front of us, if there were a minefield, and that a good artillery strike would precede our assault. When I briefed the squad leaders on the situation, I did not see that the promise of a good artillery strike, and lifting mines in front of us, encouraged them too much. So, in order to cheer myself up, I ordered all the men in all the squads to be briefed about the cheerful news and report to me on the morale of *shtrafniks*. I considered that to be one of the crucial factors for a successful battle. In my heart I had some anxiety, as if I felt that something bad would happen. I also had some stupid thought that I would be killed in the upcoming assault. I tried to chase those thoughts away and concentrate my brain on just one thing, how to complete the mission that was about to start. I understood it would begin the morning.

A group of combat engineers did indeed come to our trenches after midnight in order to lift the landmines in front of our company. They came back less than one hour later, and their leader, either excited or happy, told us that they had not spotted any mines in front of us at all. This news spread out in the company with lightning speed and cheered everyone up. The soldiers from a regiment that came with thermoses and brought us a very early breakfast. But they had to go back without emptying them, as almost all the men refused to eat before the assault. That was our habit. But no one refused to drink the hundred grams of *vodka*. Of course, that played an important role in boosting the men's morale, and so we waited for dawn in a completely different mood. My bad feelings also seemed to disappear and it seemed that it was easier to breathe. I think I even had a nap for 20–25 minutes.

I woke up as it was getting light, when there was another short artillery strike from the *Fritzes*. Almost simultaneously a runner rushed to us shouting, "The Company's Captain is killed!" Even before I completely woke up, I ordered the runner to hurry round the trenches again and tell everyone that I had taken took over the company, appointing MG platoon leader Senior Lieutenant Sergeev my deputy. The very first thing that struck my mind was whether I would be able to lead not only *shtrafniks*, but also my friends, the platoon leaders. For some reason I immediately recalled the farewell speech of an older Lieutenant, Parshin. He was deputy company commander in the academy, to us freshly graduated Lieutenants. I very well remembered his carefully thought words. "You should know how to demand obedience. Do it firmly, justly and reasonably. That is the main quality of a true commander. Remember that authority and control are always with someone. If a commander loses control, even for a moment, it would be taken over by your subordinates". I think that it was then, during that assault, and then for the remainder of my entire forty years long officer career, I tried to stick to that wise advice.

Almost before I could think about all that, suddenly our *Katyushas* and artillery opened up! The explosions covered the German trenches so densely that a wave of joy overwhelmed me. I thought that it was not a forbearing of a disaster, but a weakness of my soul, and I felt ashamed. Some fifteen minutes later the artillery strike was completed with yet another powerful salvo of *Katyushas*. Again I must say how amazed I was at the missiles that were flying over our heads, like fiery comets, and that exploded in the enemy's positions. There were huge pillars of fire and dirt shooting into the sky. It was impossible to see anything in that firestorm of steel, although the explosions were only a few, maybe 150 metres from us. As soon as the last salvo of *Katyusha* missiles had painted red traces in the sky, someone behind our trenches shouted "Forward!" before I had time, and fired a series of red flares. I had not even loaded my flare pistol! I cursed myself for slowness, jumped out of the trench and saw my newly appointed deputy, MG platoon leader Sergeev. Almost simultaneously with him, although not of one accord, the entire company stood up from the trenches. I saw it all clearly, in my strange new role of company commander. But I stayed several metres from our trench to make sure that everyone joined the assault. Answering the rallying cry of the platoon leaders, "For Motherland! For Stalin!" The *shtrafniks* suddenly answered as one, while on the move, "For the ******* prosecutor!" Apparently, they mentioned the person responsible for all their miseries!

I looked ahead and threw myself forward to catch up with the assault line. After running some fifty metres, all of a sudden something started to explode under the feet of many of my men. Fountains of dirt and smoke shot into the sky and men started falling one by one. I saw an explosion under the feet of the formidable body of my machine-gunner Pushkin. I saw a wheel of his MG flying into the air and I could not understand what was happening. We had been told that there was no minefield, but it looked as if men were detonating mines! Then I realised that those were direct hits from rifle grenade launchers, or *panzerfaust*, or some shells or rounds that the Germans were firing from some new highly accurate weapon. Probably, that was the reason for them not to plant mines in front of their defences.

Everything was so unexpected that I was lost for a moment, but then immediately I clearly understood that a mine or a shell never hit the same spot twice. I had to run forward through the places that were already hit. I ran past many of my men who got hit by that weapon. I saw that men, who were still conscious, tried to stop their bleeding, and bandaged the blood-covered remains of their feet with awful curses. I ran in front of many men, but without shouting orders that were already useless. I ran forward not in order to draw my men behind me, but rather to leave the area under the enemy's fire. All who managed to reach the German trench unharmed, rushed into it. They finished off the surviving *Fritzes* who were left alive after our artillery strike and who tried to resist. We left no living German behind us. With a really thin line we rushed into the second trench, as it was near. I no longer had any fear left, just a desire to win. Apparently, our artillery hit not only the first trench of the Germans very accurately, and the hand-to-hand fight in the second trench was short. In some places the second trench was literally full of the bodies of *Nazi* soldiers. We could see silhouettes of fleeing Germans far in front of us. George Sergeev with another machine-gunner fired well-aimed bursts at them. I saw that there were very few men left from the company. I stopped them all and gave an order to assemble round me. When I counted them I wanted to weep. Ivan Karasev and the AT-rifle platoon leader were missing, while George Sergeev was standing at his MG and was bandaging his leg.

Only Fedor Usmanov and I remained unharmed. Fate seemed to spare us. We had just come back from hospitals after recovering from heavy wounds. Sergeev answered me that his wound was "just a scratch" and he stayed with us. We had just 15 men left. It was very few, knowing that over one hundred men had stood up from our trench! Almost nine out of ten were out of action, and we did not know how many were killed! We suffered the main losses on that spot where the Germans had used something new against us. I could see the *shtrafniks* whispered something to each other and I was getting quite a lot of angry looks from them.

We had penetrated the German defences to a depth of 1.5 kilometres and we did not see any enemy directly in front of us. I decided that we could build on our success and ordered "Forward!" The third German trench was further than I thought, and after one more kilometre we were greeted with a relatively weak and disorganised small-arms fire. The terrain there had a lot of folds and was covered with low bushes. That allowed us to advance in short rushes and to stop at the assault line that I appointed next to an individual tree or a large bush. When we all reached the line of assault, the Germans must have completely lost us in the bushes and ceased firing. Or maybe they were preparing to repel our assault and were merely waiting for us to stand up.

"All of a sudden" is very rarely something nice in war! But, all of a sudden we heard the roar of engines of several aeroplanes. Those were our *Shturmoviks* flying in. I immediately thought, not as in the morning, about target marking that we knew so well from training in the academy. As my flare pistol was then always loaded, and my orderly always carried a bag full of flares, I fired several flares towards the German trench. The pilots did a great job, they understood me immediately and a series of missiles flew into the German trench and exploded there. In addition to that, our pilots greeted the Germans with several bursts from their large-calibre MGs. As the Germans had not yet regained their senses after the assault of our 'Red falcons', that was the best moment to start an assault using the remains of our company. We quickly covered the 50–60 metres to the German trenches, threw hand-grenades in, and rushed into the trench after the explosions, finishing off the survivors. My submachine-gun did quite a lot of work there, too. A hand-to-hand fight did not happen, as we finished off the Germans. They did not even try to resist, some even dropped their weapons and lifted their hands in the air. We had no mercy. We also killed all the wounded Germans. We did not want to leave them alive in our rear. Our cruelty was justified, as the following battles demonstrated. Mercy to the wounded Germans cost us much during the crossing of the Oder, but I will mention that later.

Having jumped into the German trench, I ordered preparations to use the captured trench for repelling possible counterattacks. Then I noticed two *shtrafnik* signal operators who were bringing a phone line to us. I silently thanked the chief of communications of our battalion, and of course, the excellent Valery Semykin. He did all the best things in making the communications in our battalion. Soon after that I was reporting to the deputy battalion commander, Lieutenant Colonel Aleksey Filatov. We had two deputy battalion commanders, both were Lieutenant Colonels, and both were called Filatov, Aleksey and Mikhail, so between ourselves we dubbed them the twins. I reported where I was and which forces I had with me. In addition to several men with SMGs, I had two heavy MGs, one AT-rifle and two light MGs. But I was almost out of ammo. We picked up German SMGs with full clips and a couple of MGs. We counted our hand-grenades and they were also very few, only two anti-tank grenades and about ten anti-personnel. It would be hard to repel a German counterattack.

Filatov told me that we had already captured the trenches of the German second echelon of the enemy's battalion defence sector. He congratulated us on that success. He also cheered me up with the news that I would get replacements soon, but I had to hold out for two or three hours. He told me some good news. Our company commander, Captain Matvienko, was not killed, but only lightly wounded and shell-shocked. He was staying in our battalion's dressing station, as he refused to be evacuated any further away. However, I was ordered to continue as company commander, as Matvienko was promoted to deputy battalion commander to replace the second Filatov. He was leaving the penal battalion for a higher office in the regular troops. I was officially appointed commander of the SMG Company. Incidentally, Baturin himself never spoke to company commanders in combat. They were always his deputies or chief of staff that I spoke to.

We barely managed to complete our conversation when observers reported to me that two tanks and infantry were approaching us from the German side. The two anti-tank grenades that we had were really precious. So we had to use them effectively! It was good that there were only two tanks. We defended a very small sector of the trench. We could hear a firefight to the left from us. Apparently, our neighbour was also attacking or repelling German assault, but we did not have any contact with them. The right flank was completely exposed. Exposed flanks were always considered a very dangerous situation for any unit in action, and for us this was even truer. The main thing for us was not to allow the Germans to bypass us. When men spotted about one platoon of German infantry and two tanks, they understood what was about to happen without any orders. All the *shtrafniks* had battle experience at officer level, although in that battle they were actually privates. I ordered them to bring both anti-tank grenades to me. Then I ordered one tall and physically fit *shtrafnik* to stay next to me in order to throw the grenade. The AT-rifle crew was led by that very Buslaev who beat the Germans with his rifle at the left flank of the bridgehead. All other AT-rifle crews must have been killed on the spot where the Germans fired their new secret weapon at us so precisely. Their leader, Junior Lieutenant Karasev must have died there also.

Luckily, as it turned out later, the officers were only wounded and came back to the battalion after a couple of months. Despite the dangerous situation, my brain was feverishly looking for an explanation of our catastrophic losses there, in front of the first German trench. More and more I realised that it all looked like a normal minefield. Memories of my own sad experience were still fresh. But I tried to chase those thoughts away. The combat engineers had told us that there were no mines there at all! Till the very end of the war I was bothered by those thoughts and tortured by doubts. Could I be guilty of such high losses? I could not find any peace. But six months later, Colonel Baturin revealed the mystery to me.

It happened at the battalion's Victory lunch, on the First Day of Peace, after Baturin relaxed having taken several shots of *vodka*. He told me privately that our company was deliberately sent into assault across a minefield on the order of General Batov. I thought, and not without reason, that Baturin must have agreed to it. Baturin tried to justify this by the fact that the minefield had mines that were impossible to defuse. I did not really believe that, but Batov recognised in his memoirs that his troops suffered very heavy losses there at that bridgehead. Of course, the decision was made not out of lack of experience or stupidity. I do not believe in the stupidity of people, especially if they have high-ranking positions. I rather believe in their meanness and lack of decency. Batov merely decided to solve the problem of defusing the minefield, and providing for a successful operation, by sending *shtrafniks* on the minefield. We were sent there like cattle, like useless material, although all those men were precious battle-tried officers. They could have gone into battle as officers to strengthen units of the same 65th Army.

Those thoughts only distracted me from repelling the assault of the enemy. When it became clear that one of the tanks was coming right at me and the second a little bit to the left, I left one grenade for myself, as I was an exemplary grenade-thrower in the military academy, and sent the man with another hand-grenade to my left flank. There was a rather deep communication trench next to me, which went towards the German positions. I ordered the AT-rifle crew to observe both tanks and if someone of the two of us would manage to knock out a tank, they should concentrate their fire on the damaged vehicle, finishing it off, without forgetting the second tank either. I have already mentioned that we had PTRS AT-rifles, i.e. Simonov AT-rifles with a clip for 5 rounds, which allowed for rapid fire without need for reloading. The long barrel of the rifle provided for more precise fire and advanced armour penetration capacity. I gave a hint to the AT-rifle crew to fire at the sides and the back of the tanks where their armour was weaker and where the gas tanks and engine were, but such hints were not necessary, the AT-rifle crews knew that all too well.

Apparently, the Germans acted according to their standard assault tactic. At some 50–60 metres in front of our trenches the German infantry emerged from behind the tanks and ran forward, and that was the moment when Sergeev's MGs opened fire. Men opened well-aimed and ammo-saving fire with short bursts from their SMGs, and mowed down the German infantry. The Germans were pinned down, while the tanks sped up and went for our trenches. The communication trench, in which I hid about 15–20 metres from the main trench, was a very good position. It was some 10 metres from the approaching armoured monster. Apparently, the crew of the tank noticed my men in the trench, slowed down, traversed the gun to the left and started to check the trench, firing at different sectors of the trench, firing more and more to the right, closer to my excellent position. In one of those moments I managed to make a well-aimed throw and knock out the tank's track with the AT hand-grenade. The tank driver must have sensed that the tank was slipping from his control and tried to make a sharp turn to the left, on the remains of the damaged track.

I was again lucky, just like many more times in the war. With that turn, the tank exposed its right side and the rear to our AT-rifle crew, and they immediately fired several armour-piercing and incendiary bullets into the rear of the *Panther*, and it caught fire! The tank crew tried to escape through turret hatches but were cut down by a hail of bullets from the submachine-guns of my men. I also fired several bursts at them. The dead German tankmen remained hanging in the upper hatches, while the other members of the crew tried to use the bottom hatches, but also came under our fire, and shared the fate of their comrades. When I worriedly turned to look at the second tank, I saw that it was also knocked out. I was happy that both the *shtrafnik* with the second AT-hand-grenade and the AT-rifle crews would be awarded with Orders of Patriotic War as was written in the Order's statute, and would be fully rehabilitated, even if they do not get wounded. At the same moment I realised that I would also get the same order for knocking out the tank! That would be the end of my secret infamy, in front of my family and my beloved one, for taking a picture with someone else's Order.

In the meantime, the surviving *Fritzes*, and there were very few of them left, crawled back to their trenches without standing up. I ordered a cease fire and save ammo in case of another German assault. Let them crawl away, "Those that are born to crawl cannot win the assaults!" That was my rephrasing of the famous Gorky's poem[3]. Apparently, my men did not hear or understand my order immediately, as for some time they continued to fire at the crawling Germans, who remained motionless on the battlefield, as if nailed to the ground by bullets. The communication line was still in order, I made it to the phone and reported the repelled counterattack and the two destroyed German tanks. As a reply I received an encouraging message from chief of staff Kiselev that reinforcements had already been sent to us. Would they make it if the *Nazis* attacked again?

I called for the second man with the AT-hand-grenade and both men from the AT-rifle crew, who luckily survived, and were not even wounded. I wrote a report about their heroic deeds in the battle and told them to go to the battalion staff, as they had already redeemed their guilt with their bravery in an honest battle, and deserved decorations. However, I was pleasantly surprised to hear that all three men refused to leave the battlefield, while the huge AT-rifle man even seemed to be offended with me. "Who will take care of my rifle then?" The others also refused to leave their comrades in such a difficult situation.

Of course, I was happy to hear that. If I were sending away three men from a full company of over a hundred men, the company's strength would have only

3   A line "Those who are born to crawl cannot fly" from a poem by a famous Russian writer and poet Maxim Gorky, (pseudomin of A. M. Peshkov, 1868-1936).

dropped by three per cent. But after our losses sending away three men, three active bayonets, as we would say in the Red Army from the times of the Civil War, would mean a 20% drop in strength of my company! I also had about five men wounded. It might sound amazing now, but not all men recognised that they had received wounds. I had to send away several wounded who had rather serious wounds, despite their weak protests. I did not want anything else to happen to them. When reinforcements or rather the exchanging troops came to take over our positions, we were all extremely happy. There were very few *shtrafniks* that had not yet spilled blood, and indeed, most of the officers believed that *shtrafniks* deserved to be rehabilitated and decorated for their stoicism and bravery in the battles.

However, even in that moment our joy was too early. Lieutenant Mirny, our political officer who fought together with us on the left flank of the bridgehead and won our respect as a brave officer, arrived together with reinforcements. His understanding of political work among the troops was leading them by example in battle, not just empty speeches in the rear. Our *politruk* was depressed. He knew that he brought bad news with the written order of Baturin, we had to hand our positions over to a rifle battalion and take over defences on its right flank. We were not disengaged!

Naturally, a rifle battalion with over 200 men would have an easier time defending the sector than a mere 20 *shtrafniks* had captured and had also repelled German counterattack supported by armour. We felt offended to give up our sector that cost us so much blood and sacrifice to another unit, but that was our destiny. An order is always an order. A Major, commander of the rifle battalion that replaced us, showed me both on the map and on terrain the sector that we had to defend. But in his tone and his attitude towards us I felt some sort of guilt that he sensed towards us, and his respect for the results that we had reached. From the words of the Major I realised that we would be in defence for a long time. That was the moment when I and my *shtrafniks* realised that our Army Commander, General Batov, would not release any *shtrafnik* who had not redeemed his guilt with blood or death. We had to stay in defence for over a month, receive replacements and lose our friends, many of whom, in our opinion, had already deserved to be released. However, that was only our opinion, while Baturin and Batov had a different opinion.

Some researchers and writers, after the war, tried to show that *shtrafniks* were "doomed to be killed," while penal companies and penal battalions were units that were "created to be destroyed" in battles. However, during my entire time at the Front in our Penal Battalion, that period at the Narev bridgehead was probably the only one that might confirm the radical statements of those post-war writers. *Shtrafniks* themselves had a right to think so at the Narev bridgehead.

I am not the one to judge the leadership skills and other features of General Batov. But such great military leaders as Marshal Rokossovski, Marshal Zhukov, and Marshal of Engineers Kharchenko, pointed out both the strong and the weak sides of 65th Army Commander Pavel Ignatovich Batov. They pointed to his lack of proper reconnaissance and intelligence, his lack of attention to the flanks. He had a certain degree of over-confidence that often resulted in high and unnecessary losses. It all seemed a bit strange, even to me. General Batov, holder of two Golden Stars of Hero of the Soviet Union, had huge battle experience. He had fought in the Spanish Civil War, and took part in the Winter War of 1939–1940. However, it is even stranger that Batov went through the entire Great Patriotic War as commander of the same army, and was never promoted. Also his army did not get a Guards or Shock title. I guess that it is only logical that neither Baturin nor Batov deserved the honorary title of *batya* i.e. Dad, among *shtrafniks*, like the previous commander Osipov, although they both had last names that sounded pretty much like that warm nickname.

Back then we had neither time nor the right to discuss the decisions of our superiors. In wartime a soldier, an officer and even a general does not have a right to doubt the decisions of his superiors, nor to oppose them. Any opposition in wartime can be treated as a crime, as treason. There were examples of such opposition to superiors, among *shtrafniks* who were sent to us, and no one was ever justified for it. That was why I kept my mouth shut and advised Fedor Usmanov not to spread the cursing poem that a *shtrafnik* wrote about Baturin and Batov. There follow bitter words about our Army Commander.

> *For him, shtrafnik is just a foot rag!*
> *He liberated only those*
> *That were wounded or squashed by tanks,*
> *The rest he sent to certain death!*

In those difficult days of October 1944, we had to focus all our attention on rearranging the German trenches and make them suitable for strong defence in the opposite direction, i.e. against the Germans. That meant that we had to transfer breastworks, remake MG nests, dig niches for hand-grenades and ammo, create new communication trenches and many other things. In short, there was plenty of work. Soon we received a phone line. That was again through the care of Senior Lieutenant Valery Semykin, who again stayed with us in the trenches on his own initiative. His office was to be in the staff for most of the time, while he wanted to be with us in the trenches!

I have described many practical details of our life at the front, as I think that this experience might be, God forbid, useful for future generations of history scholars. They would be able to learn about our life at the front. That is why I mention another practical detail. During fortification works we dug holes, at least one per squad, some 20–30 metres away from the main trench, for latrines. When those holes were getting full, we covered them with soil and dug new ones.

It was already late October. The nights grew colder, sometimes even frosty. Silver hoar-frost remained on the ground and dry grass for a long time in the morning. There was a simple shallow shelter in our sector of defence. My orderly found it and I was accommodated in it together with the company's clerk. Incidentally, our clerk was not a *shtrafnik*, but a regular soldier, Malkin. He had a calligraphic handwriting and could spontaneously think up funny or scary stories. He never took part in battles, always staying with the company's papers. Then I invited one former deputy platoon leader, a good friend of mine, to live in the same shelter. Soldiers dug another shelter for my deputy George Sergeev. As company commander, he and his deputy had to be apart from each other in order not to be killed by the same shell. My company was then less than a platoon. While platoons only had 8–10 men each, so the sector that we had to defend seemed too wide for us. We started to get replacements quite soon, though. After a couple of days they brought some ten rookies to us, and my company was then about a regular rifle platoon in size. It was good for strengthening our defences.

But I was upset to see one of the AT-rifle crew members there, whom I had already recommended for decoration, and release from the battalion, for the tanks that they knocked out. That was a demonstration of the 'vigilance' of our *kombat*. Both Baturin and our NKVD officer scrutinised us. They found out who fired at the tanks and who loaded the AT-rifle. As they decided that only one person could knock out a tank, they refused to release and decorate the loader of the AT-rifle. The s*htrafnik* was offended, and I was offended, too. I also felt ashamed that I had promised that diligent and brave soldier a decoration and his release. I was also ashamed that the *kombat*, who was not even close to the battlefield, did not consider my opinion, the opinion of the company commander that was there, and who had directly led the men in that engagement. So the beginning of interaction with the new *kombat* did not promise anything good. But both the *shtrafnik* and I just had to accept what, to us, was offensive.

The active battles for the recovery of that bridgehead were over. Our troops completed their mission, almost doubling the size of the bridgehead. Preparations for a new offensive and daily life in defence started. That daily life was completely different from our defence in Belorussia. Valery Semykin brought us a new table of codes, for communication over the phone, in which instead of a regular number I received a codename, "Alexander Nevski". George became "George Saakadze", and Fedor Usmanov was "Salavat Yulaev".[4] It was quite unusual, but a pleasant small thing.

The defence of the Narev bridgehead was the next part of my battle journey.

4   Famous military leaders of Russian, Georgian and Bashkirian military history.

Infantrymen armed with Mosin 1891/30 rifles in assault. The soldier in the front has a Guards badge on the right side of his chest and Medal for Bravery on the left side. He has a gasmask bag over his shoulder.

Infantrymen at rest. From their weapon – PPSh-41 SMGs – one can judge that this is a SMG platoon. Platoon leader, armed with TT pistol, is sitting with his back towards the camera.

Handing out decorations. This infantry sergeant is awarded with the Medal for Bravery, one of the most valued decorations at the front.

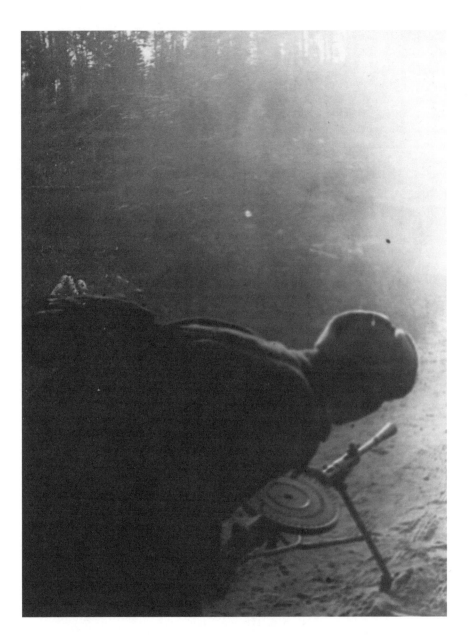

Infantryman armed with light DP machine-gun.

An infantry squad sneaking forward. The squad leader (in the background) is armed with PPSh-41 SMG.

A combat engineer is clearing a passage in a barbed wire fence.
Note the semi-automatic SVT rifle.

Combat in a ruined city.

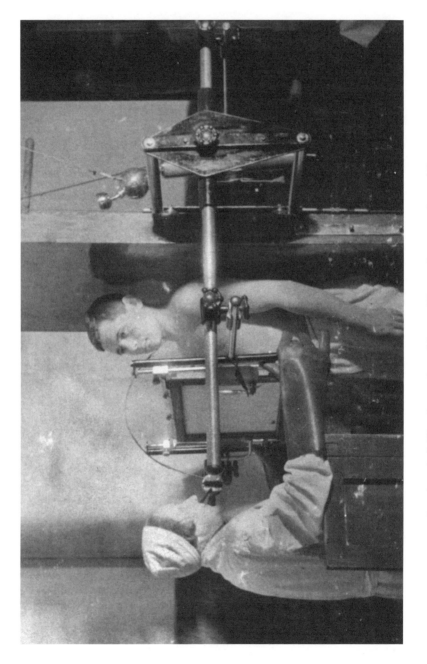

In a hospital. The doctor is making an X-ray of a recovering soldier.

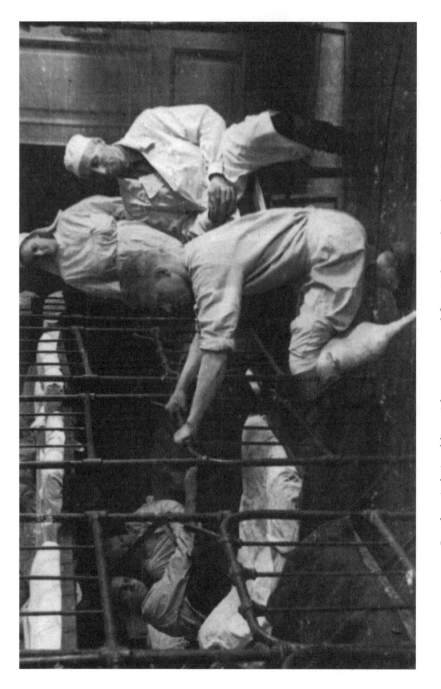

In a hospital. A soldier with an amputated foot is doing physical exercises.

A Maxim MG crew is moving into position. The Maxim MG was the main heavy MG of the Red Army during the entire war. It was heavy but did not demand much maintenance and was reliable.

Firing range practice of the PTRD anti-tank rifle. After entering service in late 1941, this rifle was the main weapon of the anti-tank rifle companies that were organic to a rifle battalion.

Alexander V. Pyl'cyn, 2002.

Major A. V. Pyl'cyn, 1946, Leipzig.

Major A. V. Pyl'cyn, 1946.

Major Pyl'cyn with his wife Rita, 1946, Leipzig
(the photo was touched in during printing).

Ekaterina Makarievskaya (mother of Rita and Stanislav), Alexander Pyl'cyn, Stanislav Makarievski, Rita Makarievskaya.

A combat engineer.

A sniper armed with Mosin rifle with PE optical sight.

Infantry attack with the support of a ISU-152 self-propelled gun.

Infantry taking up positions in a trench.

Commanders of the 8th Independent Penal Battalion. Sitting: Mirny, Kiselev, Matvienko, Baturin, Kazakov, Filatov. Standing: Vinogradov, Sokolov.

Company commander Ivan Yanin.

CHAPTER 7

In Defence on the Narev

I will try to be brief in describing the further events in our sector of defence at the Narev bridgehead, as the Germans were no longer active there. Being in defence was nothing new for me. Troops of the 65th Army were none too active either. Apparently, the commander of the Army, General P. I. Batov was satisfied with the fact that his shrunk bridgehead and his reputation were restored. In the meantime, Command of the Front was restoring communications with supply troops, and bringing order to the troops who had suffered heavy losses. They repaired the armour and other hardware, and accumulated all sorts of ammo in preparation for the next large-scale offensive. It was to be one of the most important strategic operations of the war that was later called the Vistula-Oder operation. So, we were again on the defence. After the second offensive, in which battle losses were over 80%, my company had less than one platoon, even taking into consideration the newly arrived replacements.

In those first days of setting up the defences of my company sector, the *kombat* called me over the phone. With a strict voice that forbade any objections, he ordered me to set up the CSP, i.e. Company Strongpoint. The order was so unexpected and absurd to me that I was dumbfounded for a while. Such a form of setting up company defences is proper when a company has at least three platoons, with more or less TOE numbers of men. In a CSP, two platoons are in the first trench, while the third platoon is in the second echelon. Thus CSPs are a mainstay of a rather deep defence of an entire battalion of three companies. We did not even have a company, never mind a battalion! With my small forces I could not set up a CSP without weakening our forces in the first trench, which were over-stretched anyway. I told all this to Baturin, mentioning to him over the phone that I would be able to fulfil his order only if he gave me at least two more full platoons, or when I received enough men to replace losses in the company. I realised that my answer would, to put it mildly, cause the dissatisfaction of my commander. But such was my personality!

Just as I expected, the Lieutenant Colonel replied with sharp and angry words, threatening to withhold his recommendation for my promotion to company commander. I knew well that before my appointment as company commander was officially endorsed by the Front Order, my *kombat* could easily cancel it. But I was so outraged that I just asked him to whom I should hand in the command of the company. After a long and heavy silence Baturin told me, in an angry voice, "Lead the company for a while! I will deal with you later!" And again, as if a demon possessed me, and instead of the expected "Yes, Comrade Lieutenant Colonel", I said into the receiver, "Come here, into the trenches, and you can deal with me right here on the spot". Baturin had not yet been in the trenches at the front line. He lost his nerve and almost shouted, "I know for myself where I should be and where I should go!" That was the end of our conversation.

My former company commander Major Matvienko, who had already become deputy battalion commander, asked me later, "Why did you go looking for trouble? You should have told him "yes", and then you would do everything as you pleased!" Well, I have to admit that I never had such 'wisdom'! Much later I realised that Baturin must have attended some short tactics courses, before being transferred from being a political officer to our battalion. He must have learnt about CSPs there. Then, just when he wanted to demonstrate his knowledge of tactics, a young Senior Lieutenant all of a sudden did not appreciate that knowledge of setting up defences. As I soon found out, our new *kombat* remembered the bad things quite well. There were circumstances, throughout the war, when I felt his bad attitude towards me, in fact right to the end.

In the meantime, the *kombat* had already received the Order of Bogdan Khmelnicky 1st Class, apparently, for "successful operations" in restoring the flanks of the bridgehead. Then, when he knew that the same order of the 2nd Class and the Order of Alexander Nevski had lower status than his order, he recommended all officers for those very orders. Philip Kiselev told me about this and we started writing recommendations for platoon leaders. We recommended George Sergeev for the Order of Alexander Nevski, and Fedor Usmanov for the Order of Bogdan Khmelnicky 2nd Class. Baturin passed on word to me that I would also be recommended for the Order of Alexander Nevski.

Then I had to tell Philip my stupid story of "the officer with two battle orders" and ask him to talk the *kombat* into giving me the Order of Patriotic War, at any rate, that I was supposed to get for the knocked out tank. When Baturin was given the award recommendations, he refused to sign mine for a long time, as that would mean that his subordinate would receive a decoration higher than his! As Philip Kiselev told me later, both Filatov and Matvienko actively advocated my award recommendation. As far as I understood, Philip told Baturin my story of taking pictures with someone else's order, in hospital. To be short, with joint effort they managed to talk our *kombat* into signing the recommendation. Baturin his own hand replaced the 1st Class for the 2nd in the recommendation, making an acid remark that "you should not beg for decorations, you should earn them". In his words, I did not win the duel against that German tank.

When I heard about that conversation, I realised that my official and personal relations with the *kombat* could only grow worse. However, I received the Order of the Patriotic War 2nd Class, and it was not Baturin himself but Chief of Staff Major Kiselev who handed the Order to me. Finally, the shame of taking a picture with someone else's order was removed! That cheating to my relatives had tortured my conscience for many months. Despite growing tensions with the *kombat*, I felt a huge relief. Even lack of comfort and the problems of trench life in defence did not seem so hard to me.

However, our catering situation became much worse. Perhaps it was because the Front's supply bases had not yet arrived. The rations that we received were no longer sufficient for us. Although we were on defence, and so we did not have assaults, exhausting marches, rushes and slow crawling. However, the soldiers had to go back to the front-line manner of dividing bread, sugar and all other food staples that we received. One soldier was ordered to divide bread and sugar into more or less even portions. Then a squad leader, or someone appointed, would turn his back on those portions, cover his eyes with his hat, while one of the soldiers would point at a portion and ask, "Who is getting this one?" The man, who did not see the portions, called a name and thus the food would be divided among all the men. There were no arguments or fights about others getting a larger portion. As we platoon leaders and company commanders were also eating from the same field kitchen as our men, I insisted that all officers also followed that pattern. We got used to that practice quite quickly. However, we divided our additional officer rations amongst ourselves. There was no chance of getting extra food from nature as it was already late autumn, and was quickly turning into winter. So there was nothing we could find in the forests and the local population was nowhere to be seen near to our positions. On top of all that, we had another problem which we could not get used to, so unpleasant was it.

Due to the early winter, men were issued winter hats, and those who did not have overcoats were issued overcoats, while we officers received winter uniforms. We were especially happy to receive vests made from sheepskin. All, both men and officers, were finally issued a new change of underwear. They did not send us field steam baths, though, as they did in Belorussia, and none of us had any chance of washing ourselves for a very long time. Probably because of that or because of our new underwear and uniforms not going through proper disinfection before issue, or because of some German items that were left in the trenches, we were soon attacked by another enemy, insects. To be brief, all our clothes were full of lice.

I sent requests for a steam bath but they went unheard at the battalion HQ. However, we received a rather large amount of packages of dust-pyrethrum, the most common anti-insect substance of that time. We merely put this powder under our collars and in places where we had hair on our bodies. That was not a pleasant feeling at all, but a couple of days later we were shaking our dead 'enemies' out from our long boots and from under our shirts. Unfortunately they multiplied faster than they died. It is not too pleasant to talk about, even less so to write about it, but I decided not to hide anything in my memoirs!

Finally, they sent a field disinfection chamber to a valley not far from our trenches. In simple soldier slang it was called a lice-killer. Without receiving the second change of uniforms, soldiers turned in their tunics and trousers while remaining outside in the cold in their underpants! We officers turned in our sheep-skin vests without realising that they would shrink in the high temperature! We were not too sorry for that, as we thought the vests to be one of the reasons for our insect problem. In general, that measure decreased a degree of our sufferings from lice, but it did not eradicate the problem completely. We got rid of the parasites only in winter which fortunately came very early that year. In early December we left the front line and went to receive replacements in the rear. Only there, after numerous disinfections, total shaving and washing in field and peasant steam baths, did we manage to win the war against insects. I should say that the decisive contribution in that small victory was made by our battalion doctor, Stepan Petrovich Buzun. He managed to get the so-called K soap that destroyed the insects very effectively, sometimes also taking the upper layer of skin, if the soap was applied for too long time. However, we just wanted to get rid of those enemies of humanity! And when we received new sheepskin vests we were again happy and clean. That happened much later.

In the meantime, we were still in the trenches and in addition to insects we were really bothered by German snipers and their frequent attempts to test our defences. They delivered strong and sudden artillery strikes that were followed by short assaults of infantry, sometimes up to company's strength, supported by armour. During one such German assault, I witnessed the engagement of our AA guns that were placed right behind our trenches, against German tanks. The automatic guns opened well-aimed fire over open sights, and several tanks were immediately knocked out, while the others retreated. The German attack was repelled even before they could reach our trenches. I witnessed engagements of AA guns against ground targets many times after that incident and I always admired them. Such German attacks looked like reconnaissance in force, from their side, in order to spot our weapons emplacements and to take prisoners for interrogation.

They failed to reach those objectives in our sector, but we heard rumours that in some sectors their attempts were successful. Then I thought that it was really good for me not to have agreed to set up CSP, with only part of an almost non-existent company placed in the second trench. We had enough firepower in the first trench, and the Germans never managed to approach us, even within the distance of throwing a hand-grenade. I thought that Baturin himself must have understood that, and he never again came back to the matter of setting up CSP. He never found time to deal with me, although we were gradually getting replacements. I had two platoons almost full. Senior Lieutenant George Vasilievich Razhev was appointed as a platoon leader into my company. He was a happy and open fellow and, as it turned out later, he loved women and alcohol a lot. After that our company was led only by Senior Lieutenants and was dubbed Senior Lieutenant Company by *shtrafnik* men from the Navy.

Powerful artillery strikes sometimes caused serious losses among us. People were being killed not because of their own stupidity or carelessness. However, there were cases when trenches and lightly built dug-outs took direct hits of heavy shells and mines. There was no forest next to us and we had no materials for building proper dug-outs and shelters. When direct hits happened, we often had to collect fragments of the bodies of our men. During one such strike, newly appointed George Razhev was severely shell-shocked. He could not hear anything for a couple of weeks, but he refused to leave the front line for a hospital and led his platoon although deaf.

I can well remember the death of one *shtrafnik*, Kostya Smertin. I only remember his ex-officer rank. He was either a Lieutenant or a Captain. He was one of the observers of our company. On that day, I stood in the trench next to him, and was observing German positions through binoculars. I thought that I managed to spot a well-camouflaged position of a German sniper. I warned Kostya about it, telling him not to stick out of the trench as the sniper could be hunting for one of us. My assumption proved to be true only a second later. Immediately after I sat down in the trench a bullet whizzed over my head. I was lucky, as often happened. I did not have time to order Smertin to sit down. But apparently he wanted to seize the opportunity and see where the sniper was firing from. The second bullet hit the middle of his forehead, immediately after the first, a bit above his eyebrows. He slowly went down to the bottom of the trench. He did not drop, but gently sat down. His eyes looked up and started moving quickly, while his lips whispered something that I could not understand. His face went very pale. I put a bandage over his very small wound. The blood did not flow a lot. I recalled how we were trained to put a bandage on a head that was called "Hippocrates's hat". The strange eye movements and whispering lasted for about a minute. Then, after convulsions that shook his entire body, all his muscles suddenly tensed and he went silent. He died. I closed his eyes. He was not as lucky as I was.

I felt especially sorry for him for some reason. Maybe because I did not make it to warn him, or because the last minutes of his life passed right there in front of me. I also could not understand his last words. I remembered his last name because the maiden name of my grandmother on my mother's side was also Smertina, meaning 'Death's daughter', in Russian. When he arrived in my platoon I even tried to find out about his family, whether we were distant relatives. However, my grandmother had some Khakassian blood in her and had a clearly Asian face, with narrow dark eyes and high cheeks, while this young man was from Yaroslavl and had the features of a real Russian. He looked as I imagined the ancient Russian knights looked. Even now, I can see his rapidly moving blue eyes, and his white lips trying to deliver the last words of his life to me. I saw a lot of deaths in the war, but that death I remembered especially.

In that regard I would like to note that we did not have a habit of wearing steel helmets in the battalion. The saying "caution is the parent of safety" was somehow not popular with us. It was considered 'cool' to walk without a helmet, although we all knew that they were available at the battalion warehouse, as our supply officers offered them to us many times. I don't know where this despising attitude to helmets came from, but it prevailed in the battalion, and wearing a helmet was treated almost like a sign of weakness. I think now that we officers also maintained that not really good tradition with our behaviour. It started in the battalion before my arrival. I don't think that in the case of Kostya Smertin a helmet could have saved his life. The bullet hit his forehead right above the eyebrows, and a helmet would not have protected that spot anyway. Even after Smertin's death, no one started wearing helmets. Maybe it was stupid, but it is just the way it was.

Winter was coming, and as there was no end in sight for our trench life, we started to build accommodation as best we could. We dug more foxholes, but smaller ones, for just one or two persons, as we clearly remembered the tragic death of Ivan Yanin. By every means, including night raids on a half-destroyed barn on no-man's land, under periodic German MG fire, the men managed to find bits and pieces of board and sometimes whole wooden beams. Those supplies, procured at great risk, allowed the construction of primitive shelters, just like the one that I occupied with my company's command group. Such shelters gave us an opportunity to take turns out of the sleet, or just warm ourselves and even dry our uniforms a bit.

Of course, we could not heat the shelters in a proper way, but we made niches in the walls, with a tunnel to the surface that served as a chimney. We burnt anything we could find in those primitive stoves. There were paper wrappings from rifle ammo, hay or small bits of wood that we collected from the ground at night, after looking for their possible location during the day. We also burnt the occasional bushes that we cut during the night. One thing that really amazed and scared me was that men burnt standard TNT packages, of course, without fuses! It turned out that TNT melted in a fire and burnt slowly, producing a lot of smut and also a little heat. I was afraid that by accident a single cartridge could end up in the fire, act as a fuse, and then … So when I learnt about that way of heating, I ordered the platoon leaders to control this heating process in the strictest possible manner. God forbid that a single cartridge ended up in the fire, together with tar-covered ammo wrapping paper!

Of course, our primitive shelters did not have any doors. The entrances were covered by regular *plash-palatkas*, which were thick and did not let light in. When the 'heating' was on, to write a letter home, a report or recommendation for a soldier, we had to use primitive illumination. By that time the small number of captured paraffin lamp stands had been used. So Valery Semykin gave us a hint about how we could illuminate our shelters. He gave us a whole roll of German phone cable that had rubber coating and tar-covered insulation. We hung the wire from the ceiling, so that one end would be a bit higher than the other, and ignited its upper part. Fire gradually consumed the rubber insulation and went on down the wire. One had to pull the upper part of the wire, at the right time, further from the roll. It did not produce much light, but produced a lot of stench and smut. In the morning, when we left the dug-outs, we looked like demons from hell. It took a lot of effort to wash off the awful smut mask with snow and soap. Alternatively, we soaped our faces and shaved off the smut together with our teenage stubble. In general, I do not remember that we could ever wash ourselves properly. It was good if it snowed, clean fresh snow, not yet covered with gunpowder smut. It was our joy!

I celebrated my birthday in the trenches of the Narev bridgehead. I turned 21 years old. During the war we became adults extremely quickly and it seemed that we had a long life behind us. We did not at all feel like young men, which we were in reality. Maybe it was right to count one year of service, in a penal battalion at the front, as six years of service. According to those measures I was already 27, which was quite an age! My new platoon leader, George Razhev, told me that despite my youth I received the most honourable nickname of *batya* or 'dad', among the *shtrafnik* men. Some men even called me *Shtrafbatya* or 'penal dad', for my caring attitude towards my men. I must say that this really flattered me. Even George and the other officers of the company, despite the fact that I was the youngest man among them, also started calling me 'dad' in an unofficial situation. A bit later I thought of growing a moustache in order to look older, as one older *shtrafnik* told me I was of a "shamelessly young age". I was also a bit afraid of Baturin getting to know about it. I knew that sooner or later he would hear, and probably hate me even more! However, there were no consequences for the nickname, even our *osobist* did not react at all. Maybe he did not like Baturin either!

A message about the foundation of Artillery Day almost coincided with my birthday, on November 19. It was to commemorate the heroism of the artillerymen at the Battle of Stalingrad. On that day we received a front line shot of *vodka*, so we celebrated my birthday on the same day. I was pleased to see Ivan Matvienko, my former company commander, deputy chief of staff Valery Semykin, chief of staff Philip Kiselev and Alex Filatov all coming to congratulate me with their *vodka* rations. With my trench friends George Sergeev and George Razhev, and also Fedor Usmanov, we celebrated my birthday in a nice friendly company, in a true brotherly atmosphere of front-line life. We recalled Ivan Yanin and all the others who were killed in that long and awful war, which was already drawing to an end. The end of war seemed to be near, not like a year earlier.

Shortly afterwards they brought me a letter 'from your wife' as the postman said. I realised that it was a letter from Rita. A few of my friends knew that I called my beloved girlfriend, Rita from Leningrad, a wife. I met and fell in love with her one year earlier, and our endless 'letter romance' had dragged on since that time. We again cheated the military censorship. From the first letter of names of 'friends' that were congratulating me on my birthday, I realised that her hospital had recently moved to Lochuv, a small Polish town really close to us.

In early December we were all of a sudden withdrawn from the front line. We hastily handed our sector over to a fully manned rifle company and started to prepare to disengage and leave for the rear. It turned out that Front Commander Marshal Rokossovski learnt that 'his gang' had been at the front since October. He ordered the release of *shtrafnik* officers who had already served their term in the Penal Battalion. He also released those who deserved release with their bravery and stoicism. Our joy had no limits, and those who were released were especially happy. Recommendations for release had been ready for them for a long time. It was a pity that Kostya Smertin, as well as many others, did not live to see that happy moment. They were killed when we were already in defence. I had had ready a recommendation for Kostya for a long time, as he was both brave and stoic and his two-month term of service in the penal battalion had already expired.

We quickly packed our few belongings and the next day handed over our defences to the neighbouring units. We gathered at a battalion HQ in a small house at the edge of an almost completely destroyed village. My heat was beating hard, so many things had happened between us in the previous six weeks! I went to report to a number of men in the company and to my battalion commander. I also gave him recommendations for the release of *shtrafnik* men. At a good moment, I asked his permission to leave the battalion for three or four days to see my bride in her hospital. I did not lie to Baturin that Rita was my wife, as I had told everyone else in the battalion. I recommended that the MG commander George Sergeev replace me for that time, as in battles he was my deputy.

The *kombat* hesitated a bit before making a decision on my personal request, and I thought that he would refuse. After some time he told me the name of the village that the battalion's staff, supply and support units and my company had to reach, and ordered me to be in that village two days later. He ordered me to temporarily hand the company over to Senior Lieutenant Usmanov. Of course, in that case the *kombat* was right, as George Sergeev belonged to an MG Company, and not mine. I was so happy to get this permission without any conflict that I did not lose a second of time, asked for permission to leave, and ran out of his house with only one thought, "I must make it!" I did not even have time to be amazed at this unexpected and short vacation. There was a reason for that!

It had been over a year since I saw Rita for the last time in Ufa. Then I knew I would see her there, at the front, again! I left brief instructions for Fedor Usmanov, who understood completely. Grabbing my *sidor* bag, in which I had my dry tack, bread, sugar, canned meat and other things, I was already running to the nearest road in order to hitch a lift in a car or a truck. After finding the place on the map, I realised that with a bit of luck I would be able to make it to Lochuv the same day. The very first car that I stopped was a real gift of fortune, as it was going to the rear, and through Lochuv! What good luck!

Although the car stopped quite often, we arrived in that small town several hours later. I ran to the first horse-drawn carriage. It was driven by a young small soldier in a uniform which for some reason lacked shoulder-boards. I asked the boy about where the hospital was. I was amazed that whole day, but at that point my amazement was beyond limits. With some difficulty I recognised little Stas, younger brother of Rita, who secretly went to the front together with Rita and their mother. It seemed that he also recognised me and asked me directly, "Do you want Rita Makarievskaya?" I threw myself at him, hugged his small thin body, jumped into his carriage and he slowly took me to the hospital. I just wanted to jump off the carriage and run in the direction that he showed me. Soon we arrived at a group of buildings. Stas ran into one of them, but quickly ran back out. Shy and timid, he told me that Rita could not come out as they had some lecture that was being given by the chief of the hospital, and Rita told us to go home.

Rita, Stas and their mother lived in a separate house. As much as I wanted to take this invitation, I was covered with the damn bugs that not only spoiled my life at the front but also put me in a really tricky situation there in the village. Just because of lice I was not planning to stay overnight. I just badly wanted to see my best-loved girl. Probably, that mad desire and the fact that I already knew her mother, Ekaterina Nikolaevna, made me decide to tell her about my problem straight away. I wanted to wait for Rita anyway, even outdoors where it was not too cold that day and talk with her, even outdoors.

We came to the house. Ekaterina Nikolaevna saw us from the window, and she recognised me and ran out into the street. Apparently, I blushed from shame about the confession that I had to make, so that she immediately asked me with some concern if I were sick. I had to tell her straight about my problem and tell her that I would rather wait for Rita outside. However, she understood everything immediately and made a different decision. "Come in, Alex, please don't be shy about this disease. Unfortunately, it is quite common at the front. Many wounded arrive at our hospital with it. We will take all the necessary measures straight away". When we walked in, she immediately ordered me to take off my uniform, go into a small room that was Stas's, take off my underwear and put on a white medical overall. I could lie down and rest before Rita's arrival. She started to boil my underwear in a pot on a well-burning stove, and thoroughly ironed my tunic and trousers with a red-hot iron. I was lying in a bed and could not imagine how this meeting would take place. Despite long sleepless nights, spent writing recommendations for my *shtrafnik* men, handing over the sector of defence and other business of war, I could not sleep before the most important meeting of my life!

Rita came running several hours later. I jumped up from the bed in my strange garment. The white doctor's overall was definitely not my size. Apparently, her mother told everything to Rita so she was not amazed to see me in such clothes. Rather, she threw herself at me, we hugged each other and stood like that for a long time. Rita had changed so much! It had been a bit over a year, in war that was an eternity! After my departure from Ufa she had become so much more adult. Her faded uniform tunic with shoulder-boards fitted her very well, and she had gained a bit of weight after the hunger of the siege. Instead of an enlisted man's belt she had an officer's belt, apparently from her mother. A faded cotton uniform skirt firmly covered her slim legs. We were madly happy to see each other. Almost all night, while the inexhaustible Ekaterina Nikolaevna was boiling and ironing my uniform, we talked. We recalled all the moments of our time together from the very first day that we met. Then we told stories about what had happened to us during the year, up to that happy evening. Both little Stas and Ekaterina Nikolaevna were participants of our amazing conversation and it made us even closer to each other. We have been dreaming about that moment for long days, weeks and months.

CHAPTER 8

Marriage

Our love story started one warm summer night in Alkino, a village not far from Ufa. Our regimental band was playing waltzes on the dance floor. Dances were the last thing on my mind even as a young, freshly graduated, 19 years old Lieutenant. I had two wisdom teeth cutting through my gums simultaneously. The pain was permanent and exhausting. I was hanging around the fence that hid the dancing young officers like me, who had just changed their collar-tabs from cube rank pips, to officer shoulder-boards with stars. Their dance partners were mostly fancily dressed girls, workers of a nearby dairy. Young officers did not only fancy waltzes but also serious dates with those 'milk-maids'. I saw a quietly and bitterly crying slim blond girl sitting on a bench. She was definitely not dressed up for dances. Maybe I felt sorry for her, or maybe I wanted distraction from the irritating toothache, so I walked up to her and struck up a conversation.

I found out that Rita was from Leningrad, from which she was evacuated together with her mother and younger brother to Ufa. Her father, a construction engineer, had died of hunger during the Siege. In Ufa they had a lot of relatives. The city committee of Komodo, where Lenin had spent his youth, took over evacuees from Leningrad. In order to help the new girl to recover from the near starvation of siege rations, they sent her to work as a leader in a pioneer camp that was in Alkino, next to our regiment. Instead of fancy party clothes she wore strange skiing trousers of unclear colour, a worn out blouse and wooden clogs with leather straps, instead of lacquered shoes. So the poor girl was crying from frustration that her clothes did not suit the beautiful music of the military orchestra. Probably she also cried out of self-pity. We spoke for a long time. She calmed down and my intolerable toothache also seemed to ease a bit. I saw her off to the very gate of the pioneer camp. There, an angry woman, 35–40 years old, started to scold her for leaving the young pioneers who were not at all angelic without supervision. I had to plead for her. That was how I got to know Rita's boss. Probably it helped the poor girl a bit, as this big lady started to treat Rita in a nicer way after our conversation. We agreed on a date the next day, and several days later I felt that I could not wait for the next date with her.

Previously, I did not avoid any sorts of duties, sentry, kitchen or other services, and even found a certain charm in all those monotonous sorts of jobs. I was charmed at being responsible for the battalion, a sentry or even the kitchen. But from the moment that I met Rita I started to hate all those sorts of duties, as they deprived me of the possibility of seeing that charming girl on a daily basis. It was always interesting to spend time with her. In short, I fell in love with her, head over heels, from the first sight. But one day she did not come to the bench that we used to meet at. All upset, I still managed to notice an address written with a stick in the sand, "Ufa, Tsuryupa Street". I just had to wait for a good moment. In Alkino we had a humorous saying, "You have money – fun in Ufa, no money – sit in Chishmy". Chishmy was the nearest large railway junction. Soon I managed to get some free time and I found Rita in Ufa. I was always a timid boy but then for some reason I got brave! I introduced myself to her mother and all her aunts, as all her male relatives were in the army, at the front, and managed to make a good impression on them.

I went back to the regiment and several days later, without any initiative from my side, I was sent to Ufa to a local timber mill on the Belaya River, to procure timber for the needs of the regiment. I spent two weeks on that trip. During that time my feelings towards Rita grew into real love for that fragile, blonde, and grey-eyed girl from the siege of Leningrad. At that time she was working as an assembler at the Ufa factory that made phone sets. She also found time to go to the nursing courses of the RSRC, the Russian Society of the Red Cross. But we spent most of the evenings in a good theatre in Ufa. The actors had been evacuated to Ufa from Moscow and Kiev.

Her mother, a military doctor with battle experience of the Civil War and the Finnish War, was enlisted into a newly formed military hospital. Rita was also enlisted there as a nurse. Her 15 years old brother, little Stas, was also working in a factory somewhere, getting a worker's ration card. I tried, like a real gentleman, to find a reason to buy some treat for Rita. But the only thing one could get in Ufa in those days, without ration cards, were sticky candies and a beverage that was called 'bread soufflé' and did not remind one of any sweet pastry at all. All good things have to end some time. My timber-harvesting trip to Ufa was soon over. I went back to the regiment in Alkino. We then saw each other rarely. Soon after, Rita informed me that the hospital was fully manned, and that she was to be sent to the Front in a matter of days.

I ran to my company commander Senior Lieutenant Nurgaliev. In our eyes he was an older officer, about forty years old, calm and steady. He permitted me to go to Ufa for one day, but to report back to him that evening. I barely made it to see Rita and her family at their home. They were packing up the last of their belongings. I managed to help them get on the train. But before the train left I had to say "goodbye" to them, as I had to make it back to the regiment. That was the first time that I saw Rita and her mother, Ekaterina Nikolaevna, in military uniforms. And that was the first time that without timidity I kissed my female soldier on the lips, wiped away her tears and barely held back my own. As it was late, I ran to the train that was going to Alkino, the train was already on the move. I jumped on it and soon we disappeared from each other's sight.

I could not rest for several days. Among other things, I was bothered by the thought that she, an eighteen years old girl, not fully recovered from the siege, was already going to the Front. Meanwhile I, a grown man almost twenty years old, stayed in the rear, although many officers had already gone to the Front with replacement companies that we had trained. Yet again our regiment commander, a *frontovik* Major Zhidovich with a typical long scar on his left cheek, turned down my application with a laconic order. "Ten days of home arrest for an untimely request". Home arrest meant refusal of leave to Chishmy or Ufa as well as withholding 25% of the monthly wage. We joked that the money went to the defence fund. Breaking the insubordination rules, I ran directly to the regiment commander in the morning. But he replied in an even more laconic manner, "No hurry! We will all be there sometime". However, soon destiny responded to my tenth request. They started forming a team of officers, for a reserve officer regiment of the military district, for posting to the Front.

... Human destinies are sometimes unpredictable! In 1960 I was an airborne Colonel, serving in Kostroma and was undergoing treatment in Yaroslavl garrison hospital for surgery on the removal of my thyroid gland. A medical inspection was supposed to decide whether I was fit or unfit for further service in the airborne troops. In that hospital I met the former commander of my reserve regiment, a retired Colonel Zhidovich in hospital pyjamas. I recognised him from the typical scar that went across his entire left cheek from the temple to his ear. From a distance it looked like a side-whisker. Strangely enough, he not only recalled me, but almost immediately recognised in me the stubborn young Lieutenant who had bothered him so much with his requests to be sent to the Front. He, my then-commander, as it turned out, also volunteered for the Front. He took over a Guards rifle regiment, but was heavily wounded in the very first battles. He then spent long years in hospitals and remained to serve in the army until his retirement in Yaroslavl.

I stayed in the hospital, before they found me unfit for service with the airborne troops. So we would spend long evenings indulging in memories of Alkino, our battle experiences, and life after the war. He told me about the destiny of his deputy commanders in the reserve regiment. Major Rodin, a strong and handsome officer, was killed during his second posting at the Front. Lieutenant Colonel Neklyudov, with his short tidy beard and refined manners, looked like a typical representative of the old Imperial Army to us young Lieutenants who had just received shoulder-boards. He was rather older, so he was not sent to the Front and was discharged from the army immediately after the end of the war. We had a time of nice memories in that hospital in Yaroslavl ...

But back then, in 1943, when Rita left from Ufa, she and I started an intensive correspondence, a real 'letter romance'. I learnt from her letters that she was in Tula, where their hospital was stationed on Krasnoperekopskaya Street. Much later, when I was already at the Front, Rita wrote to me that their hospital had became an organic part of the Belorussian Front. That was how a merciful destiny gave us the chance to be on the same Front and to have a second meeting, one that lasted our entire life. Just like many other young men in love, I found a passion for writing poems and I wrote entire letters in poems to my beloved one.

Even now, many years after the war, I still believe that our love was the talisman that kept me alive. It led me away from deadly dangers in my encounters with the realities of war, with its bullets, mines, tanks and bombs. I cannot help mentioning another 'test' that Rita herself put me through. From summer 1944 she wrote to me that she had already been married and even had a child. I answered her that if all that was then in the past, it would not prevent our love, and her child would be our child. I almost believed her letter, although I could not understand how and when it could have happened. She left Ufa in August, and it had not yet been a year. Even when we met in Lochuv the question was still hanging in the air, although I did not question or doubt her love for me, or my love for her. Early in the morning, without getting any sleep, I put on a clean and ironed fresh uniform and started my journey in order to arrive at the village on time, and not to upset my *kombat*. Being late was not my habit.

I unfolded the map and found two small villages on it, Buda Pritocka and Buda Kuminska. Both were close to the highway between Warsaw and Brest. Kalushin I knew from my time in the hospital, and Rembertuv, which was a suburb of Warsaw, to the east from Vistula River. I pointed out the two villages to Rita, as I thought that we would stay two or three weeks there, or even longer. According to the order of Front Commander Marshal Rokossovski, that was the place where we were supposed to release the *shtrafniks* who had already served their term in the penal battalion. We would then receive replacements, arrange them into battle-capable units, and train them for the new battles. Rita told me that their hospital, just like all others, I think, had a group of amateur artists, and as she was a former student of a ballet school in Leningrad, she was the leading dancer in the dancing group. Thus, during periods of lull at the Front, when the hospital did not have that many wounded, that amateur artist group would 'tour' the nearest army units that were resting or receiving replacements. Such tours were set up by the political department of the Front. Who knows, we thought, maybe their amateur group would make it somewhere close to us. Although during the entire war our penal battalion never had any visiting artists. The assumption was further strengthened by the fact that their ensemble was scheduled to visit the town of Sedlec, to the east of Kalushin.

As they say in such cases, "I knew it!" By the end of the day I reached the villages that my *kombat* pointed out to me and met the new political officer of the battalion Major Kazakov. He had been appointed to replace Lieutenant Colonel Rudzinski, who was taken away from the battalion by our former *kombat* Colonel Osipov. I was a bit amazed to see several other political officers who must have arrived at the battalion shortly before, but had never visited our trenches at the front line. The *kombat*, when I reported to him, just grunted with satisfaction. He did not even ask me about how my 'vacation' went and ordered me to accommodate my company in the village of Buda Pritocka. I went to the village, where I met Fedor Usmanov, George Razhev and, still 'attached' to my company, the MG platoon leader from MG Company, George Sergeev who had already settled in the village. AT-rifle company commander, my old friend Pete Zagumennikov and mortar platoon leader Michael, or as he was called, Musya Goldstein were also in the village.

In fact, all my battle friends were again next to me. My orderly was an older former Captain Nikolai. I don't remember his last name, unfortunately. He found the house of a lone Pole called Krul, whose name, for some reason, I do remember. The Pole was very proud of his last name. It did not mean rabbit, i.e. *krolik* in Russian, as I at first thought, but king, i.e. *korol.* The house did not look beautiful, but we got a large room for sessions of the military council of our company, as Fedor Usmanov said. Two smaller ones were for me and for my orderly. Pan Krul was lonely for some reason, he did not have wife or children, but a whole dozen male and female peasants worked on his farm. They had not been sent to Germany for slave labour, as we got used to see in Belorussia or Ukraine. Then, in December 1944, we noticed a lot of hares running in the fields, and I decided to use my marksmanship and treat myself and my friends to hare meat.

As early as in secondary school I was one of the first students to fulfil right away the requirements, and pass the norms, of the "Voroshilov sharpshooter" badge, 2nd Class. When I was a newly graduated Lieutenant and held one of the first training sessions for my platoon, I wanted to demonstrate to a poor soldier that it was not the rifle that was to blame. With his rifle, I hit the telegraph pole porcelain isolator from about a hundred metres, standing without support. The porcelain isolator burst into pieces and the wire hung loose in the air in full view of my surprised men. To be honest, I was also shocked to see such a result, although I understood that I had set a bad example to my men. I should not have damaged the telegraph line and I also risked my reputation. What if I had missed?

So, on December 14, 1944, one of the most important days in my life, at around 4 pm, after a lunch that was neither tasty nor filling, I went hunting with my TT pistol that I had instead of a Nagant, and killed a hare after several attempts. With that hunting trophy I went back to camp, and there I saw Nikolai helping to take overcoats from three young female soldiers. My dear Rita was among them! A slim Tatar girl with a nice body and a pretty Asian face, Zoya Farvazova, and a harmonica-player, Lusya Pegova, came together with Rita. All the girls were young, their faces red with frost, and excited to see us! I had already mentioned in the battalion, that Rita was to be my wife, so apparently that was the reason why no one except me was amazed to see her in the battalion, while I was crazily happy.

My friends from the battalion came running and decided to arrange a "front line wedding", as our *de facto* marriage relations had to be made official by a marriage ceremony. I was a bit worried about Rita's reaction to that, but she looked at the other girls and agreed. Nikolai had already taken the skin off the hare, and started cooking hare ragout with a huge amount of onion and lard. As it turned out, the dish was perfect although none of us ever had had real hare ragout. The only thing we knew about it was a joke that said, "for a hare ragout you need at least a cat, but a rabbit is better".

The news about our wedding spread around my friends with lightning speed and they all gathered in the room of our "military council". Both the chief of staff Philip Kiselev and deputy battalion commander Ivan Matvienko as well as Aleksey Filatov, whom we called Alex, despite the fact that he was about ten years older than me, came to the wedding. Probably, the reason for us to treat Filatov as a person of our own age was his open and happy personality and young looks. The guys quickly gathered all that was necessary for the feast. Some brought the food that they had saved from their officer ration, some brought pickles and smoked ham, while Valery Semykin somehow managed to get a huge chunk of US-made butter from our supply officer Seltzer. Excellent Polish Monopolka *vodka* and even bottles with some foreign wine appeared on the table. Apparently, officers were saving it for a special occasion, which happened to be our front line wedding. I was looking at Rita from time to time. She looked a bit shy, easily made contact with my friends, but showed that she was ready to act as a bride. By then I had come to conclusion that her previous marriage was an unpleasant episode from the past for her and she was ready to become my real wife on that day. Apparently her mother, Ekaterina Nikolaevna, had already blessed that important step in her life.

Our wedding was both happy and exciting. We had two harmonicas playing. Lusya could play very well, while the other was played by Musya Goldstein. We had a gramophone, with records of *Rio-Rita*, *Sparkles of Champagne* and *Waves of*

Amur. Those melodies reminded me so much of the dance floor in Alkino. We danced in Pan Krul's room that was too small for us. That amazing celebration was not long. Both girls, Lusya and Zoya, either understood all the delicacy of the situation, or they had agreed beforehand. But they started to leave, explaining that they were ordered to return to the ensemble by midnight. No good reasons could make them stay. We even tried to tell them that they should not leave so late at night.

Incidentally, George Razhev, a rather loving guy, had already fallen in love with Zoya Farvazova and was awfully upset to hear that she was not staying. Those slight but brave girls were not even afraid of walking to the highway through the forest, to hitchhike on a truck, although in those days we were afraid of the provocations of the Polish *Armeja Krajowa* that had failed in the Warsaw uprising so bitterly. George Razhev seemed to be mad with Zoya. He cited a recent shell shock, which did not stop him from drinking as much as the others, but he did not want to see the girls off. Another George, Sergeev, a silent and reliable guy, took the mission. He saw the girls to the highway, and flagged down a car that was going to Sedlec where the girls had to go.

… By the way, in 1984, George Razhev whom I had found among other battle friends, wrote to Rita and me. In the very first letter he wrote, "Of course I remember you well, even very well. I remember your bandaged head after the battle on the Oder, and your pistol holster that was hanging almost at knee level. Only you followed that fashion in the whole battalion! I remember Rita from that Polish hut where you became close to each other. Of course, I also remember how that other girl dumped me and left".

A lot of other things happened to George Razhev. They were all about women and alcohol. He was just such a guy. Speaking about my "pistol holster that was hanging almost at knee level", all of us officers, not only young ones, tried to follow front line fashion to the degree that we could afford and our superiors allowed. On the recommendation of several ex-Navy *shtrafnik* men I was wearing my pistol holster "Navy style" and seriously believed that it was more convenient in battle. Even our *kombat* Baturin, whom we perceived as an old man, and his relatively young, slim and handsome political officer Kazakov also broke uniform regulations. Instead of winter fur hats they wore *kubanka*, the traditional headgear of Cossack troops, with red tops, like on a general's *papakha* hat. We, younger officers, saw this and also made *kubanka* for ourselves. There were both tailors and material available. It was just like the fashion for special long boots from *plash-palatkas* that we wore the previous summer …

In the meantime, our wedding feast was over and all my friends left quickly, wanting to give us as much private time as possible. While we were partying, Nikolai prepared a wedding bed for us, as he sincerely believed that we were already a real husband and wife. I sincerely believed in turn that I was not the first man in her life. She had written to me that she already had a baby! But I would become her new, real husband. I was extremely shocked when I realised that she lied to me, both about being married, and having a baby. Of course, I was not a virgin myself, but as an officer, I had pledged not to take her virginity from any girl, till the end of the war. If such a thing were to happen, then it would only be after marriage. One could get killed in the war, so why make a girl unhappy, even widowed. A girl should keep her honour, and her virginity. It was a rather common opinion among officers of that time, although our concept of female honour is sometimes considered an old-fashioned remnant of an 'uncivilised', 'wild' and 'uneducated' society. And there I was, in such a situation, at the front. I felt so sorry for my dear Rita, while at the same time I was so happy that she really wanted to and did become my wife. Not a "PPZh", 11, that was not fashionable, but just a common thing in the dangerous times of war. Rita became my real wife, a devoted battle girlfriend, my sister-in-arms and wife for the rest of my life, and the mother of our future children. We lived happily together for exactly 52 years.

... It happened on December 14, 1996, the same winter evening as 52 years before, that I said my last goodbye to my Rita at her graveside. She had already had two heart attacks and did not survive the third. In 1996 we already had two sons, four grandchildren and a beautiful great-granddaughter. 'War' caught up with my battle girlfriend, a front line medic of the Great Patriotic War over fifty years after the Victory, as it caught up with many of my front line friends. By that time we had lost over ten veterans from the battalion's men that I managed to find ...

Back then, in 1944, the Victory was still in the future, and no one at the front knew if we would live to see it, although everyone hoped. In December 1944, the ice-bound Vistula River and the Polish capital Warsaw, as well as the whole of Poland beyond the Vistula, were under the boot of the *Nazis*. Bloody battles were still ahead of us, as well as the border of *Nazi* Germany. The slogan, "Let's finish off the *Nazi* beast in his own lair", sounded as a distant future to us. Crossing the Oder, and the Battle of Berlin, were still too far from us.

Rita started packing to go back to her amateur ensemble on the morning of December 15. She was worried that her absence, as the leading dancer, would be a complication for their first concerts, although she did not know when they would start. I talked my wife (I was so happy and proud to say this word!) into waiting a bit and going to our *kombat* in order to introduce her to Baturin and ask him to register our marriage, i.e. put stamps in my officer ID and her Red Army soldier's book. When we came to the *kombat*, Philip Kiselev, chief of staff, told us, that he could have done it himself. But the *kombat* kept the stamp of the battalion with him all the time, not trusting it even to the chief of staff. That contradicted a regular army tradition. So, Philip went to report our request. After several minutes a round belly that looked like a meatball emerged from the half-opened door. Then Baturin himself appeared on the threshold. As it seemed to me, he looked at us, both standing at attention saluting him, with a dismissive glance, and instead of congratulations, he bluntly said, "I have no marriage registering agency here. You will register your relations, if they are serious ones, after the war". He was already walking away, when he told us over his shoulder, "if you survive".

I felt really uncomfortable. Of course, you cannot complain at or be offended with the strictness of your superior at the Front, and in an army in general. But deliberate rudeness, a neglectful attitude to subordinates can be more painful than the enemy's bullet. Demanding good performance, and sometimes even cruelty, are necessary in the army, and even more so at the Front, but that was not the case here! Most likely, it was the routine rudeness of a bureaucrat. I had to take it all, I could not do anything, it would have been front line insubordination. But when I looked anxiously at Rita, I was amazed! She had the same happy look, shining eyes and a smile on her face. I could not prevent myself but kissed her on her pretty lips, and thought that she was a really strong girl, and how easy it would be for me to be with her, even in the hard situations of our life!

Phil Kiselev, deputy battalion commanders Matvienko and Filatov, hugged us both, and shook our hands. Valery Semykin who all of a sudden also happened to be around, even said something like, "Well, kittens! (I remember his words precisely!) Live in love and accord for long years after Victory!" He kissed us both. He called us 'kittens' also in his letters after the war. Thank you, dear battle friends! Your words from your kind hearts compensated for the bad impression of rudeness from Baturin and neutralised my offence with him. Those words of yours were with us all the time, both during our short life at the Front and our long peaceful life, after the war, that lasted over fifty years.

After that unpleasant incident with the *kombat* we ran back to our hut that had become our wedding palace. We grabbed Rita's *sidor* bag that had all the necessary theatre clothes, a beautiful Ukrainian peasant blouse and skirt, as well as red long boots for the *gopak* and shining gipsy clothes, and some other personal belongings. After that we ran to the highway through the forest in order to hitch a lift to Sedlec. We both had mixed feelings. Rita was a soldier and I wanted to send her away as quickly as possible so that her superiors would not be mad with her. But even more I wanted to spend another minute with her. But there is time for everything, and several minutes later Rita was already waving a scarf at me from the back of a departing truck before it disappeared beyond a turn in the road.

I came back home to the house of Pan Krul and my orderly Nikolai, who was already packing our belongings and the gramophone with its records. He reported that we were transferred to the next village, Buda Kuminska. He also said that it was the order of our *kombat*. I did not immediately understand what the logic of the transfer was, but an order is always an order. It turned out that it was just easier for the *kombat* to have all company commanders in one spot, although the newly formed platoons remained where they were. It seemed reasonable for him as he did not have to send runners so often and it would be easier for him to control us company commanders. In principle, it was a right decision.

I departed from a not too hospitable Pan Krul without any special feelings. I was accommodated in a nice apartment building of an elderly Polish woman. It was especially tidy for a wartime village. Her 17 years old daughter Stefa was cleaning the house thoroughly and zealously. She was a rosy, blooming beautiful girl with puffy cheeks and an attractive body. When I called all my platoon leaders for a briefing, I noticed that George Razhev was looking at her with a very special look. During our entire stay in that village he used any reason to come to my apartment and try to talk Stefa into at least taking a stroll together. But Stefa was a decent girl and paid attention to me, as I was their main guest and superior to all other officers. I noticed that the Poles always paid special attention to their superiors. Stefa even knitted warm gloves for me and gave them to me through Rita during one of her visits.

I have mentioned relations between men and women in the war, several times. Those relationships were of such a variety of destinies, meetings and chances, as well as their consequences, that I would not dare to make any generalisations. I often saw that dating at the front did not involve any really deep feelings, but was a mere 'call of the flesh'. Perhaps it was some sort of pity from women, towards men who had been at the front for years and had not had women's company. Who knew if those physically strong and powerful men would survive the coming battle, perhaps not even having experienced romance. Pity is typical for women, and it is even stronger in war. So I could understand George when he failed to date the beautiful, young Polish girl Stefa and then switched his attention to a Russian woman. She was a repatriate as we called women who came back from German slavery or concentration camps. Stafa was thin, starved, unattractive and noticeably pregnant. When I learnt that she had already been staying with George for two days, I asked him if he was safe on the venereal disease side, and whether he cared that she was pregnant. He replied in an offended manner that "a satisfied man does not understand a hungry man". George was three years older than me and I did not try to moralise with him on the matter, although there were reasons for that later on. I understood that I no longer had the right to be a judge in that sensitive matter, and honestly did not miss it at all.

The landlady and her charming daughter Stefa received Rita very warmly. They treated Rita with special attention and respect. I guess they took her as the wife of a Russian Captain. They addressed her only as "*Pani Kapitana*". When Rita was leaving, I again saw her off to the highway and a car soon took her away from me, just as before.

Even before the start of the offensive on Warsaw that we were expecting any day, Rita visited me again January. Her mother, Ekaterina Nikolaevna, was a respected doctor in their hospital and Rita herself was a good and devoted nurse. The chief surgeon of the hospital was well disposed towards them. I guess that was the reason why it became possible for her to get short leaves to visit me. Another reason was probably the lack of wounded in the hospital, during the lull at the Front. In any case, as I thought, her marriage was taken seriously in the hospital, unlike by our *kombat* Baturin. There had been very little time since Rita's last visit to me, at Buda Kuminska, and our battalion starting the offensive towards Warsaw.

CHAPTER 9

The Vistula-Oder Offensive

"You are a lucky boy, Alex!" Those were the words of my Siberian grandfather Daniel. I recalled them, when I managed to make it in one day from Lochuv to the highway, close to the Polish villages that were pointed out to me by the *kombat*. My grandfather himself was a lucky person. According to his stories, in his youth he hunted bear with a spear eighteen times, and was quite successful every time. I can remember myself, that when I visited him as a boy, in his small village of Sagdy-Biru in the middle of the *taiga*, not far from Birobidzhan, he came running back home from the hunt, quickly harnessed his horse to a sled, and went back to the *taiga*. The next day he brought a large dead tiger that filled the entire sled. Its tail was dragging on the snowy road. That was the first time that I saw a real tiger, but a dead one. So I guess I inherited being lucky from my grandfather.

It was still light when I reached the Polish villages and easily found the battalion staff. There were the familiar faces of our supply and staff officers, and the nice smell of some fried food. Apparently it was suppertime. First I found chief of staff Phil Kiselev, and learnt from him where *kombat* Baturin was, and went to report to him, happy that I was on time and did not have to look for excuses for being late. I have already written in the previous chapter about how our meeting took place. There, in those villages, my life both before and after our front line wedding, in addition to the final victory over the lice, was also important for all us. We were busy both with the release of *shtrafniks* and the formation of new units. I spent a lot of time writing to the *kombat*, or his political officer Major Kazakov, the most detailed character references for *shtrafniks*, and rewriting those that did not seem complete or convincing,

Formation of the new units also took place in a different manner. In order that the officers from the companies of the battalion did not 'relax', the *kombat* ordered us to receive replacements of *shtrafniks* in all companies. We had to form the platoons, although they were quite small. After that we brought them all together into one company under the commander who would have the honour of leading them into battle. I was not alone in my opinion that the main shortcoming of the new method meant that platoon leaders did not know each other. Such links are so important in battle! But an order is an order.

Many of us guessed that Baturin introduced that novelty in order to prevent officers having spare time to express their dissatisfaction with his attitude towards the men. He had demonstrated his attitude during the offensive operations on the Narev bridgehead. Of course, it also did not allow officers much time to relax, or to release their stress, during the lull after long and intensive battles. Especially given the fact that they could treat their stress with *bimber*, the Polish moonshine that Poles had in abundance. Officers could trade it for 'war booty', such as watches, lighters, cigarette cases and so on. So everyone could get as much of that poison as possible. There were not many drunkards in our unit but, alas, with some exceptions. In general, we had time for a lot of things, rest, writing letters, and conversations about the meaning of life, including the features of our new *kombat*. Of course, there were no singing nights like those that we had in Belorussia. The general mood was not fit for songs, as we were expecting a new offensive, and assumed that it would not be any easier than the previous battles.

While the battalion was outside the battle area, the new *kombat* established a new catering order for officers. Previously, we all ate from the same field kitchen and pots with the other soldiers. Only our additional rations made our menu different from the food of *shtrafniks*. From that moment on, all the officers of the battalion ate separately from *shtrafniks*, in a so-called 'canteen' in a slightly smaller room. They cooked food separately for us. I cannot say that it was much different from the food of the company's field kitchen. We no longer ate from mess kits, but from aluminium plates or bowls. Of course, it was some sort of improvement. Our resourceful and energetic catering officer, Moses Seltzer, sometimes managed to bring variety to our menu by serving us fresh milk.

It turned out that our Lieutenant Colonel Baturin had a weakness for milk. While we were fighting the heaviest battles, to expand the Narev bridgehead, he managed to obtain two milk cows. He always took them with him when the battalion was moving from one sector of the front to another. So from his 'noble' table we sometimes received coffee or tea with milk. The *kombat* and his deputies were served food from a separate kitchen, and they also ate separately from us. However, almost all his deputies, except for the political officers and supply officer, longed to be with regular officers like us. I don't think that the *kombat* really had any delicacies there, except for milk, but that distance was kept strictly and we never ate with him. Nevertheless, we received the novelty as something proper. Probably, it was really something necessary, but it was hard for us to judge. Our previous *kombat*, Osipov, never tried to keep a distance between us and it did not harm our morale or discipline.

We also noticed that one of our new political officers, a Captain Vinogradov, was eating together with the *kombat* and his new political officer Kazakov. His function was as propaganda officer of the battalion. We had such an officer in our army, too! He was a slim, not well built, untidy officer. His high voice was almost a squeal, and his manner of making absurd gestures, which looked like throwing his hands in all directions while talking, often caused dislike and irritation from the other officers. All those qualities contradicted his office so much, that often his propaganda had an effect completely opposite to his words. Vinogradov was one of those demagogues, with their uselessness in the battalion, that were not only disliked by front line officers, but who caused feelings of antipathy bordering on hatred. His stupid moralising speeches, on every matter, caused irritation, and often direct opposition to what he was preaching. For example, he preached that we should not only quit drinking the Narkom's *vodka* rations, but even strong tea. We should quit smoking and forget about women. Officers openly despised his boring political speeches, or 'political moralising', as they called his messages. In order to make Vinogradov mad, we openly drank strong tea and Polish *kawa*, simultaneously smoking cigarettes or hand-rolled *mahorka* cigarettes!

We always wondered where Baturin was getting such officers. Could it be that they were his former subordinates, who had hidden in the rear the whole war, just like Baturin himself? Vinogradov did not have even a Medal for Merit in Battle, the lowest of all battle decorations. And that strange officer dined with the *kombat* sometimes. We thought that they had either served somewhere together, or were close to each other in some other area. Maybe they were just very similar persons. Well, forget about Vinogradov, but his proximity to Baturin did not help the *kombat* to gain respect among us officers.

... Going a bit ahead in the story, I must say that the 'works' of Vinogradov, and not only his words, did not at all correspond to his moralising and teaching. When the issue of the next State Bond Loan was announced just before the end of the war, I think on the 3rd or 4th of May, that propaganda officer had been bothering all the officers. He convinced them that each one should sign up for the loan, with at least three months pay, as "this is necessary for the near Victory". We all did so anyway, turning in the bought bonds to the Defence Fund. When we asked the financial officer of our battalion, Kostya Pusik, about Vinogradov himself, we found out that he only spent one month's pay on it. Such was the real face of our *politruk* propaganda officer. To complete the picture, in the very first days after Victory, our 'saint' was the first one in the battalion to fall sick with gonorrhoea. There were several cases after him, too! What a saint! But all those things happened much later, after January 1945 ...

As I have mentioned, we had started decentralised formation and battle training of all units. Each company created several rather small platoons. I have already mentioned the weak and strong sides of the new method. Of course, I guess no one's goal, except for Vinogradov, was to completely stop consumption of alcohol, especially since we often had 'legal' reasons to celebrate. We celebrated each decoration or promotion. Sometimes at yet another *sabantui*[1], as Fedor Usmanov called such parties, it was considered extremely 'posh' to consume pure alcohol instead of stinking *bimber*. We sometimes treated ourselves to it. There were many spirit refineries in Poland, and the Poles made good business from selling us that pure alcohol at a high price. As a rule, we would drink it pure. It was considered 'low class' to mix it with water and we merely chased it with water. In such cases we would pour 100 per cent alcohol into a cup and set the second cup with water next to it. Sometimes we tricked people, and secretly poured spirit into the second cup, too. One could only imagine the condition of a person who had swallowed the burning 'fiery liquid' and then tried to chase it with water right away, but would keep getting the same burning sensation in his throat. However, the one responsible for the trick always held a glass of water at the ready, in order to help the victim at the right moment.

One month before, on December 18, I turned 21. The new commander of the Front Marshal Zhukov, who had just replaced Marshal Rokossovski, signed an order that must have been prepared by his predecessor, on my promotion to Captain. Soon we celebrated my new Captain's shoulder-boards, as well as the promotions of some other officers. We felt especially sad for Marshal Rokossovski who was leaving for the 2nd Belorussian Front. We loved the Marshal almost as sons love their fathers.

In the meantime, the reinforcements were arriving, although not in any great numbers. Apparently, the lull at the Front and lack of large-scale military opera-

---

1 *Sabantui* – a traditional Bashkyrian festival, dedicated to the beginning of agricultural works. As an idiom it means any large and happy celebration.

tions did not allow for the courts-martial to 'create' *shtrafniks* for us. I think that was the first time we started having another category of *shtrafniks*. They were former officers who had been sentenced at the beginning of the war, or even before it, and had already served a major part of their sentences in prisons or labour camps. As we understood it, they were not sent to the Front, under guard like criminals, to the detached penal companies. Instead, they arrived there exclusively voluntarily, but with the escort of some guards. The whole country was feeling the approach of the end of the war. Many convicts who still had a feeling of patriotism in them, understood that the long-expected and already inevitable Victory would come, and then they would be released. Many were even hoping for an amnesty on the occasion of Victory.

Those men who stayed in prison avoided fighting and dying in the war, unlike millions of their countrymen. So they would have a hard time returning to a society that had been burnt by war, but which had defeated the enemy, in a deadly battle that lasted almost four years. It would be hard for the convicted to live among those whose relatives did not spend the war in prisons, but were killed in battles for the Motherland. Millions sacrificed their lives for the victory over *Nazism*. Such logic brought many former officers to apply for the exchange of their remaining prison term for being sent to the Front, even as *shtrafniks*. There were quite a few who were given that opportunity, but others were not. They arrived continually until the beginning of the Berlin operation.

In general, formation and training of the company went on as usual. Battle training was quite stressful. As usual, in the training process we paid special attention to all those who had low levels of marksmanship and marching training, and to *shtrafniks* who were former officers of supply branches, as well as pilots, tank officers and others. We paid even more attention to the former convicts, who were physically weaker than the others. Many had not held weapons for a long time, only seeing them in the hands of their guards. There were only 7–10 men in each platoon, which gave platoon leaders an opportunity to have some individual training sessions with *shtrafniks*. They used other *shtrafniks* with infantry experience as assistants. In general, the trainees understood that Suvorov's famous 'science of winning', and its famous slogan "hard in training, easy in battle", was true for their situation. Some *shtrafniks*, who had previously considered themselves to be 'goners', had already started to realise that they would not be used as cannon fodder. They knew they were being trained to fight professionally, in order to kill the enemy more efficiently, and stay alive themselves. That helped them realise the necessity of extremely intensive training, as we said, "until they sweated their guts out". Often we did not need to force anyone into training. Nevertheless, the staff of the battalion set up really good control for the training process. Deputy battalion commanders and chiefs of branches were always in the companies and platoons.

The training was equally hard for the *shtrafniks* and for us, their officers. It was around that time that we found a good place for a firing range in a quarry. There we fired live ammo from all types of small arms, and fired at an abandoned and burnt-out German assault gun from AT-rifles. We even set aside a whole area in a nearby forest for live ammo practice with mortars. During a certain period, the firing range was guarded from all directions and our mortar crews trained in delivering indirect fire into that area.

In general, one could envy the resourcefulness and endurance of unit commanders and chiefs of branches of the battalion. The main stimulus was of course, not the strict control from the staff and leadership of the battalion, but a desire to avoid leading untrained soldiers. Of course that was no fault of theirs. Company commanders were also quite excited about learning to ride. Who could know when we would need it? That all started with some officer from our battalion taking strong and good riding-horses with all their harnessing and saddles from somewhere. Our *kombat* approved that with great enthusiasm, as he must have spent many years of service in the cavalry. Baturin chose a beautiful, calm and quiet bay stallion for himself. I got a young, restless and wilful dappled grey horse. It would constantly move its sensitive, mobile ears and would often show its large young teeth to demonstrate its discontent. When I saw how skilfully our *kombat*, despite his large belly, got on to his horse and seemed to be at one with it, and how he pranced in front of us. I envied his skills for the first time. I also became excited about learning to ride a horse, although I understood that I could never ride a horse as professionally as our *kombat*.

I must say that it turned out to be a hard task. The first days of the exercises brought neither pleasure nor results. After two or three hours, of daily intensive training sessions, all my 'saddle parts' hurt a lot. But I had my goal set, so every following day, although without any real desire, I again mounted my horse. Without understanding the difference between trot and gallop, and with my lack of skill, I sometimes really exhausted my horse and myself, too. One of my *shtrafniks*, apparently a former cavalryman, saw my lack of skill at horse-riding, and all my difficulties in training, and volunteered to be my teacher and driver. He treated the horse skilfully and gave me lessons. Then the horse started taking me more calmly. Meanwhile, I felt more comfortable in a saddle and could use the stirrups better. Soon, shortly before the New Year of 1945, Rita managed to visit me on 'vacation' for a couple of days, and when she knew that I had my own 'personal transport', she begged me for permission to ride it. Although Rita had never been on horseback in her life, to my amazement, she could handle the wilful horse very well, and loved riding a lot.

We celebrated the arrival of New Year 1945 at one common table. The *kombat* himself, all his deputies, staff officers, chiefs of different branches and officers from line units, all those who were free from duty, were present at that party. It was the first time that we had had such a big party. The only other time for such a big celebration was Victory Day, May 9, 1945 in Berlin. It was the first day of peace after the war that we were all so tired of, but also used to, however paradoxical that might sound.

However, in those days the Victory was still far away. Ahead of us were heavy battles for Warsaw, a hard way to the border of *Nazi* Germany, and then on to Berlin. No one knew who would make it to the end of the war, or who would forever rest in Polish or German soil. I hastily wrote several verses about my battle friends, for the New Year celebration, and they were very warmly welcomed. Even Baturin, who was quite greedy for praise, applauded me. It also turned out that the birthdays of Peter Smirnov, who had just come back from the hospital, Alex Shamshin, my namesake and of the same age, as well as the deputy battalion commander Ivan Matvienko, almost all coincided with the New Year. That was how we celebrated the New Year of 1945, as we all knew for sure, it would be the Year of Victory!

As we learnt later, on January 20, Stavka was planning to start the operation of the liberation of Warsaw, as well as the whole of Poland that was still under the *Nazi* yoke. But in his letter, the British Prime Minister, Winston Churchill, begged Stalin to start the offensive from the Vistula as soon as possible, in order to divert German troops away from the Ardennes. There the Western Allies were in a hard situation. Stalin answered that call for help and Stavka changed the beginning of the Vistula-Oder operation to January 12. Literally only several days after the New Year, we started to hurriedly gather our decentralised small units into platoons of one company, under the command of Ivan Beldugov. He was a stocky, blonde officer, with a wide face and large forehead. He seemed a very calm person among us, but his calmness could any moment explode into sternness and sharpness.

Officers with strong *shtrafbat* experience were hastily forming platoons in his company. They were Captain Vasily Kachala, Senior Lieutenant Alex Shamshin as well as the recently arrived Senior Lieutenant Alexei Afonin. He was a modest and cheerful officer, who seemed very young to us, but was in reality four years older than Shamshin and me. Alexei was wide-shouldered, thickset, and as it turned out, a hellishly enduring person. The harder the situation the more stubborn and determined he was. That always boosted the morale of his men. When I got to know him better, it turned out that we graduated from the same 2nd Far East infantry academy in Komsomolsk-on-Amur. We had climbed the same hills and mountains, eaten food in the same cadet canteen, and guarded the same buildings. However, he was commissioned as a Lieutenant a bit earlier. Alex knew the Far East very well, which made us close friends. He served at Lake Khasan immediately after the events of 1938[2]. Then he served in units of the Far Eastern Front, and after graduating from the academy he went to the Central Front. He was badly wounded at the Battle of Kursk and they took him to hospital as far away as Novosibirsk. It took him a long time to recover from his wounds, and then he graduated from courses for company commanders, and finally was sent to the 8th Detached Penal Battalion as a platoon leader.

I was always amazed that I, a lieutenant without any battle experience, was appointed first penal company commander in 1943. I guess it was someone's mistake, but *kombat* Osipov corrected that mistake, letting me lead a scout platoon. However, Alex, older than me, with real battle experience, a wound, and completed courses of company command became just a platoon leader. He was not the only one. My friend Peter Zagumennikov also came into the *shtrafbat* as a platoon leader, after leading a rifle company at the front and being wounded. It was obvious that they tried to get battle tested and experienced officers to lead units in an Officer Penal Battalion, while I must have been a random exception to the rule.

2   Battles between the Japanese and Soviet troops raged on Lake Khasan in July-August 1938, and in them (just as in battles on the Khalkhin-Gol river) the Japanese suffered a crushing defeat. The results of these two conflicts were one of the main reasons that held Japan from declaring war on the Soviet Union in the hardest year of the Second World War. As the result, the battles between the Soviet Union and Japan only started in August 1945.

But, as they say in the Army, "the ways of the Lord and superior officers are mysterious"!

We had very little time left for knitting the units together. That was when all the weaknesses of their separate training and formation showed up. As early as January 11, the company marched on foot to the Magnushev bridgehead that had been captured the previous summer. That was on the western shore of the Vistula to the south of Warsaw. The company marched into the bridgehead on a well-worn wooden bridge in the darkness of the night of a new moon. The ice on the Vistula seemed to have been ploughed up from bank to bank by a huge plough. Those were the traces of bombardments and air raids. Our company of *shtrafniks* started the offensive from there on January 14, together with the troops of the 61st Army, thus opening the Vistula-Oder strategic offensive.

I don't know why, but Beldugov did not get a deputy company commander, as for example, Yanin did with Matvienko. I was ordered to go, together with his company, as the reserve company commander. That was some sort of a shift for him. It was a new system of our *kombat* Baturin. According to his system I was not part of the fighting company but was supposed to be next to the company, with my runner and two *shtrafniks*, so that I could take over the company if necessary. It was extremely uncomfortable and unnatural. I always had a feeling that I was not necessary or not competent enough. I would have preferred to be demoted and be a deputy of a company commander as my official job, rather than be with the company without any role, and not being part of his decisions.

First the company received a mission to capture a hill. From it the Germans had repelled all attempts of our units to advance, with 'hurricane' fire. Both Beldugov and I came to the conclusion that we should use a small brook, with bushes on its shores which ran into the Pilica River. I remembered its name as it sounds the same as my last name. We would bypass that ill-fated hill and attack it from the rear. Beldugov gave this mission to platoon leader Vasily Kachala. He managed to bypass the hill unnoticed by *Fritzes* and surprised them by an attack from the rear. It was an attack in which the main element was surprise, and the result of the entire engagement depended on it. Either all the men would be killed on the open frozen hillside, or they would capture that 'damn hill'! The battle was furious, and as the Germans shifted their attention and fire to the rear, Beldugov got his company up for a frontal assault. The hill was captured and the first platoon to reach its top was the platoon under Alex Afonin. Losses were still quite low and we managed to reach the Pilica River.

Many years later I learnt that a young Dragoon of the 5th Cavalry Division Konstantin Ksaverievich, his real *patronymic*, Rokossovski, received his first military award, the St George Cross[3] for a daring raid behind the Pilica River. It is a pity that we did not know it then.

After the hill was captured, all units of the regiment that our company supported also joined the offensive. Soon the entire 23rd Rifle Division that our company co-ordinated closely, started the offensive towards Warsaw. They reached Wlochy station in the southern suburbs of the Polish capital as early as January 16. After that our company disengaged and the infantry with armour continued the assault. Warsaw was fully liberated on January 17. Of course, we felt

---

3   Traditional name of the Russian "Sign of Distinction of the Military Order".

offended. We had come all the way to Warsaw but the honour of capturing the city was not given to us. I guess someone thought it was wrong for *shtrafniks* to liberate even part of the Polish capital. It was the same in Rogachev and Brest. There, too, we were not allowed to enter the most beautiful city of Europe, as some believed, the capital of the first liberated Western country. We were the means to provide for the success of other units, and that explained everything.

We were given permission to see the beautiful city as late as January 18, when we entered the city after the 23rd Division of the 61st Army. The first impression that we had was of the awful destruction in the city. Those were results both of the failed uprising of the Poles and the results of deliberate destruction of the best, the most beautiful buildings, by the Germans. We could see signs in Russian on the walls of the buildings, such as "mines defused", or signs on poles along the road, "checked. No mines found", with the name of the combat engineer who did the check. When we were on Marhsalkovskaya Street going to the city centre, we noticed several groups of combat engineers with dogs that were continuing their dangerous job of defusing mines in the city. The dogs were sniffing for the explosives, and I thought that it was very hard for them, as the whole city smelled of gunpowder and dynamite. After that occasion I knew not only the medic dogs and AT-dogs[4], but also about the faithful assistants of our glorious combat engineers.

At that point we were stopped by a military patrol that was already present in the city and did not let us go further than that wide, once beautiful street. Then, it was blocked with the debris of collapsed buildings and burnt-out German tanks. It turned out that the further part of the city had not yet been cleared from mines. We turned to the right and next to the Vistula's bank, almost next to the destroyed bridge, we saw a badly damaged, once fancily decorated building. On its façade we could hardly read the Polish words, "Emission Polish Bank". We did not understand the meaning of the word "Emission" but we realised that it was a bank. As the guards were not there and the doors were wide open, we decided to step in.

My goodness, there was so much different money in the basement! Both Polish *zloty* in thick stacks, and also lying chaotically on the floor, with accurate holes drilled through them. Apparently the Germans did that to make the currency unusable. We saw whole printed sheets of money, with only one side printed, and German occupation *Reichsmarks*. We thought then that the money could no longer be used. But it turned out that some of us who were more experienced, stuffed their pockets with it and then used it a lot in trade with Poles. It turned out that they were very anxious for money. They were convinced that the bills with only one side printed were the new Polish currency. Some, the most 'skilful', managed to buy not only food, but also other valuable things, including jewellery. When I saw those who stocked themselves with money and made good business with them, I might have felt sorry that I was so timid. I did not take a single bill even as a souvenir. However, I did not envy those 'lucky guys'. In the bank, we merely laughed at the abandoned millions and kicked those millions with our feet. After that excursion in the bank we went to the gathering point in the western part of Warsaw. At every step we could again see the vandalism of the *Nazis* who had

---

4   The Sovet Army used significant numbers of trained dogs for delivery of messages and
     ammo, as well as evacuation of wounded from the battlefield on light sleds. Some dogs
     were successfully employed in an anti-tank role.

turned the major part of Warsaw into a heap of ruins. Our officers and *shtrafniks* who had taken part in the Battle of Stalingrad, compared the ruins of Warsaw to Stalingrad.

Either because I did not take an active part in the battles for Warsaw or because Baturin understood, or someone gave him a hint, that appointing me as a "shift commander" during battles was unreasonable, he ordered me and several other officers to travel on independently. Each of us was told where we were supposed to arrive and at what time. I don't remember the names of the villages and towns where I had to travel in different ways. But from the gratitude certificates of the Commander-in-Chief, Stalin, for liberation of different Polish towns, my route went through Sohachew – Lowich – Skernevice – Tomashuw – Konin – Lencica.

The *Fritzes* fled, either from the amazingly strong blows of our troops, or from the name of Marshal Zhukov who had become our Front Commander. The Germans were also very much afraid of Rokossovski's name, too. The German retreat after they lost Warsaw looked more like a rout. But often there were significant German forces left in our rear in the forests, and they continued to fight. We had to allocate quite a lot of troops for their liquidation. My comrades and I, and others too, travelled mostly by hitching lifts on trucks and sometimes in Polish horse-drawn carriages. Our horses, that we had dedicated so much time to, somehow were of no further use to us, so yet another idea of our new *kombat* proved to be pointless. Several times, when military vehicles did not stop at our request, we had to use a more secure way of stopping them, i.e. firing our pistols at the rubber tyres. Of course, that 'hitch-hiking method' was dangerous. If we had hit something other than the rubber tyres, we would have been court-martialled. But for some reason I was not afraid of a court-martial. Once, a Major jumped out of the car that I hitched in that way, with a gun in his hand and threats to send me to a penal battalion for that trick. I showed him my ID of a Captain from the 8th Detached Penal Battalion. He was dumbfounded, but then we made peace, and they took us safely to the destination that we needed.

I liked to stand in the back of every truck that agreed to take us and expose my face to the wind. My cheeks and lips would get numb from the cold stream of air. The numbness reminded me of my dear Far East of Russia, and my childhood experiences in the winter. Then, I used to travel home, or back to school, in the open doorways of trains on the 40 kilometres from Obluch'e secondary school.

On February 20 or 21, I arrived in the town of Kutno. The battalion staff was already stationed there, along with mobile supply units that had carriages and trucks. The town looked very cosy to me. It was completely untouched by a war that had been especially harsh in the territory of our Motherland. I was amazed by the facts that the electricity and sewage even worked in Kutno. Apparently, the Germans had spared that city for some of its merits, or they were fleeing so quickly that they did not have time to spoil it. In compensation, there were many signs, e.g. "Pst!"or "Be silent!" with the drawing of a finger pressed against lips. We also had posters like that and even road signs that said, "Don't talk!" Meaning, "Blabber is a find for a spy", and so on.

I happened to stay in a neat house with a red-tiled roof behind a strong fence. The house belonged to a local veterinary doctor, who was married to a relatively young and beautiful woman. She offered me a bath after she accommodated me. What bliss it was! I had both aromatic soap and a thick and fluffy towel! Not my light cellular army-issue towel, that I had washed so many times! The landlady was exceptionally attentive and accommodated me in a room with a good bed, a sofa, and a large writing table with a table lamp and its green cover that made the atmosphere in the room extremely cosy.

I asked around where the officers from my company were staying. It turned out that in addition to George Razhev and Fyodor Usmanov they had just sent Junior Lieutenant Kuznetsov to my company. He had newly arrived at the battalion and was a rather nice, but short and slim person. He had already received a nickname of 'Grasshopper' due to his fragile body, high weak voice, and ability to blush like a girl in his worst moments. I wanted to get to know him better, especially as I did not want to stay alone in that house with such a cute landlady. Her husband had just left to go somewhere on his veterinary business. I also made the decision because our 'Don Juan', George Razhev, had already offered me his company during my stay in that house. I realised that he had already noticed the beauty of the landlady, and that his accommodation with me could end in some scandal or harassment from him. I did not give in to his requests, citing my desire to get to know the 'Grasshopper' better.

We spent several days in Kutno and there they told me a story of a *kobeta*, the name that they used for a young woman in Poland. She was a pretty girl with a gorgeous body and lived as a wife together with some German officer from a *Waffen-SS* punishment team. The woman lived with him, proud of being a woman with elite status in that small town, and who even had a child with the *Waffen-SS* officer. He was a two-year old boy with amazingly red hair and crossed eyes. But the German officer fled west without taking her or their child with him. I saw the boy, and had no other name for him but "bastard" and "*Fritz*'s descendant". Our hatred was of the *Waffen-SS*, people of "Aryan" status, and was very strong against everything German in fact.

I understand these days that I was wrong in some ways. But in those days hatred was deeply rooted in our minds, there was no other way. I can also recall the slogans that we had, e.g. "you cannot beat your enemy unless you learn to hate him with all your heart", and "If an enemy does not surrender, he should be destroyed". Both posters, newspapers and movies, and even strong publications of Ilja Erenburg, and other famous writers, rallied us to "Kill Germans!" So we learnt to hate and destroy them. Of course we understood that we should kill those who came to the land of our Motherland with a sword and a torch. But despite logic our hatred spread out to all Germans, everything German, except for the legal war booty that we took. Men even did not want to change their canvas belts for German belts with aluminium buckles that read, "*Gott mit uns*"! i.e. God with us.

One more event took place in Kutno. They managed to catch *shtrafnik* Kasperovich in Belorussia, the one who had deserted from the battlefield at Narev saying that he was leaving to repair the damaged phone line. So, there in January 1945, he was for some reason again delivered to the battalion. Apparently, I guess, someone wanted to arrange a show court-martial for him, or probably the public execution that he deserved. That would be a warning to admonish all other *shtrafniks.* I guess we all, commanding officers and *shtrafnik* ex-officers, thought so at that time.

As the deserter could not be left unguarded, the *kombat* decided to put him into the attic of the house where the staff were staying. The guard was also a *shtrafnik* who was strictly warned about his punishment if he decided to execute the deserter himself, whatever the circumstances. Kasperovich believed that he was invincible and started provoking the guard by imitating an escape attempt. He broke up part of the tile roof and started throwing the tiles at the guard. The guard took it for some time, then tried to make the deserter come to order. Finally, he gave up, and fired at the deserter, wounding him in his shoulder. The wounded prisoner had to be transported to the nearest field hospital and held there under guard. Even in the hardest years of the war it was believed that a wounded or sick prisoner could not be tried or executed. While he was in the field hospital, there was no trial, and I don't know what happened to him in the end. There were other events that distracted me from the story.

In mid-February, the *kombat* gave me a mission to go to our supply units that were still in the Polish villages where we had stayed before the offensive towards Warsaw. I did not understand why Baturin ordered me to do it, relieving me from the strange office at Beldugov's company. My task was to give directions to the workers of our supply units where to go in order to join the staff and the bulk of supply units of the battalion. As I learnt later, the two milk cows were also there and I was supposed to bring them, as without them our Lieutenant Colonel felt quite uncomfortable. I don't know if he had a stomach ulcer or some other disease, but I understood that the delivery of the two cows was an important part of my mission. However, the *kombat* did not stress that I had to lead the supply column personally. There were enough trucks to transport all the battalion's belongings and the personal belongings of officers, including Michael Goldstein's harmonica and my gramophone and records.

I gave directions to Sergeant-major Fermanyuk, giving him a map with the route to Kutno. After that I decided to visit Rita in her hospital without permission of my *kombat*, on my own responsibility. I hoped at least to see her, as her hospital was still in Lochuv, despite the advance of the front line westwards. However, everything did not go as I expected. Rita threw herself at me, hugged me and all of a sudden asked to go with me to the *shtrafbat.* Apparently, she had already discussed this matter with her mother, and to my astonishment Ekaterina Nikolaevna supported this idea. I could not know how my *kombat* Baturin would react to this, but agreed to this 'double game', as I thought it would be hard to talk the chief of hospital into letting Rita go. Quite unexpectedly for me, the chief of hospital, Captain of Medical Corps Nisonov, received us immediately, and heartily congratulated us on our recent front line wedding. Almost immediately he gave us a go-ahead for that, ordering some of his workers to process the proper papers. As Rita told me, such an easy and non-conflicting solution of our seemingly very complicated matter was explained by the following. She told both her mother and the chief of the hospital that she would go to her husband wherever he might be and whatever it would cost her. They understood her decision!

There we were, with a vacation ticket or an order to "report to the new place of service, unit No. 07380". Literally the same day Rita packed her belongings in a bag pack and was ready for a 'honeymoon trip to *shtrafbat*'. She whispered to her mother and little brother, kissed all her girlfriends, waved her hand to the cheering crowd of the doctors, nurses and even some wounded and off we went to look for a car to hitch a lift. We reached a railway station and were amazed to know that trains were already running to the front line. The only thing we had to do was to climb on an empty freight train, and go west, pressing our bodies together to keep out the cold, not knowing what adventures we might have or what lay at the end of our journey. I was constantly checking the map to see if the names of the stations coincided with the direction that we needed. Luckily, we were going in the right direction. However, the train did not reach Kutno as the railway station was not yet restored. So we continued our journey on trucks and cars.

The battalion staff were not on the previous place, but had already left. Luckily, Fermanyuk arrived there at the same time with his small truck column. We received information about the route of the battalion staff from the local military commandant and continued the journey together. From the map we could see that the border of Germany was near. It was the lair of the beast that tortured our country for three years, and that now had to pay for its crimes. Although we had waited for that moment for several months, it was still unexpected. We crossed a plain bridge across a plain river, and saw a large stand that read, "here it is, that cursed Germany!" and immediately after the bridge we saw a standard German road sign saying "Berlin so many kilometres". A large frozen old goat was tied up to the sign. One of its front legs was pointing in the direction of Berlin and there was a wooden sign attached to it, saying in Russian, "To Berlin!!!"

We drove a bit further and saw several vehicles standing at the entrance of a village. Military personnel were there too. We stopped and went on foot with Rita and Fermanyuk, to ask if we could drive further. When we walked closer, we were dumbfounded by a horrible sight. There were five or six naked corpses lying across the road, among them women, a teenager and even a child of six or seven years old. Apparently it was a family. They were lying face up. Their bodies were pressed into the ground and flattened. Judging from the marks of track links on the ground, several tanks drove over them, or one tank drove over them several times. It looked like a Soviet tank driver's revenge on the Germans, for the crimes they had committed in our country. Possibly he revenged himself for his own dead family. However, those dead bodies were lying too accurately and submissively. It seemed that he first shot them and then put them on the road in that horrible line.

Rita turned away from the sight, and hid her face on my shoulder. Her body started to shiver from cries she barely held back. I took her back to our trucks and tried to calm her down, but she only repeated through her sobbing, "Why? Why did he do it? Why?" I thought that the tank driver that did such evil was full, not only of revenge, but inhumane hatred that could be understood, but not justified! Of course, the war went through the lives of each one of us, like that, as a blood-covered German jackboot. We all knew about the atrocities of SS men, torturing and killing women and children, burning them alive and hanging them. One must not forget and forgive those crimes, even centuries on. But we were not *Nazis*. We must not act like them!

We bypassed that horrible place, driving across a field, as the road was still frozen despite some thaw. We travelled on, staying silent for a long time. Rita continued to sob. I was occupied by thoughts of that awful sight. Of course, we hated *Nazis* without any limits. It was extremely hard to remove that hatred from our hearts, especially when we finally made it to the land of our enemies. There it was, that cursed Germany. It was a subconscious border that we all longed for. Many died before reaching it, in battles in Belorussia and Stalingrad, in Ukraine and in foreign Polish lands. They died waiting for us to come. They lay in swamps and forests, at the bottom of rivers and in snow-covered fields. Who knew if they would ever be found? They would never know that we had reached that 'source of evil'. We remembered all our fallen comrades and at that very moment, when we were entering the enemy's land, we told our fallen friends, "you are also crossing this border, because without your sacrifice, and the last step you took in your lives, we would not be here." We also remembered the words of the oath that we made at the graves of our friends, "take revenge!" Our endless longing and striving for the Victory that was already near, was the embodiment of our oaths. But it was not a 'wild' revenge that we wanted, such as we had just seen.

It was hard to hold an army that had fought for almost four years, from such atrocities. But we were not fighting against the German people, just against the German Army, aggressive and criminal, that had killed millions of innocent Soviet people, women, elderly people, and children! We were fighting to destroy *Nazism* and their troops that embodied the inhumane and bloody Hitler's *Neue Ordnung*. We also remembered the words, "Hitlers come and go, but the German nation remains". However, I guess that the cases of 'wild' revenge that we had just seen were not unique and this forced the Stavka of Supreme Command to issue the strictest order on tough punishment, up to execution, for releasing their hatred towards *Nazis*, on the peaceful German population. As time showed, this order produced results very quickly. One could judge the effectiveness of that order from the fact that several men were sent to our battalion for robbing civilians, and for other crimes against the German population.

Going forward in the story, I should say that those were mostly men and officers who had never killed Germans in battle but who were aggressive and dissipated in their treatment of German civilians. The real temptation was living Germans! Not at the front line, where no one knows who will kill whom, but there, in the rear, where one can do whatever he pleases without any risk to their own lives. There were some men who ended up in our battalion due to their crimes against civilians. Some were officers from the supply units. Some of them arrived even after the Victory. Those things really happened.

We continued our journey in silence, each one of us occupied by thoughts. Many villages were empty, the local population having either fled under the influence of false Goebbels' propaganda about the Soviet people, or they were evacuated by force. It was behind the Oder that they had nowhere to run and white sheets were hanging out of every window as a sign of surrender. There, in the part of Germany east of the Oder, there were very few locals. We saw more refugees coming back from German captivity, exhausted and in threadbare clothes.

We caught up with our staff after Beldugov's company had been thrown into battle to repel counterattacks of the *Nazis* at Stargard. Strong German forces were trying to break through there from Eastern Pomerania. They were surrounded by troops of the 2nd Belorussian Front under Marshal Rokossovski. The enemy managed to shift the balance of forces in his favour for a short time. On February 17 the Germans launched a powerful counter-offensive from Stargard that forced our troops, including the 61st Army, to withdraw. Beldugov's company was again thrown into battle to repel German assaults. The 23rd Division of the 61st Army had already fought at the approaches to Warsaw. Strong reinforcements, thrown there by Marshal Zhukov, broke the stubborn resistance of the *Nazis*, jointly with troops of Rokossovski, and again resumed the offensive on March 1. Meanwhile the penal company finished off the remains of Stargard's garrison. The city was free. I did not make it in time to take part in those engagements, but as officers told me later, it was a heated battle that lasted several days and resembled the encirclement battles at Brest. The battles were as heated and desperate there as at Brest. The Germans did not have a chance. Our losses too were really high.

I got to see Stargard some time around March 10. It was a large town, like many German towns where the *Nazis* put up stubborn resistance. It was almost completely burnt down and destroyed. Before that I had found the *kombat* and reported about the arrival of the supply units of the battalion, at their full strength, without losses. I did not mention the cows, as it was interesting for me to know if he would himself ask me about them. But the *kombat* did not ask anything. I guess he realised that without losses meant cows too. Of course, I used the moment of his good mood and reported that my wife was transferred from her hospital to our battalion. I introduced Rita to him, and she reported to him in strict accordance with all manuals, that she had arrived at his disposal for further service and handed the *kombat* her papers. I quickly asked the *kombat*, in order to deprive him of time to react, to send "Junior Sergeant Makarievskaya to the battalion dressing station for disposal of Captain of Medical Corps Buzun". Apparently, Baturin did not expect such a course of events, and just shrugged his shoulders. Then he ordered me to pass the word to Stepan Petrovich Buzun to give a set of responsibilities to Rita. Thank God for that! Everything went quite well.

Beldugov's company had become noticeably smaller after Stargard, and was licking its wounds. They advanced in the second echelon of the rifle division, behind the armoured troops, towards the Order River, in the direction of Stettin. They were marching directly behind the rifle regiments, always ready to be engaged, as it had happened at Stargard. The *kombat* found a job for me again, ordering me to form a company from the arriving *shtrafniks*. Then I had to either replace the fighting company at a critical moment, or join it at that moment.

Part of the staff and rear units of our penal battalion, as well as the units that provided support to the company during the offensive, changed their location once every two to three days, depending on the speed of advance of the front. The bulk of the battalion's dressing station was also in that group. Meanwhile, the other part, led by medical assistant Ivan Demenkov, was with Beldugov's company. That was why the main doctor of our battalion, Stepan Petrovich, was so happy to have an experienced nurse in his dressing station. He thoroughly prepared her for her new tasks, which were quite different from the tasks in a permanent hospital. There she would have to deal with bandaging the wounded on a battlefield.

The battalion continued to march behind the divisions of the first echelon of the 61st Army, sometimes almost catching up with their forward units and sometimes falling 5–6 kilometres behind. Some time around March 15, when the Division stopped, confronting strong resistance of the enemy, we arrived in the suburbs of Altdamm, on the eastern bank of the Oder across the river from Stettin. There I received an order to hand over to Beldugov's company, not a complete company, but at the best a half-company of one and a half platoons. I should point out here that I refer to the company by its commander's name. I don't remember its official number but the numbers did not have any meaning any more, as only one company was in battle during the period.

As Alexei Afonin, a platoon leader in Beldugov's company, reminded me in his letter that he wrote in 2002, our half-company caught up with the others at dawn, in the area next to the outskirts of Altdamm. There the *shtrafniks* were preparing for the assault of the town. The one and a half platoons that I had brought were already armed, and were quickly distributed between the under-manned platoons of the main company. Grasshopper's platoon was fully incorporated into it, while Junior Lieutenant Kuznetsov himself replaced the wounded Alexander Shamshin. That was the baptism of fire for Kuznetsov. As I found out a bit later, it was also Rita's baptism of fire as she, as it turned out, convinced doctor Buzun to send her to the front line. Buzun also went to the front line and created there his dressing station, where his medical assistant and nurse in fact became part of the company.

I was again without a job, as I did not have any orders about where to go after I handed over my half-company. Naturally, in anticipation of serious battles, and also because Rita was already with me, I independently made a decision. I voluntarily assumed the role of shift commander, which I had already played during the capture of the suburbs of Warsaw. Beldugov agreed with my decision in an appreciative way. As a result, I ended up next to the company commander and platoon of Alex Afonin, while Kuznetsov's platoon was on the right. Ivan Beldugov briefed me on the mission to assault German positions over the lines of the rifle units of the division. Again we had to lead an assault and break the enemy's resistance and go into battle in a built-up area.

Altdamm was a town made of a single wide street, parallel to the river, with stone buildings along it. The eastern part of the town was facing us, with barns and yards of the main street, and we captured it quickly, 'at one breath', although the Germans put up strong resistance and we had significant losses. Ivan Demenkov was bandaging the wounded and pulled them into the 'rear' some 50–60 metres from the assaulting area, into the yards. He had Rita as assistant. She quickly and skilfully ran and sometimes crawled between the wounded.

The other side of the street was hitting us with devastating rifle and MG fire from the numerous cellar windows that the *Fritzes* had turned into a whole series of gun-ports. Their concentrated MG and SMG fire pinned the company down on our side of the street. Beldugov sent a runner to the regiment of the rifle division that we were supporting, and asked to bring 45mm AT-guns to destroy those targets over the open area, but for some reason the guns never arrived. Probably they did not have those guns anywhere near. Our attempt to take out the MGs with hand-grenades came to nothing. The distance to the gun-ports was quite large and it was quite hard to hit them, and we did not want to waste hand-grenades. Firing AT-rifles at the windows also did not give the desired effect.

I was depressed by the worrisome feeling of helplessness of the company, and my own personal uselessness in that situation. I was also unsure that the houses on our side of the street were abandoned by the enemy. What would happen if the company were to start the assault anyway and the Germans opened MG fire from behind, at our backs? I, just like the company commander Ivan Beldugov, was hastily looking for an exit from this situation. It turned out that the company commander also came to the same conclusion, to revisit the captured houses. He ordered Kuznetsov to go through the houses with part of his platoon. As it turned out, it was not in vain. On the second floors and the attics of the buildings, they found and destroyed the secret MG nests of the Germans.

By the way, that was the time when I saw Rita crawling towards us. I felt uncomfortable, as her place was with the wounded, and not here, in the middle of a hellish firefight! I shouted at her, gestured, then whispered, all of which was quite stupid of me, as she could not hear me anyway! I tried to make it clear to her that it was a very dangerous spot. But at the same time I felt some sort of joy and pride at her fearlessness on the front line! I had a thought that now I would not be ashamed to tell Baturin that I had brought Rita to the battalion, without his permission.

The successful result of checking the houses on our side of the street made us sure that this measure was both necessary and timely for our further operations. However, it was necessary but not sufficient. We had to decide how to capture the houses on the other side of the street. During the moment when I was confused and at a loss, as I did not know what to do, or maybe because I had insufficient battle experience, Alex Afonin and *shtrafnik* Yastrebkov crawled up to me. Yastrebkov had just been transferred from my half-company. They proposed an extremely bold but, it seemed to me, completely impossible idea. The idea was for Yastrebkov to take all the available hand-grenades with him, and then play 'the defector' in the straight sector of the street. When he had reached the other side of the street, he would press himself into the walls of the buildings so that the Germans would not be able to hit him from the gun-ports. He would then throw one or two grenades into each window and thus suppress the MG nests that pinned down our company. For the Germans to believe that he was a real defector, he would emerge on our side of the street shouting, "nicht schiessen!" Then, with his hands in the air, we would all open fire at him, but aiming high, in order to miss him for certain.

I could not immediately agree, but not because I did not trust the *shtrafnik*. He volunteered for this almost suicidal mission and we understood him well. Apparently, he saw no other choice in this situation. I remembered him from the period of formation of my 'half-company'. I believed he was a reliable man, as he had a lot of infantry experience before getting to the *shtrafbat*. He used to be a rifle company commander and there were ribbons for three battle decorations on his tunic. While we were forming the company, he was a squad leader and exhibited skills and resourcefulness many times.

I guess there was not a single person in the war who would not be afraid of getting it from a bullet or shrapnel in battle. But I guess that in this situation the *shtrafnik*, a former officer with a stable commander's consciousness, felt personally responsible for the outcome of the battle. He must have been so consumed by the battle, and so concerned for its outcome, that the matter of personal safety and well-being was no longer important to him. I noticed that some of my fellow officers also behaved in that manner, for example, Yanin, Semykin, Sergeev and others. I noticed that I too sometimes behaved so. Apparently, Yastrebkov also did the same thing.

Nevertheless, I could not agree to his proposal, as those men were not my subordinates. I gave it thought and advised Afonin to report the suggestion to the company commander first. The latter approved it, agreed, and gave the most detailed explanation of the mission to the other platoons, so that all the men would understand the trick, and provide for a proper and plausible imitation of fire on the 'defector and traitor', also firing at the gun-ports.

We gathered two gasmask bags full of hand-grenades for Yastrebkov and he stuffed his pockets with them, too. He chose a good moment, crawled forward, jumped up, threw away his submachine-gun and with lifted hands, holding a piece of white linen, shouted as loud as he could, "Nicht schiessen! Nicht schiessen!" Jumping from side to side and stumbling, he ran to the buildings on the other side of the street, while the company opened fire at the 'defector'. We were all so worried about that brave man! Would this crazy idea work, or would he die in vain before reaching his goal? We were all extremely happy to see that he reached one of the buildings on the other side of the street, and pressed himself against its wall. Barely catching his breath, he literally pressed his body into the wall and slowly made his way to the nearest window. He threw two hand-grenades into the window, one after another, and after they went off he then ran to the next window. So he moved from one window to another, taking out the deadly German MGs one by one.

Soon a red flare signalled the beginning of the company's assault. The first platoon to stand up was the one under Afonin. Then the rest of the men from the company joined the assault. *Shtrafniks* rushed across the ill-fated street, finished off the German MG nests that were still returning fire, surrounded the houses, and did not let the Germans slip away. Some of them tried to hide in barns, or flee toward the Oder through gardens and fields. The success was staggering! Afonin's platoon found a small village nearby, and saw a platoon of *Fritzes*, who were rushing to Altdamm, to help the ones that were being destroyed by Beldugov's company. Platoon leader Afonin found a solution quickly. He took his platoon there, in order to cut their road. *Shtrafniks* first pinned down those *Nazis* and then forced them to surrender. It was a rare case when *shtrafniks* took prisoners, but there we captured about twenty Germans alive.

Almost immediately after the penal company, the units of the regiment from the 23rd Division attacked in their sectors, and the city was captured by mid-day. The rifle units were consolidating our defences on the shore of the Oder, while the penal company that had completed its task was disengaged. Altdamm was captured! That happened on March 20.

Our losses were still significant. As Rita told me later, she managed to evacuate and bandage many wounded from the battlefield. When I asked her how many, she replied, "I don't know, I did not count them". When I asked Senior Lieutenant of medical corps Ivan Demenkov about it, he told me that she evacuated about twenty wounded. Great job, Rita, you did not fail them. I am proud of you! Rita told me later that she also saw the 'defector' scene and was also worried for this desperately brave *shtrafnik*.

The battalion's staff arrived by nightfall. Our *kombat* ordered Beldugov to leave the *shtrafniks* who had already deserved the right to be released from the battalion, and hand over the rest to my company. So I was the next officer to lead the company into a new battle. I could not understand why other company commanders never went into battle, but an order is an order. I noticed as early as in the Narev battles that Baturin had a special 'liking' for me. We were transferred to a suburb of Altdamm. There we started the formation of the company that was already a routine for us.

I had some spare time, too. I chose a small house for myself and stayed there with Rita. Afonin, Kuznetsov and all the other officers of the battalion stayed nearby. Not all the dead bodies of Germans had been removed from the streets. It was already late March and the sun was warm, so that we did not wear overcoats and sheepskin vests, but only *kubankas* and winter hats, instead of visor hats and *pilotka* side caps.

Rita looked much more mature, prettier and even a bit chubbier. It was much later that we realised that she was pregnant. Back then I asked her if she was scared there at the front line.

"It was scary, but I did not think about it then," Rita said.

"Could you kill a German, a living person, there, at the battlefield?"

"I guess I could, I don't know."

Then I gave her a small war-booty Browning pistol that we called a lady's pistol. I proposed she tried to shoot a dead *Fritz*, pointing at a corpse lying in the roadside ditch. We walked up to it, and Rita fired at the dead enemy, almost without aiming. The stomach started to get smaller, and a disgusting gas came out. The enemy's dead body does not smell good. Then Rita said, "If I have to, I will shoot an enemy who is alive. I will not miss".

We also underscored the results of the company's action in the Vistula-Oder operation. Captain Ivan Ivanovich Beldugov received the top battle order of those times, the Order of the Red Banner. Afonin and Kuznetsov received the orders of Alexander Nevski, while *shtrafnik* Yastrebkov received the Order of Glory 3rd Class. He felt sorry that it was not the Medal for Bravery. Beldugov recommended him for it, but Baturin either due to kindness or with some hint, recommended Yastrebkov, who was almost rehabilitated as an officer, for a soldier's Order of Glory. Several other men received decorations. As for me, I was not in the TOE of their unit, and naturally did not receive any award. Rita, on the other hand, was recommended for the Medal for Merit in Battle, by our battalion doctor Stepan Buzun, and we were both extremely happy.

Several days later we got to know that the sector of the 1st Belorussian Front was shrinking, in anticipation of the decisive offensive towards Berlin. We were to move much further south. I was forming the company, and preparing for the march, when the commander of the 2nd Belorussian Front, Marshal Rokossovski, suddenly drove up to the battalion's HQ. He already had the reputation of a Marshal who would often visit troops in the field. Here, he drove to the sector that his 2nd Belorussian Front was about to take over. Or maybe he knew that 'Rokossovski's gang' was stationed right there and wanted to visit it. At least, that was what we wanted to believe. I was again unlucky. Just as back then at Zhlobin, I did not understand what was going on, and did not go up to see the famous general. But Rita described to me what happened there.

The problem was that there was the strictest order not to send women to penal battalions. And there came Rokossovski. A tall and handsome man, he got out of his car. "What it this? What is this woman doing here? Wife of a company commander? What difference does it make? Get her immediately out of here!" A woman remained in his car at the same time! Her pale and beautiful face was well known to the whole country from the movies, in which she always smiled. Rita decided to object to the Marshal. She would do anything to stay with me during that difficult time. She said, "There is another woman here besides me, Comrade Marshal", and put her hands together in front of herself, as if in prayer. Then Rokossovski glanced at her already noticeably large belly, and all of a sudden waved his hand, saying, "All right, you can stay, Sergeant".

Soon I got to know that my company was to take part in the crossing of the Oder, in one of the sectors of the Kuestrin bridgehead, to the north of the one already captured by the troops of the 1st Belorussian Front. They urgently transferred us there.

CHAPTER 10

Over the Oder to Berlin

After a long and exhausting march we concentrated in a pretty little German village, a few kilometres from the Oder. The village mostly consisted of two-storey stone buildings. There were no villagers left, they had all managed to flee beyond the Oder. There was no damage visible in the village. The Germans had left everything behind, the furniture, beds with soft mattresses that were a 'must' in any German house, and all the cutlery. In short, our accommodation was cosy and even luxurious. All the officers of the company stayed in one house that had 3–4 rooms. Rita and I took one room, the platoon commanders, the Sergeant-major and the company's clerk took the others.

Supply personnel quickly set up an officer canteen, in Baturin's style, next to our house. Rita and I were constantly aware of the strong smell of food. Rita became quite selective in food, as some dishes made her sick. After the visit by Marshal Rokossovski, who pointed out her growing waistline, we had no more doubts that she would soon become a mother. A new, as yet unknown feeling grew in me, too. Soon the entire battalion knew that Rita was expecting a baby, and all the officers in the canteen gave her their portions of the tastiest herring, as Rita started to like salty food. Our battalion doctor, Stepan Buzun, came to visit us once, and instantly told us that due to Rita's pregnancy he forbade her to work at the front line. She could only assist him at the battalion's dressing station. He added that he had received approval of this decision from the battalion commander.

When we had settled down in the village, and found out where our battalion commander was accommodated, and where HQ was, we noticed that there was a woman living in the same house with our *kombat*. At first we thought that he was living with a German woman who had stayed behind, and not fled. She was a rather short chubby woman with a slightly swollen, but quite pretty face. As we found out later, she was Baturin's wife, not a 'field and campaign wife' from the military, but his real wife. I have no idea how our battalion commander managed to bring her over from Russia, but she was neither an officer nor a soldier. We knew that many high-ranking officers had their wives sharing all hardships and dangers of the front line with their husbands. Many men saw the famous actress Serova in the car with Marshal Rokossovski, who was dating her at that time. After the war I learnt that General Gorbatov's wife was also with him in the war. The conditions of life for our battalion commander, when our battalion was only engaged by single companies, also allowed him to have his spouse with him. I felt some relief. From that moment on, Rita and I were not the only object of envy for some officers, and Baturin started treating us much better too.

In the meantime, formation and battle training of the company continued. We all understood that crossing the last large German river between us and Berlin, the capital of *Nazi* Germany, would be our last and decisive battle after crossing the Oder. Our battalion would still have the manpower to reach Berlin. This is why I would like to tell, as much as my old memory will allow me, about the men with whom I went into this last deadly battle, about their personalities and appearance.

As I have mentioned, the MG platoon attached to my company was formed again under George Sergeev. He was assisted by another platoon leader of the same MG Company, Senior Lieutenant Sergey Sisenkov. I have written a lot about George Sergeev and his personality. He seemed to find the most dangerous spots in battle and went there because not a single German expected it. That was his supreme logic of survival in war. He was not mad in his bravery. It was a combination of cold calculation, confidence and tactical skill. His two colleagues from MG Company, both Sergeys, Sisenkov and Piseev, were his good followers. They tried to copy George in everything, and although they did not always succeed, very often they acted by just copying their fellow officer. I was very happy to have Sergeev, that reliable officer, at my side.

My first platoon leader, at that time, was again George Vasilievich Razhev. He had become nervous, easily losing his temper, and was hard to calm down. I also noticed that he had started to drink a lot, which caused a lot of unnecessary tensions between us, and strained our relations. His behaviour forced me to take measures, and consider the importance of military discipline. Of course, I came to the conclusion that discipline, full obedience to a superior, regardless of his rank, was an absolute necessity. However, it should not be a blind and submissive obedience that excluded personal initiative. It had to be obedience with good heart and will, to complete missions and tasks better, faster, safer, and not just in the name of your commander, but in the name of victory over the enemy. One absolute necessity in war is not an obedience of the 'do whatever you want to me' type, but rather a willingness to do what is needed to be done. In general, I managed to control, although with difficulty, that uncontrollable officer George Razhev.

The second platoon leader was a newly arrived Lieutenant Chaika. He was a slightly chubby, large-headed officer of medium height. He seemed old to us, although only 35 years of age. He had unusual white hair and was bald in many places, with attentive blue eyes and thick eyebrows. He had a rather soft voice, seemingly unfit for an officer. His speech was always calm and slow, while his words were very convincing and weighty. He was immediately elected party organisation secretary of our company. Our company's party organisation consisted of communists, who were permanent personnel in the company, as well as the commanders, the Sergeant-major and the clerk. One could see that Chaika had a sharp mind, and decisiveness that was hidden behind his seeming simplicity.

Junior Lieutenant Semenov's first name was Yuri. His wide and boyish face was so abundantly covered with freckles, as if someone had painted his nose and cheeks with light brown paint and never washed it off. He did not have battle experience, and acted timidly in many situations, although I never saw him completely losing control of the situation.

My deputy, or *ratyer* shift commander, in accordance with Baturin's leadership style, was Captain Nikolai Aleksandrovich Slautin. His previous office was commander of the 2nd Rifle Company that had never been formed. He was short and round like a barrel, or a 16 kilogram weight of pig iron, although one could not call him chubby. The Captain made an impression that he was himself made of pig iron, especially his fists. He was of tough temper, silent and a bit rude. In a case when words were not enough, he could use obscenities or his heavy fists as an argument. He did not take an active part in forming the company, although he was always in the company. I understood that he would not take part in the crossing of the Oder, and would only be appointed to replace me if I were out of action. I saw three options for me being out of action, to be heavily wounded, killed, or drowned in the Oder. My only desire was that he would not have to replace me!

George Yemelyanovich Kuzmin was leader of the AT-rifle platoon attached to my company. After his arrival we had three Georges in the company and we received a joking nickname of 'three George Company'. He was only one year older than me, but he looked much older as he was extremely serious-minded. He had a good sense of humour though.

I did not yet know how to use a platoon with those heavy weapons, when crossing such a wide river. An AT-rifle had to be carried by two men. I still had time to think how to use them. Deputy platoon leaders were appointed from among *shtrafnik*, former line officers, as usual. Unfortunately, I do not remember their last names, except for one. He was a tall Georgian man, with a charming smile and vast battle experience. His last name was either Gaguashvili or Gogashvili. He had a joke that he fought the war four years without breaks, although he had to recover from wounds in hospitals three times. As he said, "When Goga is in a hospital, Shvili is fighting, when Shvili is in a hospital, Goga is fighting".

I can very well remember another short, well-built, round-faced man with narrow Asian eyes. He seemed to possess the power of a bull and the calmness of an elephant. I remember yet another *shtrafnik*. He had dark colouring, with his face shaved so clean that it looked blue. He had an amazingly kind face and dark eyes. He was a decisive and active soldier, and despite his seeming kindness, immediately took the platoon in hand, which was a great help for the inexperienced platoon leader Junior Lieutenant Semenov.

I remember one squad leader, a former Captain Lieutenant with an interesting last name, Redki. He was appointed squad leader for his energetic and extremely cheerful attitude. He was always telling jokes and stories about his battle and civil life adventures. One could hear that there were a lot of exaggerations and lies in his stories. At the time I did not pay attention to this, thinking that his cheerfulness would not let him down at a tough moment.

When the company was almost completely formed, and the arriving *shtrafnik* soldiers no longer changed the number of platoons in it, an older *shtrafnik* with a strange name, Putrya, arrived in the company. He was so thin and exhausted that I was even amazed that he was sent to the front. He seemed old, although he was under fifty years of age. During a long conversation with me he told me that he was sent to our battalion after spending several years in jail. He was a *technician-intendent* 2nd Rank, a rank abolished in 1943. He had been a department chief of a large army warehouse near Moscow. He was sentenced for hiding several pieces of soap that were not in the army books. The auditors, who were checking his department, found an extra box full of soap bars, some of which Putrya had already exchanged for bread for his large family. According to the laws of war, he was sentenced to several years of jail. His conscience tortured him all those years. He was spending the war in a prison cell, not at the front! So he applied for a penal battalion. He told me that he would prefer to die at the front, for his country, than live with the reputation of a criminal, who tried to get rich stealing soap from soldiers. Finally, his remaining term was replaced with a shorter term in a penal battalion.

I had had several former criminals in my company before. They too were transferred from jails and labour camps. Their number only grew at the end of the war. At first, I spared one of them. He was rather young and had been serving at the kitchen in his camp, so I sent him to our kitchen. I was not surprised by his arms that were almost completely covered with tattoos, or his gangster slang and manners. He convinced me, that before the war, he had worked as a cook in a restaurant in the southern part of the USSR, and that he could cook a decent dinner even from simple soldiers' food.

But then came Putrya, with the sad eyes of a person who was prepared to die. His thin arms looked more like the legs of a bird, and I thought that he would not be able to hold even a light SMG, not to mention a machine-gun or an AT-rifle. So I decided to send him to the kitchen instead of that tattooed *shtrafnik*. It would not expose Putrya to the dangers that lay in front of us. Besides, I spared him because he could not swim, just like me. You had to see the joy in his eyes, and the new hope that appeared in the smile that he held back. I also remembered the phrase that Putrya liked to repeat in every situation, "your own dry tack is better than someone else's cake"!

The former criminal with the tattoos, did not hold back his anger when I transferred him to Chaika's platoon. For the first time during my entire service in a penal battalion I heard some sort of threat. He said, "OK, Captain, let's see who gets a bullet first". I never was a too self-confident person. However, I could be decisive and insistent if I had to, and that phrase from a criminal only strengthened my faith in the correctness of my decision. When you do business and bear responsibility for it, you should not hesitate. After completion of a mission you can analyse the situation, look for improvements and think of your mistakes. However, in those days I did not think much of that small incident, and from my point of view that was not a threat, but rather a hope.

In general, most of the men in the battalion were aware of all the hardships of the coming mission. They were sad and concentrated, even depressed, at the uncertainty and inevitability of the approaching battle, at the very end of the war. It was a natural reaction. We all knew what the past had been. Many were killed but we were lucky and had survived. But who knew what tomorrow might bring. We commanders also understood that we had to go into battle with the men, probably into a suicidal battle. And I also had to lead them. Of course, they all thought that their future, to a great extent, depended on me, and my battle experience and skills. It is not a paradox that I thought almost completely the opposite. It was my life that depended on how they would fight the battle, and how they would fulfil my orders. That was exactly why I paid great attention to training the men in handling weapons and making them keep in good physical shape. I must confess that all of us had quite sad thoughts while preparing for that last strike. We called it 'a penal strike' for the enemy.

I do not remember many *shtrafniks*, but I remember one former Captain, a pilot with an unusual last name, Smeshnoi. He was a tall, relatively young, blonde officer with the face of a calm Russian peasant. I knew that his wife was also at the front, serving in a large staff as a code officer. Two of their children lived with their grandmother in a small town, somewhere in Russia. This Captain was a *frontovik* with three Orders of the Red Banner and had been a squadron commander. He ended up in the penal battalion when he was flying new fighter planes to the front from a factory, and one of the planes crashed. One of the subordinate pilots of Smeshnoi made a mistake, losing control of a plane and crashing, destroying the plane and himself.

Smeshnoi trained himself the best he could, in those days of intensive infantry training, exercising short rushes, and crawling on the ground, till he dropped. As he himself said, "till my arms and legs hurt". He was persistent and patient, learning and trying everything. He was in an SMG platoon, but learnt to fire an AT-rifle and MG very well. He wanted to know everything, as he thought he might need every bit of knowledge and training in battle. He even learnt to fire the captured German *panzerfaust*, firing at a burnt-out German tank. "You have to learn everything. Without a skill you cannot even make a shoe!" He would say. It seemed that this Captain worked twenty-four hours a day. The Captain also said that he would give all his fancy pilot rations to the infantry. He said that pilots had a lot of difficulties but they did not have even ten per cent of the physical stress that an infantryman had. He described the difference between the war of a pilot and an infantryman. "You just take off and fly where you have to, and act according to the situation. And that's it! Here, on the ground, you sweat so much before you actually reach your target"!

Once, his wife, also a Captain, completely unexpectedly came to visit our battalion. I managed to arrange for them some private time together. Later, she spoke to me with a soft voice, trying to keep calm with visible difficulty. She did not beg me to spare the life of the father of her children. Instead, she asked me about one single thing, to help him to survive if he were wounded. I remembered that modest and wise woman for a long time. I admired her decision to leave her children in Russia and serve at the front, to be closer to her beloved husband, and contribute to the common Victory. "My dear Rita is just like this woman", I thought.

It was only my company that was training so hard for the coming battles. The other units of the battalion had less training, and so officers had time for other things. At that time, after the strict order forbidding the robbing of the German civilian population, we received permission to send parcels home. Our officers who were not busy with preparing for the crossing, and the senior officers of course, tried to legally get German goods for those parcels. We, the younger officers, did not have time for that, and we did not need all those material things. We had a feeling of extreme dare-devilry. Many of our feelings were overwhelmed by the expectation of the coming battles. Those feelings were suppressed and kind of numb. Even then, at the end of the war, we were full of energy, despite all our wounds and the fatigue that had accumulated for years. We just had to get a good sleep and then we were again full of energy. We were a bit depressed, as we missed our Russian birch forests and our Motherland, and our mothers and sisters who had had to stay there. But even homesickness was hidden, under the main burden of how to prepare soldiers for the coming battles, in the best way possible.

The rest of the battalion had more time for other things, for jokes and tricks that were common in wartime. I mentioned that I could not understand what our *Smersh* officer Gluhov was doing, but in the spring of 1945 he started to pay more and more attention to hunting for German souvenirs. He confiscated German pistols from officers, or German decorations and cigarette boxes with fancy carving, and even round German chocolate bars. One time, when a small group of officers gathered for a smoke break, commandant platoon leader Senior Lieutenant Slava Kostik, noticed Gluhov walking in our direction. So Kostik took a round box out of his pocket and pretended that he was eating something very tasty. Gluhov walked up to him and, with his usual manner of begging, asked what Kostik was eating. Lieutenant Kostik demonstratively hid the box behind his back, and answered that he had several unusual candies left and he would not share them with anyone. Of course, this only intensified Gluhov's interest, and he started to beg Kostik to share the sweets with him. Then Kostik, seemingly reluctantly, opened the box, which had several small objects wrapped in foil. Gluhov greedily grabbed one of them, unwrapped it, and put it in his mouth. You had to see how his face twisted as he started to chew that 'trophy of war!' He spat it out with obscene curses, and angrily asked, "What the hell was that?" Kostik calmly replied, with everyone else laughing out loud, "That was a German anti-haemorrhoid pill that you put in your ass, Herr Oberleutnant!" I don't know what sort of relations they had, as they were both permanently at the battalion HQ, and officially had similar functions. Maybe they were even friends, but after that cruel trick Gluhov never again asked anyone to share their German sweets, even if it was an open bar of German chocolate.

In the meantime, the days were passing by quickly in intensive battle training. The company was growing. We already had about a hundred and twenty men in the company, almost forty men in a platoon, not counting the attached AT-rifle and MG platoons. The courts-martial were quite busy! We carried out fire range practice, intensive marches and tactical exercises, from dawn till dusk. The days were already warm, and we took off our overcoats, padded jackets and vests. However, we still wore the *kubanka* hats that some wore tilted according to a fashion of those days. Both Baturin and his political officer, Major Kazakov, only took them off several days after the Victory, when they were both ordered to report to Marshal Zhukov's HQ. Of course, almost all of us followed their example, although officers who had winter hats had long before replaced them with side caps and visor caps.

Some unclear event happened to George Razhev. Baturin unexpectedly replaced him with Lieutenant Sergey Piseev, whom I knew as a talkative and good-hearted guy. I was even happier to hear this news as I had more and more conflicts with Razhev, for all sorts of reasons. So our company ceased to be 'the three George Company'. We had three officers with the name of Sergey instead. I learnt about the real reason of Razhev's departure much later.

A Major soon arrived from a Division in whose sector we had to fight. I think its number was 234th Division, from the same 61st Army of General Pavel Alekseevich Belov. We got to know that a small scout party from our new division had already managed to swim across to the opposite bank, and carry out very basic reconnaissance. The scout party came back almost without losses, while the leader of the scout party, a Sergeant, was recommended for the Golden Star of Hero of the Soviet Union. Many officers started to say that if we managed to complete the mission, and survive, then we would also have a chance to get the top military awards. By that time, we already knew that for crossing such large rivers as the Dnepr and Vistula, many men and officers were awarded with that high decoration.

We were told that the night before the crossing they would bring enough strong tar-covered rowing boats to the river. We could only guess which night that would be. The rowing boats were built by the same engineer battalion that was supposed to build a bridge, immediately after we secured a bridgehead. Of course, I was again nervous about not being able to swim, but I was calmed down by the fact that no one was ordering me to swim across the Oder. Spring was already warm and the ice had gone from the Oder in early February. But the water was still extremely cold, about +5 degrees. Other information about the Oder also made us apprehensive. The depth of the river was then about 10 metres. But now, at the time of the spring high water, it was even deeper. It did not make much difference to me anyway. The width of the Oder in our sector was about two hundred metres, and the current speed was over half a metre per second. We calculated the approximate speed of boats on the river, and even measured out 200 metres with strides on the ground. We calculated the time for crossing the river, in order to see how far we would be taken by the current, and which route we had to choose. It was about 100–150 metres! We were also happy to know that in our sector the river only had one course, and split into two courses some five kilometres down the river.

The type and the difficulty of the mission became clearer as we approached the crossing time. I noticed that the new moon was there and that the nights would be dark. I guessed that our leadership would use the darkest time, which would be between April 10 and 20. That was exactly what happened. Soon we received the order of one-day readiness. On the night of April 14, the company marched on foot with all weapons, ammo and hand-grenades to the bank of the Oder.

A Captain, a representative of the Division, was our guide in the darkness. He strictly warned us about not smoking, and not turning on flashlights, even for a short time. It was the first time that, in addition to platoon leaders, squad leaders also received flashlights with red and green filters. It was the first time in my memory, that all signals for leading the combat were supposed to be given by signals from flashlights, not signal flares, as in the past. We had signal flares, too, but we were supposed to use them on the bridgehead, on the solid ground that we had to reach first.

We marched quickly, following the pace of this fast and slim Captain, so the last ones in our column even had to run in order to keep up with us. No one talked. All were silent, thinking of what lay ahead of us. Even before we reached the Oder proper, the Captain made a "Stop!" signal with his red flashlight in front of a long building. He gathered the platoon leaders and allowed smoking under cover of the long barn or warehouse, using *plash-palatkas* and sleeves for camouflage. Then he took us officers to a nearby trench. There was a Major with an overcoat hanging over his shoulders and a stick in his hand. He was still recovering from a wound. He was the representative from the Division HQ and another Major, *kombat* of the shooters, as we dubbed rifle units.

They explained that the men had to be brought into the trench immediately, leaving the heavy weapons in the trench. From a nearby ravine they would bring the boats, on which we would, as the Major with the stick said, "Capture the Oder". There was one boat for every four men. When I asked why they had not brought the boats beforehand, he answered, "The Germans would hole them, they fire at our rear quite often!" The Germans confirmed it themselves, delivering a short but intensive artillery strike. That happened immediately after the company entered the trenches. It was a relief that we had made it to the trenches, because we would have definitely suffered losses behind that barn. We were not hit in the trenches. "Now the *Fritzes* will be quiet for about three hours. You should use this time to bring the boats", the Major said.

We were given one guide for a platoon, and the platoon leaders took their units to pick up their boats. Two hours later the boats had been brought and hidden behind the long barn. However, the boats were so heavy that some of them had to be carried by six men, and physically stronger *shtrafniks* were sent to pick up the remaining boats. The *kombat* told me that he had a special boat with oars for me. Their Sergeant and his scout party had used that boat for their mission and came back, so that was a lucky boat!

Behind us, the sky grew grey in the east. All the years of the war, both in Belorussia and here, in Germany, we still lived on Moscow time, so dawn was three hours later than in Moscow. It grew noticeably lighter only by six o'clock that morning. I asked the local *kombat* to help me to reconnoitre both banks of the river. Our bank could be very easily seen, in depth, from the German side. So we had to crawl on the ground, in order to bypass the sections of a communication trench that had been destroyed by a recent artillery strike. Finally, we reached the first trench that was dug directly on the bank. It turned out to be uneven, flat in some places and raised in others.

A high metallic railway bridge over the Oder on our right, immediately caught my attention. Judging from the map, the railway led to a rather large town, the name I do not remember. I think it was Frankfurt-an-der-Oder. I thought, that after a good artillery and air strike on the German defences adjacent to the bridge, we could run across the bridge and capture a bridgehead. But the *kombat* must have guessed my thoughts and told me "the bridge is heavily booby-trapped by the Germans". So, there was no other way for us, we had to cross that damned German river in rowing boats!

I studied the terrain as best I could, and distributed sectors of the trench between the platoons, immediately making a decision not to take the AT-rifle platoon with us. I ordered that platoon to support us on the river from the bank, firing at the German bunkers and other weapon emplacements that would be found. After some consideration, I made the same decision about the MG platoon. Both the Goryunov MG and the Maxim that we had were quite heavy. Our 'dread-noughts' could barely remain on the surface under the weight of the machine-guns and their crews.

George Kuzmin, an AT-rifle platoon leader must have been glad to hear the news, although he did not show it at all. Even if he were happy, he was happy not only for himself but also for the entire platoon, as he had the strongest and bravest men. Sergeev, an MG platoon leader, remained quiet for some time. He asked me who would be my deputy instead of him, and offered to take at least two or three MG crews. Then he tentatively asked me, almost whispering, "Are you completely sure about your decision?"

I calculated where we would land on the opposite bank, if we made it at all, and was happy to hear that it matched the calculations of the division HQ. The place that they ordered us to reach was some 150 metres down the river from the place where we were. I ordered the MG and AT-rifle platoons to move to our right flank, across the river from the spot where we were supposed to capture the bridgehead.

I still don't understand why my deputy stayed with the battalion HQ. But he and Sergeev stayed on our bank on my orders. So I appointed Lieutenant Piseev my deputy for the time of the crossing, as he at least had some battle experience. We spent the day in the second trench. For *shtrafnik* soldiers the day was mostly one of rest, as they only checked their weapons before the battle. Those who could sleep compensated for the previous and the following sleepless nights. We commanders had more things to do. We spent the whole day studying our bank, defining spots for bringing the boats to the river, and establishing signals, etc. We did all this together with the Major from the Division HQ. It was only relatively dark, as some factory was burning near to us, and the Germans were firing illumination flares into the sky.

When complete darkness fell at midnight, after yet another German artillery strike, the platoon leaders took their men to pick up the boats, relying on the famous German punctuality. Men from the MG and AT-rifle platoons also went there, although they did not yet need the boats themselves. They just wanted to help the riflemen in order not to go to the ravine twice. We also needed some extra men just in case. At around three o'clock in the morning the boats were on the shore, including the one that the Major kept for me. It was indeed a light boat, made of aluminium, with good aluminium oars that the Sergeant had used on his scout mission. It was indeed a 'boat for heroes', although several bullet holes in it were carefully filled and insulated. That boat made me more confident.

The wooden boats were too heavy. Apparently, they were made in great haste from wet wood, but where would they find dry wood at the front, and were thoroughly waterproofed with tar, which was quite an achievement in front line conditions. The soldiers carefully hid them behind the slightest folds of the ground, hillocks and in shell craters. They treated the boats as their last hope of survival. Every boat crew carefully studied their sector, and found the best route for taking their boats to the water. Some boats did not have oars, and the oars that we had were uncomfortable. So, many of the men decided to use small entrenching tools instead of oars, as everyone had those.

I think that all of us had some feeling of jealousy or envy. Again the regular infantry was staying behind, while *shtrafnik* officers had the honour of going ahead of them, and capturing a bridgehead. From it, the Division would be able to continue towards Berlin, thus completing that long war. Most certainly, we would not be able to reach the opposite bank safely. The Sergeant scout made it to the other bank secretly, without disclosing himself, and also left quietly, while we had to storm that bank.

That's fine, it was not the first time! We had to 'bank' on our luck! At least several of my company of over one hundred men would make it to the opposite bank, and there was not a single case when *shtrafnik* men failed a mission! Even if they captured only a small bridgehead, they would hold on to it till the last man. The *shtrafnik* soldiers did not have a way back, there was neither ground nor water behind them. Everything was just in front of them. A single soldier would not be able to do anything in this battle, but even if at least one of my three platoons could manage to get a foothold, then I would be able to say that it was again our victory!

The *kombat* spent almost the entire day with us. But I did not get to see the regiment commander, although the bridgehead was supposed to be captured for his regiment. He gave me a radio set and two radio operators, both regular men, but not from the penal battalion. They were supposed to stay with me all the time and transmit signals about our progress on the mission. In my mind I had already made a crew for our boat of heroes. I needed my orderly, two radio operators, and a *shtrafnik* who would assist the radio operators, and row together with my orderly. We needed a good speed in order not to fall back behind the platoons.

Platoon commanders sent their runners and reported readiness. One of them reported that my reserve was securely accommodated in a good dug-out. I was surprised, as I had not given orders about any reserve. I asked what sort of reserve he was talking about. It turned out that he meant the squad of that cheerful ex-Navy officer Redki. He was from the platoon that was now under Piseev's command, after Razhev's departure. They were the squad that was formed mostly of former Navy officers and for which I had special hopes. The Navy had a reputation of stoic soldiers! I ordered the runner to take me to the dug-out and when I entered it and illuminated it with a flashlight, I saw all the former Navy officers in it with their leader. When I asked him about who appointed him commander of reserve and what sort of reserve it was, he started to tell some vague lies such as he had also told to Sergey Piseev. That was the moment his bravado went and his cheerfulness gave place to the usual fear after telling a blatant lie. Any lie is humiliating, while in any war it is unacceptable and unforgivable. Often the price of a lie is lost blood, in many cases the blood of others, but not the liar himself.

When the other men in the dug-out realised what had just happened, one of them, called *moryak* Sapunyak, sailor Sapunyak, as his last name rhymed so well with his military trade, exploded with curses. "You bastard, damn you!" and confidently added, "Comrade Captain! Such bastards were executed on the spot in the Navy. Let us deal with him ourselves". I realised that all the men knew what had just happened. They had just been used as a cover for the cowardice and betrayal of one bastard. The ill-fated dug-out became full of awful curses. I immediately took away Redki's weapon, dismissed him from the office of squad leader, and appointed the still outraged Sapunyak instead of him. After that I took my pistol out of my holster and ordered Redki to walk out of the dug-out. I did not yet know what to do with him, or what sort of report to write. Who would escort him to the battalion HQ? I wanted a court-martial to take care of the case.

Who could have guessed! As soon as he walked out of the dug-out, a German shell exploded right above him and killed that liar and coward on the spot. "God's judgement!" I thought, and I was happy that he had walked out first, in front of me and the other *shtrafnik* sailors. Secondly, I was happy that I did not have to worry about what should be done with him. Probably those thoughts were cruel, but I admit having them. One of the men walking out of the dug-out saw the dead body of Redki and even said, "a dog deserves a dog's death!" and I did not reprimand him. In that case, destiny severely punished a deserter who was trying to flee from the battlefield, through a lie. At that time, we did not yet know what lay ahead of us, minutes later on that dangerous night.

Soon after midnight I calmed down after that incident and from another. My mistake was in not determining the real qualities of a subordinate. Through runners I ordered the boats to be brought to the river. My *shtrafnik* men jumped out of the trenches, and ran to their boats using the darkness of a moonless night. They froze motionless under the bright white light of German illumination flares and took cover from German shrapnel. Some of the boats were already damaged by splinters. The men tried to insulate the holes, that they found by touch, with some pieces of material, even cutting pieces off their overcoats and padded jackets. We had already lost several men killed and wounded, whom I had ordered to that ill-fated dug-out. But the order to prepare boats for launching came long before dawn, just as I expected. We had to 'take to the seas' on those boats.

Again runners brought a message that we were to start the crossing five minutes after the beginning of the artillery barrage, with a green flashing of lights. The artillery barrage was to start at 5.30 am. It was supposed to be short, and was supposed to last the time that we needed to cross the river. After that the artillery fire would be shifted to the depth of the German defences on a signal that we were supposed to transmit over the radio. However, unfortunately things rarely went as they were planned.

I was praying for at least a light fog over the river that would prevent the Germans from spotting our crossing right from the beginning, and prevent them opening fire. The artillery barrage opened up before dawn. The strong roar of our guns cheered everyone, and soon our first boats were in the water. My words that the faster we moved the less chances the Germans had to hit us, were naïve and unconvincing. But I saw that our boats were moving quite quickly. The fog was quite near, but only covered some parts of the river, and was there for only a short time. That night was the third or the fourth after the new moon, and a thin crescent appeared in the sky only after dawn. That was a good coincidence for us.

The German artillery and MG fire intensified. Our AT-rifles and MGs behind us also intensified their fire. We could see tracer and incendiary bullets flying well above us, and this cheered us up, just like the artillery fire. At that time I did not understand why we did not have air support, and only much later, after the war, I realised that all the air force was supporting the main strike of the Front, from the Kuestrin bridgehead.

Black cold water seemed to boil from the explosions, devouring both boats and the men that swam next to them. As it turned out later, some boats were so overloaded or were so heavy, that they merely started to sink under the weight of four men with weapons. Then *shtrafniks* left their weapons in the boats and swam next to them, holding on to the boats and fighting convulsions in their muscles in the ice-cold water. I do not know how many of them survived swimming in the cold river, or how many drowned without even being hit by German bullets. But many of those brave men continued to swim towards the German bank. They swam much slower than we expected, so the current took them away from the planned bridgehead. Some of the men gave up and were floating on the surface, some were floating face down, already dead.

My mind only paid attention to the number of the boat crews that could be seen on the surface of the river, in the fog and weak morning light. The men feverishly rowed with oars, entrenching tools and their hands. The water seemed boiling from explosions and bullets and from their rowing. Some of the men no longer had their *pilotka* caps. Not because they were hot, but because they used them for plugging bullet holes in the boats.

My light boat was moving faster than the others, and even before we reached the shore I ordered the radio operators to transmit a signal to the artillery to shift fire. At the same moment I realised that we were under the well-aimed fire of a *Fritz*, possibly a sniper. My radio operator screamed with pain as his shoulder was hit by a bullet. I myself sensed that an explosive bullet hit the upper part of our aluminium boat and my left wrist was badly scratched by its splinters. Men that were in the boats were firing at the approaching bank. I even noticed that an MG was firing from one of the boats!

Two or three boats, that were approaching the opposite bank, were destroyed before my eyes by direct hits of German shells. They flew into the air together with the soldiers in them. Thank God, the boat with the MG was not hit. The Germans also fired *panzerfaust* at us. I did not see how many boats were destroyed in the middle of the river, I was only looking ahead. Several boats reached the opposite bank and men rushed forward, covering their breasts or stomachs with entrenching tools as if they were small shields, and firing SMGs on the move. We captured the first metres of the enemy's bank. But how few boats made it, how few men I had! Only about twenty men! When I looked back I did not see any more boats or men in the water. That meant that we were the only ones who had made it. What about the others? Could it be that they were all killed? I did not have a single platoon leader on the bank with me. What happened to them all? For two of them it was their baptism of fire, while Sergey Piseev would have been a good support to me as he already had battle experience. One comes across the phrase "the river became red with blood", in books about war. I can imagine that this river must have become red, or at least pink, as about one hundred of my men were killed in it. But in my memory the colour was dense black.

When I jumped out of the boat on the bank, I yelled to the radio operator, "send a message that we are on the beach". He shouted back, "I can't! The radio is damaged!" I grabbed my signal pistol and fired a green flare high into the sky. That was the signal for our troops to understand that we had made it and were fighting on the bridgehead. At that moment I was again sorry that our air force was nowhere to be seen, although the sky was clear and everything could be clearly seen. I could clearly see the opposite bank, which meant that they could see us too. The flare was also a signal for our AT-rifle and MG crews who remained on the opposite bank to shift fire to our flanks and deeper from the bank. I think there were two or three German tanks emerging from there.

Then, on the left bank, events unfolded with a lightning speed. A German shell or *panzerfaust* round flew by me with a hiss. Pilot-Captain Smeshnoi immediately rushed from the left to our right flank, shouting something that I did not hear. I also noticed ex-Navy officer Sapunyak and even noticed his unbuttoned tunic with a striped Navy shirt under it. He ran forward, taking not only ex-Navy officers, but also the other men who had reached the bank. Some of the men ran after pilot Smeshnoi. I also ran after him. Our two small groups ran forward. I don't know if we shouted "Hurrah!" or the worst obscenities from our wide-open mouths. But *shtrafniks* ran on and destroyed the German forward security in the first trench, losing several men. Three or four men fell on the ground just two or three metres from the German trench. Our pilot Smeshnoi must have spotted a German grenadier with a *panzerfaust* from the boat, and was running straight at him. The German was apparently shocked by such an unstoppable rush, missed Smeshnoi, jumped out of his trench and ran for his life. But Smeshnoi got him with a burst from his submachine-gun. I fired a red flare and with my whistle gave the signal to stop. I had to give my men some time to catch their breath and reload their empty weapons. The three German tanks seen in the distance continued to approach us.

I counted thirteen of us in the trench. We continued to fire at the fleeing *Nazis*. It was too little, but we controlled that patch of land! Now our task was to hold it even with our weak forces. I could see counterattacking German infantry behind the tanks. Can we hold? How many are there? All of a sudden one German tank stopped and started to smoke. It turned out that Smeshnoi took the weapon of the German grenadier and knocked out the German tank with the German grenade launcher. Excellent job! His effort in learning to use that weapon was not in vain. Then two more *panzerfäuste* hit the second tank. First its turret was jammed and then it also caught fire. My men had reloaded their weapons and opened intensive fire on the German infantry that rushed at us from behind the tanks. Many Germans were killed, while the rest turned back.

At that moment my men spontaneously, without my command, having mistakenly thought some gesture of mine was a signal, jumped out of the trenches and ran forward. I saw that Smeshnoi was also among them. The Germans were fleeing. Many of them dropped their weapons, but none of them lifted their hands in surrender. I think that they understood that it was useless to surrender to us desperate Russians, and they were right. Suddenly, as my hero pilot ran past the dead grenadier, the German who was pretending, or was just wounded, came to life, and emptied the entire clip of his MP into Smeshnoi's back. He fired, until I finished him off with a long burst from my SMG.

I ran up to my pilot, turned him face upwards and saw that his already motionless, but bright blue eyes, reflected the morning sky, the sky that he loved so much and to which he dedicated his entire life in the armed forces. His chest had been terribly injured. His mouth was open, as if in a loud victory cry. Many bullets had ended the life of that brave man, stopping his heart in a second. For a moment, I put my hand on the eyes of Captain Smeshnoi, sensing the warmth that was departing from his body. But I could not stay by his side, much as I wanted to. I then understood my men's desire in previous battles, to finish off wounded *Nazis*, never leaving a living enemy.

But then I had to make an immediate decision what to do. We captured the second trench. I had only twelve men left, and I was a thirteenth. And that was not counting the radio operators who stayed with the boat on the bank. I again gave the

"Stop!" signal and shouted orders to the men to take up defensive positions. I decided to send a message to the *kombat* by the two radio operators, one of them was not even wounded. Without a radio I did not need them there anyway. I also did not know when they would send a new radio to me. I decided that I could send two or three heavily wounded *shtrafniks* with them. I quickly wrote in my message report that we had captured the second trench, holding our defences with 13 men, and saying, "we need air support". I had not a single platoon leader. I appointed *shtrafnik* Sapunyak my deputy. I reported Air Force Captain Smeshnoi killed in battle, "after displaying outstanding bravery and unmatched heroism". I wrote that he was an Air Force Captain. Smeshnoi had already paid the price for his return of rank, redeeming it with his blood! Unfortunately, I could not remember his first name, either Valentin or Viktor.

After making the decision, I ordered the evacuation of two heavily wounded *shtrafniks* to the boat, in order to send them to the rear for medical treatment. They would not have survived there. Before we managed to carry the wounded to the bank, I leaned down to the radio operator, when suddenly, again suddenly! I did not even hear, but rather sensed a loud bang at my right ear and I immediately fell into a bottomless black hole. Much later, when I regained consciousness, I thought that it was a lie about your life flashing in front of you the moment before you die. It was not like that at all. I think the only thing I thought was, I am killed. That was it. As it turned out later, I was hit by a bullet in my head which was later described in hospital, as a wound certified as a "penetrating bullet wound of the right temple area. The wound was received in battle at the Oder River on April 17, 1945". I think that it was a German sniper who got me.

Apparently, the men who were around me saw that I was still alive. They put a simple bandage over my wound, and lifted me from the water. I guessed that, because I was all wet when I regained consciousness. Then they put me in the same boat and pushed it away from the bank. It is interesting how this was interpreted by the observers from the opposite bank, who told Rita about my 'death'. George Sergeev who was already wounded himself and observed our battle through binoculars, said, "I could see it very clearly. He fell into the water. He was killed". My 'kitchen' soldier Putrya told Rita, "Daughter, this is it. I saw for myself. He fell into the water, and the boat dragged him on".

Indeed, I fell into the water but I was immediately lifted by my men and put into the boat. I do not know when I regained my senses, but the sun was already quite high in the sky and I felt the warmth from its beams. Warm sun was probably the reason for me regaining my senses. I wanted to take a look at my wrist-watch and saw that my hand was covered with blood. I had not had time to bandage it on the bridgehead. The watch was damaged by the bullet that hit the side of our boat. Thus the watch stopped at the moment of our landing. I realised that, judging by the sun standing high, it had already been two hours since we had left the bridgehead. We were floating close to the left bank, down the current, some five kilometres from the spot where we crossed

The wounded radio operator tried to row with one hand instead of an oar. The oars got lost somewhere towards the opposite bank. The second radio operator was dead. One of the two *shtrafniks* had already died. The second one, wounded in his stomach, begged us to give him water and then shoot him, as his life could not be saved, and he did not want to die in awful pain. I could understand him well, but I always remembered that 'there is always hope' and one should not lose heart even in the worst circumstances. I tried to talk him out of his desperation as best I could, even more so that we were almost on the opposite bank.

My mind and sight gradually cleared up. I could see more clearly. It was useless to look at the map, as we were off-map already. I could clearly see the course of the river splitting into two streams. With not yet completely cleared sight I managed to see that we were indeed approaching the right bank of the left course of the Oder. It was an island, maybe a small one, but who controlled it? Was it in our hands or still in German hands? I had a German whistle with a built-in small compass, and I automatically looked at its hand, although it did not help me at all.

Together with the wounded radio operator we managed to bring the boat to the bank. We even managed to pull its prow on to the bank covered with grass from the previous summer, so that it would not be dragged away by the current. I almost fainted with strain. I ordered the radio operator to pull the boat further to the bank if he could. I decided to go, or rather creep, on a reconnaissance and see whether the Oder and destiny had taken us to friendly troops or not. I told the wounded radio operator that if he heard firing that would mean that I had had bad luck. I decided not to surrender in case the island was controlled by Germans. I told him his best choice would be to float on and then he would surely meet friendly troops. I knew that I was giving him a vain hope but that was the best I could do for him. I also ordered him to guard the wounded *shtrafnik*, never give him water and keep his ears closed for his second request, too. The soldier confirmed that he understood my order.

I barely made it out of the boat. With awful difficulty, sometimes at the edge of passing out, I was creeping in this wet island, covered with bushes and thin trees with no leaves. It seemed to me that I crept for a very long time, feeling that my whole body was burning from fever. I felt very sick and threw up several times. God knows how long it took me to creep the hundred metres that seemed so far. Then, before me, I saw a breastwork of a trench on the elevation. A German helmet was lying on it upside down. "Well, this is it. Bad luck", I thought. Nevertheless, I decided to creep forward thinking, "I will not give up".

While I was creeping to the trench, I noticed that artillery shells were flying over the island in both directions. This conceived some hope in my damaged brain. I took out my TT pistol, put one cartridge into the barrel and crept on. I decided to shoot myself if there were Germans in the trench. Then I gave it a thought and decided no, the first bullet would be for the first German that I saw, and then the second one for me, so that they would not take me prisoner. Years of war brought up in me a complete unacceptability of captivity as an alternative to certain death.

So, there were three, two, one and a half metres left to the breastwork. I could already see a German canteen on the edge of the trench, but I could not see the German who would get my bullet. Just one more movement, and all of a sudden a winter hat with our red Soviet star on it emerged over the breastwork! The star was red, not khaki as we got used to. Then, as if in slow motion, under the hat I saw the beautiful face of an Uzbek or Kazakh or Kalmyk soldier with wide cheeks and narrow Asian eyes. Apparently, he got an awful scare at the sight of this face of a Soviet Captain covered with blood with a pistol in his hand creeping from the enemy's side. The next second after he saw me, he ran away along the trench, while I crept up the breastwork with my last bit of strength and fell on the bottom of the trench, again losing consciousness.

I regained my senses after being dragged into a dug-out. There was an officer with the same rank, a Captain, who ordered the nurse to bandage my head. While I was still conscious, I tried to tell him to first find the boat on the bank, with a heavily wounded officer, I called this *shtrafnik* an officer, and a radio operator. "Help them!" They even washed my face and skilfully bandaged me. The Captain calmed me down and said that both wounded had been already bandaged and sent away to our shore in a boat. They promised to evacuate me soon, but they could not do it immediately as the Germans opened fire on that sector of the river. My consciousness came and went all the time. In that strange glittering condition, either in delirium or in reality I thought that they fed *pelmeni* to me! I don't know even today, was it a hallucination or a reality.

Later that afternoon, when the sun had already set over the western bank of the Oder, the fever in my body became almost unbearable and they took me to a boat. I remember that there was a Sergeant-major with a moustache in the boat, and he started rowing very hard. Indeed, that stretch of the Oder was under German fire and one bullet even slightly scratched my leg, but then I did not care about it anymore. I do not remember how they brought me to some dressing station. I had again lost consciousness. I only regained my senses for a short while in the hospital, when they were patching up my wound, and that was it. I finally regained control of my constantly slipping consciousness only when Rita found me in the hospital.

I will tell the story in her own words that were recorded by a journalist.

Rita was walking down the stairs to the canteen and was not seen by the officers inside when she heard the voice of George Sergeev. He, as she knew, was supposed to cross the Oder the next day and to whom she had said farewell the day before. "I saw it clearly. He fell face down in the water. He is gone, gone. But how can I tell her about this?" Only then Rita realised why our mutual friend Misha Goldstein asked her to give her pistol to him, literally forcing her. "Give it to me, I will clean it! Just give it to me!"

Rita did not cry. She was not just a woman who had learnt about the death of her husband, she was a Sergeant. She tried her best to walk straight and calmly as she went out of the canteen. When she got out, she saw the replacements loading on a truck, together with the 'spare' company commander, my 'shift' Nikolai Slautin. He was going to the front line in order to replace me, the dead company commander. Then she ran to the truck and grabbed its side, begging them, "my dear friends, kind friends, please, take me with you, hide me. I have to see him one last time!" The men lifted her into the back of the truck, and hid her under their bodies as the truck rushed to the Oder under a hail of German artillery and mortar fire.

The Oder was burning. The opposite bank, to which, as Rita already knew, I had made it together with twelve men who were all that were left of the company, was burning under constant German fire. This bank of the Oder was also burning. It was covered in shell craters and German shells continued to explode all around.

At the very bank she saw Putrya, the old man that I always felt so sorry for, when he ended up in our battalion for the lost box of soap. Putrya was weeping, "daughter, that was it. I saw for myself, he fell into the water, and the boat dragged him on". But Rita suddenly decided, "if the boat dragged him, why is he crying then? There was at least some hope!" She started to creep under fire from one shell crater to another. She asked all the men that she came across, did they see "a beautiful, tall Captain with a black moustache?" Rita spent two days and two nights in those craters. She could have moved faster, but in almost every crater there was a cry for help. "Sister, little sister, help me!" She would bandage the wounded and then creep on, and ask on, and finally she heard the answer, "tall, beautiful, with black moustache? They took him to the medical battalion. It is unlikely that he will make it, he has a heavy head wound".

Then she stood up, under fire, and ran to a truck on which they were loading the wounded. Again she grabbed the truck by its side. She could not ask for a ride in that truck, the wounded were even standing on the sides of the driver's cabin, and many were still expecting evacuation. To walk would mean to miss me, so she grabbed the side of the truck with her hands of a former ballet school student, with the weak hands of a girl who survived the Siege of Leningrad, and hung on the side of the truck for three kilometres. Hanging on that truck with her hands, she not only brought herself for me from the battlefield, but also our son. He had already lived in her for several months. He was born soon after the Victory and that day when we wrote on the *Reichstag*, Alexander and Margarita Pylcyns.

She looked for me in the medical battalion for a long time, because there was no 'beautiful' officer with black moustache there. If she had looked in the mirror, she would not have recognised herself either. Grey hair changes even twenty-year old people. I was bandaged like a mummy and she recognised me only by my lips. I was unconscious and could not reply to her kiss. Rita spent almost two weeks in the hospital. They all mingled into one long exhausting day without any details or faces remembered. It was for that work, during those two awful weeks, that she received her Order of the Red Star. Rita only remembered one thing. She donated blood by a direct transfusion. It was only then that she lost consciousness. I regained consciousness in the evening of that day. For some reason I was not amazed that she was next to me.

Probably, I regained my senses from her leaning over me and feeling her tender, caring and worried look at me. Of course, I was not too amazed and thought, "Where else could she be?" although I did not yet understand where I was and how far in distance and time I was from the Oder. It became a grave for most of the men from my company. They wanted to survive so much, before the end of the war, and wash off the stain of guilt, getting rid of the *shtrafnik* title, and becoming fully qualified officers again on the eve of the long expected Victory. That river that was covering Berlin almost became a grave for me, too.

Thoughts about the grave did not leave me for a long time. Of course, no one wanted to lie in a strange land after death. Relatives would never be able to come and put flowers on your grave. It was almost the same with drowning in the depths of a strange river. I managed to avoid both those fates. It was destiny, happiness, and again my unbelievable luck. When I found out how my Rita ended up there, I was not too amazed. I admired even more, the faithfulness, the bravery and decisiveness that she exhibited in that hard situation. Several days later I could already stand up, while Rita was working away days and nights in the hospital and had just a few seconds for me.

There, in the hospital, I was amazed by the unique will to live of one wounded soldier. Just like me, he was wounded in his head. His room-mates noticed that the soldier was knocking on the wooden side of his bunk bed with his fingers, for a whole day, but remaining unconscious. One of the wounded, apparently a signals operator, realised that the soldier was using Morse code and wanted to deliver a message, even though he was wounded and unconscious. Someone advised replying to the wounded man, in Morse code, saying that his message was received, and that the wounded man would fall silent. The signals operator tapped on the hand of the wounded man that his message had been received. The unconscious soldier indeed became silent. His heart stopped beating fifteen minutes later. All that time he remained alive with a mortal wound, just wanting to deliver a message, to fulfil his duty. He fulfilled it and only after that he died. One can hardly imagine the will-power that kept him alive for that day!

During the first years after the war when a lot of books were published about the war, I came across a description of that case. I decided that the author must have been in the same hospital with me, or probably someone told him that amazing story. I think that the case was unique.

Several days later I started talking Rita into coming back to the battalion with me. First of all, I did not want her to be treated like a deserter, as she had just run away from the battalion! Secondly, I wanted her to report to the battalion HQ where I had been, thirdly to know what happened on that patch of land that cost us so dear, and fourthly, to ask them to pick me up! I wanted to make it back there before Berlin could be captured! I don't know how she had made it to the battalion or how she ended up in that hospital, but we immediately went to the chief doctor of the hospital and asked for my discharge.

Rita already knew him well. He was Major of Medical Corps Borovikov, as I double-checked on the wound certificate in my file. He had just handed the Order of the Red Star to Rita, so she bravely walked into his office, dragging me with her. Unexpectedly for us, the Major agreed quickly, saying that he could entrust me to such a nurse, and issued my discharge certificate immediately without any red tape. We had only several seconds to pack our things. We went into a sunlit yard to find an elegant four-wheel carriage, with shock absorbers, was standing there, with a calm young horse harnessed into it. We did not waste time, received bread and canned food for two days, from our food supply officer, and departed.

The journey was amazingly pleasant. I don't know if I ever had such a pleasant and carefree ride with such a charming driver! I was amazed how easily Rita could control the horse, although she had never dealt with one before. Rita told me the latest news from the battalion on the way. The main news was that the bridgehead remained under our control. It turned out that after me being wounded the *shtrafnik* repelled two or three Germans counterattacks. In the evening, combat engineers built a pontoon bridge for the infantry and light artillery, and our heroic ten *shtrafniks* were reinforced with that very replacement that gave Rita a lift to the Oder. The rifle units started enlarging the bridgehead that had been captured by us.

When Rita came back from the hospital, at first no one believed that I was alive. Everyone thought that I was killed. Some of my friends secretly told Rita that a death certificate and posthumous recommendation for the Golden Star were ready for me in the battalion's staff. I had a twofold feeling. Of course, it was nice, but as I was still alive, I wanted to receive the same Order but on active service. However, the one who deserved this highest award more than any of us was my *shtrafnik*, Captain Smeshnoi! Even if he were to become the only *shtrafnik* from our 8th Penal Battalion that would receive that award, he would be a great exception! I think that he deserved that high award with his heroic death.

However, I was most happy from the fact that I was alive and to know that my Mom would not receive a death certificate about her last surviving son. She would not want me to get an award posthumously. And there was I riding in a carriage on a bright spring day. Trees in full blossom were on both sides of the road, and it was amazingly beautiful! It was so beautiful around us that sometimes it even seemed that there was no war going on! A few times we met groups of women and men, and even children who had just been liberated from German slavery. They were starved, exhausted people, but with happy smiles and lively looks. Many of them waved their hands to us and shouted words of gratitude.

At some place that I did not know, we crossed by pontoon bridge the wide, alien and tricky expanse of the Oder that was by then quiet. Finally, I asked Rita where we were going, and how we would find our battalion. She said that she knew part of the road as she had received a map with a route of the battalion from Fillip Kiselev, our Chief of Staff. The route of the battalion was written on that map with a thick red line going to a small German town. There we were supposed to ask the military commandant for further instructions if we could not find our battalion.

I don't want to describe all the details of that long journey. We left the hospital on April 28, I think, and caught up with the battalion on May 1, somewhere behind the town of Freienwalde on the northern outskirts of Berlin. I will only describe the most important events of that journey. Almost every house, in almost every window had large white flags of linen as a sign of surrender. Some German children had already appeared in the streets, while the German adults always tried to get them into their homes when our military trucks or tanks appeared on the streets.

Sometimes we met long columns of tired and depressed German prisoners of war under the guard of Soviet soldiers. Civilians looked at those columns with grief in their eyes. For some reason, I did not see a single German *Frau* trying to give food to any German POW, as the Ukrainian and Belorussian women did when the Germans took large columns of our Soviet POWs into Germany. Well, every nation has its own understanding of humanity.

We decided to stay overnight in a small German town that evening and chose a rather decent looking house, as our military personnel were not accommodated there. I cannot say that the Germans were too happy to see us, but apparently we were not the first Soviet soldiers to stay there. German civilians seemed to take this as a responsibility, and took the responsibility as punctually and seriously as all other things in their life.

We stayed in a room that was given to us. It had everything we needed, table, chairs, and two wide beds with thick feather covers. There was a bowl on a small night table with a metallic jug with water for washing. Germans slept under thick feather beds, but we thought that they were too much. We preferred regular blankets, it was not that hot and we were not yet used to feather beds.

We asked the landlady to boil water for tea. An older German woman with a numb face without any expression nodded as a sign of understanding our German that was far from perfection. She only said "*Jawohl*", and left. Later, during my time of service in Germany, I realised that *Jawohl* was one of the main words in conversational German. In the meantime, we unpacked our food supplies, opened a can of American spam and put some sugar on the table. The landlady brought us two cups of hot water, and when she saw the sugar, asked if we wanted to have coffee. From her eyes that greedily looked at the sweet white bits of lumped sugar, we understood that she did not offer coffee out of pure hospitality. Of course, we made a deal and gave her half of the sugar that we had. Apparently, she did not expect us to be so generous and her face suddenly came to life; with a changed voice she said several times, "*Danke, Danke schön*", and even bowed to us. As we learnt later, Germans had not had real sugar for a long time, using *Ersatz* saccharine. In the morning the landlady herself displayed initiative and brought us two cups of hot coffee when we were ready to have breakfast. However, this was also *Ersatz* coffee and tasted pretty much like the coffee that we had in the Far East, barley and acorns, from which our mother baked us black pancakes in the hungry years. But it was not water but a drink that was served out of hospitality.

We thanked the landlady and left, feeding the horse with oats before departure. We found oats in a bag under the seats of the carriage, and Rita told me that it was Valery Semykin and Moses Seltzer who had taken care of that. All day we came across columns of captured *Nazis*. Many of them had surrendered. We passed crowds of refugees liberated from German slavery. Tanks and SP guns, columns of trucks with soldiers were passing us. For some reason none of the soldiers were excited to see a young female Sergeant and a Captain with a bandaged head. No soldiers shouted "Air alarm! Frame!" Apparently, they were in a bad mood. Berlin was still resisting, and they were going there.

We spent the second night in a small town or a village. Those small towns were not too different from each other. If a house had not been destroyed by war, it was almost sinking under the blossom of the surrounding garden. The bulk of the houses were made of stone and almost all of them were covered with red tiles. The burghers lived quite well. But they wanted to have an even better life, so they supported Hitler and his *Drang nach Osten*. Now it was time for them to pay for their *Drang*.

We woke up early. We were impatient to leave, so after a quick breakfast we started our journey and several hours later reached the last town that was marked on the route of our map. The very first old German man told us where to find a commandant. We were so amazed to see that it was an officer from our battalion, my old friend Petr Zagumennikov who was commandant in this town! We were all so happy to see each other. Petr even offered to have a drink to celebrate this meeting, but I had strict orders from the doctor and Rita also forbade me to drink, so I refused. Petr felt sorry about this, but he understood my condition and did not insist on drinking. We spent a couple of hours with Petr and had a second breakfast. Petr explained to us that he was appointed commandant of the town temporarily, and a permanent commandant was to replace him soon. After that he would again show up in the battalion. He took our map and pointed out the villages through which the HQ of our Penal Battalion was supposed to proceed.

We received replacements of food and fodder for our one-horse-power carriage and continued our journey, which was already almost over. We decided not to stop anywhere overnight in order to reach our dear home, our 8th Detached Battalion, as quickly as possible. We spent the night on the road with the monotonous sound of hooves clattering. When we reached yet another *Dorf* in the morning, we saw a sign at the German *Kirche*. The simple sign on a wooden desk made with an axe was on an accurate German road sign pillar and it said, in Russian 07380 – the number of our field post, and then "Baturin's household".

We could not doubt it, we were almost home! It was already May the First! However, there was no festive atmosphere in the streets. For Germans it was a regular Tuesday, full of worries and troubles. They must have known that Berlin had lived its last hours. Battles had raged in the area of the *Reichstag* already. The Germans had a sign of grief on their faces. A good many of them carried black mourning stripes on their sleeves, either for their dead relatives or for Berlin. Probably, they already knew about the suicide of Hitler and Goebbels, although we did not yet.

We were following road signs in the northern outskirts of Berlin. Those were areas of summer cottages. Every garden was green, with trees and bushes in bloom. But there the fragrance of flowers was not strong due to the smells of war. It seemed to me, that one could not only see the traces of recent fighting, but even the wind from Berlin brought both the smoke and smell of gunpowder. There was, too, the sweetish sickly smell of exploded TNT from artillery shells and mines. It even seemed to me that I could smell the stench of decomposing bodies. Those smells of war haunted us for a long time after the war, both waking and in dreams.

We could already hear artillery fire in the distance. It sounded like a nearby thunderstorm. Waves of planes were flying towards Berlin one by one. The days of Berlin were numbered. As we learnt from Petr the commandant, battles there started from April 26. Our road to Berlin was hard and long. Easy victories make a victor arrogant. We, that gained the near Victory with awful losses, highest heroism, strain of all our strength and self-sacrifice, we, the surviving men, only had the highest of pride. Pride of achievement and pride for the fact that our blood was not spilled in vain. From the very first days of the war we had a holy and unshakeable faith that "Our cause is just, the enemy will be destroyed, and victory will be ours".

With this optimistic mood and almost philosophical thoughts we reached the HQ of our dear Penal Battalion. I was so excited that my heart beat too fast and I had a strong unusual headache. The officers who were at the HQ saw us and literally pulled us down to the sinful earth. They hugged us so hard that our bones almost cracked, kissed us, and shook our hands. Fillip Kiselev must have noticed our fatigue. Rita managed to tell him that we were on the road all night, hurrying to get to the battalion. He saw my pale face and the sweat on my forehead and ordered everyone to leave us alone. "You will hear all the news later!" he sharply said and added, "now your orderly will be 'almost' Lieutenant Putrya. He volunteered for this for several days".

From this phrase I understood that Putrya was also rehabilitated, although later I learnt that Baturin reluctantly signed the order for rehabilitation, explaining his stubbornness by the fact that Putrya had not yet spent the entire month in the penal battalion that replaced his term in jail. How exact of him!

That happy 'almost Lieutenant' took us to the underground floor of a well-built house that was allocated for us. The room was ready. He had prepared clean towels and all we needed to wash ourselves after the long journey. As soon as we were ready, Putrya served us lunch and two full cups of milk. It turned out that he had been anxiously waiting for our return for 24 hours.

After lunch I noticed that my headache grew weaker, so I decided to report to Baturin about my return, otherwise it would be a violation of military ceremony. Just like many other officers, Baturin was staying in the basement of a large building, although this basement was well decorated and furnished. Apparently, it had served as a comfortable bomb shelter to one of the local *Nazi* bosses. Many others did the same, as they were scared of a random shell flying in. It was safer in a basement. Later I learnt that accommodation in basements was an order of our *kombat*.

The *kombat*, who received me in a rather reserved and cold manner, listened to my official report on arrival. Without saying a word of appreciation about our action on the bridgehead, he told me to have some rest, and come to his place in the evening together with my wife. I was a bit shocked by such a cold reception and turned to the exit from the room. I was hoping to hear at least a word of praise on the way out of the room, but left without hearing a single word. It was just like the previous summer after my return from the hospital at Warsaw. However, that time he did not know me at all, but here we had had so many contacts both at Narev and after it. I thought that this was just his style of treatment of subordinates, which did not at all fit my concept of political workers or commissars, which was the office that Baturin had just had.

Rita, both Georges, Sergeev and Razhev, and some other officers were waiting for me, among whom was one of the assistants to Kiselev, Nikolai Gumenyuk. He was in charge of decorations, and was waiting for me outside. He walked around me a bit, as if he wanted to say something, but left without saying a word, as it appeared that he could not find a minute for us to talk one on one.

I did not fall asleep for long, but managed to have some rest and I felt better. Rita was already preparing for the evening visit to Baturin. She prepared my parade tunic that had been lying idle in our supply column, and sewed on a white collar-liner. Then she ironed her own tunic, and attached the Order of the Red Star that she had just received in the hospital, and the medal that she received for the battles in Altdamm. It was the First of May Day and Baturin held a reception on this occasion, and he invited us. Rumours spread out fast that unlike the celebration of the New Year, this reception would be in a rather close circle of the *kombat*.

When we arrived, in addition to the *kombat* and his wife, we saw political officer Kazakov, and all the other deputies, the battalion commander, almost all the staff officers, both Georges, the same Sergeev and Razhev, as well as our battalion doctor and company party secretary Chaika. He was also wounded in the waters of the Oder but made it ashore. He refused to go to the hospital and just like George Sergeev was undergoing treatment with our battalion doctor, Stepan Buzun. There were some other officers whom I no longer remember.

As it should have been, the *kombat* gave the first toast. He spoke about May the First Day for a long time and then switched to the recent battles on the Oder. I learnt that only four men remained unwounded from those *shtrafniks* who captured the bridgehead, among them Sapunyak who took over the command after me receiving the wound. I was so happy to hear that! Baturin said that those four men were rehabilitated without "spilling redeeming blood" and were sent back to their units or to officer reserve regiments. Underscoring this long speech that did not really fit a 'festive' table, the *kombat* also spoke about the decorations. He started by saying that Captain Smeshnoi was posthumously recommended for the Golden Star of the Hero of the Soviet Union. He then mentioned that I was recommended for the Order of the Red Banner and promotion to the next rank, with which "one large star will replace all other ones on your shoulder-boards". He expressed himself in a really strange and complicated manner.

Captain Nikolai Gerenuk privately told me the story in much simpler terms. First, the posthumous recommendation for the Golden Star of the Hero was prepared for me. But as soon as Baturin learnt from Rita that I had come back from the hospital, and that I was alive, he immediately ordered the change to the recommendation, "according to the will of the company commander", for Smeshnoi. I thought, maybe our *kombat* received an order that the top military award of the Soviet Union can be given only posthumously in a Penal Battalion? Or maybe Baturin did not want, just as before, someone in the battalion to have an award higher than his own? By that time he already had the Order of the Red Banner. I guess he received it also for crossing the Oder.

An unexpected incident took place at that reception, the same night, after a couple of toasts. The guys were just drinking to my return from the hospital, and telling me how much they missed me. They told me how Rita had looked for me and about how great our love was. At that moment one of our friends stood up and spoke out to the two speaking officers. "You don't even dare to say their names!" According to him, those two guys had already agreed who would be first to try to 'console' Rita. As Rita recalled, I became extremely pale and fainted at that moment, and the guys barely managed to catch me. Indeed, for some time I fainted from an awful headache that suddenly struck me. I had drunk a little, despite the strict prohibitions of the hospital doctors. I did not drink *vodka* or spirit, but I think they poured some French cognac, to celebrate my 'resurrection', that was quite common among the war booty.

The friend who started the scandal was the same George Razhev, who was becoming more and more nervous and ready to start a fight. He was also quite drunk even before Baturin's reception. His sick imagination, heated up by alcohol, painted some perverted picture from one sentence that he misunderstood. Two of the officers were discussing how sad they were about my death and what they could do to console the young pregnant widow. During those last days of the war George managed to make numerous scandals both among line officers and officers on the staff. All those scandals started when George was drunk. The next day he was no longer in the battalion.

However, the *kombat* had made a decision to send him away a bit earlier. His sudden replacement, by Sergey Piseev, was explained in a letter from Razhev's father, a Colonel who had a high-ranking position in the 5th Shock Army. It was assaulting to the south from us, from Kuestrin bridgehead. The 'good dad' must have learnt from his son that our penal battalion was preparing to cross the Oder. He sent a request to the commander of the 8th Detached Penal Battalion not to send his son into the last battles so that he, who had already been wounded and shell-shocked, would not be killed at the very end of the war. Of course, one can understand a father, every parent wants to spare and protect his child. He had such a chance, as we had officers for four companies and only one company went into battle.

The last scandal of Razhev must have overfilled the 'cup of patience' of the generally calm Baturin, and George was sent away from the battalion, to his father, so quickly that he was gone by the next morning. He left without saying "goodbye" to anyone. I think he felt ashamed. Many years later, after the war, when I was looking for my old battle friends from the Penal Battalion, I found George Razhev in Penza, and we maintained correspondence till his death. Our joint life at the front, and all the dangers that we had gone through together, are stronger than bad memories of scandals, like the one that he made at the reception on May 1, 1945, in Berlin. Then his letters stopped coming. Several years later I received an official answer to my query from the local military commissariat in Penza. "Captain (Retired) George Razhev died on May 14, 1993, and is buried in the Alley of Glory of Penza". Apparently, he had 'breakdowns' only in our penal battalion, and he lived the rest of his life decently.

During those days the battalion HQ several times moved to new locations around Berlin. Small units of our battalion were no longer sent into action, although we were still receiving replacements of *shtrafniks*. The war was drawing to an end, but courts-martial continued to function. Maybe, they were in a hurry to fulfil some sort of a plan that they had.

We had a touching farewell from my faithful Putrya, who departed from us with tears of real sadness in his eyes. After that he left for a personnel section of the Front or to an officer reserve regiment. He left the penal battalion as a Lieutenant, and I even gave him my shoulder-boards, removing the extra stars from them(!). He must have been almost immediately discharged to reserve after the Victory, and I am happy that I assisted in saving his life. He would not have survived the crossing of the Oder.

My first orderly was killed in battle on the bridgehead at the Oder. Then Putrya left the battalion after completing his term. By order of the *kombat* all the officers received orderlies from the ranks of the arriving *shtrafnik*. I received artillery Captain Sergey as an orderly. I don't remember his last name exactly but I think he was called Kostryukov. He was a blond Muscovite of medium height with a refined face. He was a person from an educated family. He played the piano very well and was generally very well educated in music and literature. I don't remember what he did wrong, just before the end of the war, or why he ended up in our battalion.

It happened that the new replacements did not get to go into battle, although we had six or seven hours of battle training with them every day. Their destiny was such that, almost immediately after the Victory, they all received amnesty. Sergey gave me his address in Moscow. During my first leave, in late 1946, when Rita and I were travelling to the Far East, and were in Moscow for the first time, we visited him on Kropotkinskaya Street. That was the incomplete foundation of the Palace of Soviets. The Cathedral of Christ the Saviour now stands there. Sergey was not at home. Despite his term in the penal battalion, he continued active service in the Army, somewhere not far from Moscow. It was nice and touching though, to see his relatives, who knew about us from his stories.

Berlin fell on May 2. As we knew later, that was just one week before the Victory. On May 4, Baturin and Kazakov somehow managed to get permission for us all to go to Berlin, to the *Reichstag*. Again, like in Rogachev, Brest and Warsaw we did not take part in the assault on the city, but provided for its assault at the price of many lives. Just as in Warsaw, we entered burning Berlin like tourists.

It took us a long time to get to the *Reichstag* on the streets of Berlin, as they were in many cases blocked by the ruins of collapsed buildings, destroyed tanks and guns. As far as I understood, chief of staff Philip Kiselev was in the same car with Baturin, and somehow managed to find the route in that alien destroyed city. Berlin, the capital of the Third *Reich*, left a gloomy impression on all of us. It was not only because of the destruction of war. Most of the streets were boring and straight, and the entire layout of the city seemed too precise and boring to us.

The array of buildings looked at us, as if with distrust, with windows that were missing their glass. Some of them also had white linen hanging low, like flags on a mourning day. Those were a sign of surrender. Behind windows that had the glass preserved, or if windows were covered with something, we could see life going on. Many doors were missing, together with parts of adjacent walls, and the houses looked like the toothless mouths of old men. The remaining walls looked dirty and grey. Sometimes we occasionly saw people looking out of the windows or appearing in the streets. They too looked worn out and grey. They were mostly women, old men, and curious children, just as in all countries.

In some places we came across surviving men from the *Volkssturm*, and teen-agers from the *Hitlerjugend*, who looked lost and depressed. They were caught by our patrols and taken to the gathering points of POWs. They had been hoping to defend their *Reich* to the edge of destruction. Many of them sacrificed their lives, just for the sake of the crazy ideas of their insane *Fuehrer*, while some tried to hide in basements, change their uniforms for civilian clothes, and hide in the mass of civilians.

I remember that we entered the city from the Spree River and got stuck in front of a destroyed bridge. Metallic frames of the bridge were sticking out of the water, and over them we got across the river, right to the square in front of the *Reichstag*. We approached the building. While still at some distance we could smell the smoke coming from the smouldering *Reichstag*. Smoke was still streaming from some of the windows of that large dark building. It did not look magnificent at all! The red banner, our Soviet banner, was flying high over the skeleton of the former glass dome! That was not a mere flag, it was the Banner of Victory!

The wide staircase of the main entrance and numerous columns were covered with many bullet and splinter hits. A young Lieutenant met our small group at the entrance and Baturin spoke to him about something. He ordered us to wait and entered the building together with the officer. Soon the Lieutenant came back and permitted us to enter. There were very few men in the hall that we entered, while our *kombat* was standing next to a short, but slim, Colonel, unlike our chubby Baturin. The slim Colonel was telling Baturin some story, using vivid gestures.

... As I later found out, that Colonel was commander of the regiment that assaulted the *Reichstag*, and had now been appointed its commandant. A twist of fate made me meet the same Colonel thirty years later. I was chief of the ROTC course at the Kharkov Road College and was leading exercises of students in a unit in Cherkassy, Ukraine. Before the students were sworn in, I was recommended to invite Hero of the Soviet Union Colonel Fedor Matveevich Zinchenko. Both his face and his gestures seemed very familiar to me, and when he introduced himself as commander of the regiment that assaulted the *Reichstag*, I immediately recognised him as the first Soviet commandant of the *Reichstag* ...

Back then in 1945, when we entered the *Reichstag*, its walls, columns and other architectural decorations were largely destroyed and heavily smoke damaged. Every surface was covered with the signatures of Soviet soldiers. It had been two days since the fall of the *Reichstag*, but the walls were completely covered with both short and long messages at unimaginable heights. The signs were written in chalk, and with pieces of brick and burnt coal.

Petr Zagumennikov, who was already back, helped me to pulled some lumps of concrete close to the wall. I climbed on them, while Rita and Petr supported me from both sides so that I would not fall. With a half-burnt Far East – Leningrad – Berlin sign we put up signatures for both of us. Rita's last name then was still Makarievskaya, but she did not have any doubts about the correctness of our autograph on the wall of the *Reichstag*.

We stuffed our pockets with debris of plaster, pieces of stones and bricks as souvenirs, both for ourselves and for the others who did not make it to the *Reichstag*, and also for our descendants. It was a pity that I did not preserve them, or the spoon twisted by the bullet, and not even the bullet that they cut out of my buttocks after the war, one year after I received the wound at Brest.

For some reason, in those days we did not want to keep the things and souvenirs from the war with its horrible events. We remembered the war from our wounds, both physical and psychological, the wounds of our souls. It seemed to us that this memory would be more than enough for the rest of our lives.

We were expecting the surrender of Germany every day, and I recalled that back in 1944, I wrote a poem which had a line saying, " the salute of Victory will come like thunder in early May!" But the spring was already in full swing, May already started, and Victory was not there. Our deputy chief of staff, Valery Semykin, laid lines with earphones to Baturin, his deputies, Kiselev, Rita and me, and some other officers. Radio operators were supposed to turn them on as soon as they received news about the Victory.

The moment came during the night of May 8! Some time after midnight a radio operator rushed into our room and shouted, "Victory, they surrendered! Hurrah!" The Victory salute started before we could put on our clothes. Everyone was firing pistols, submachine-guns and machine-guns. I think I even heard loud bangs from an AT-rifle. The only weapons that did not fire were mortars. Hundreds of flares of all colours, calibres and smoke shot into the sky. Tracer bullets filled the sky all over the horizon. There was no more need to spare ammo!

People were hugging, kissing each other, many cried, without being shy about their tears of joy.

We even heard artillery fire from the nearest village, where an artillery unit was stationed. I guess they were firing blanks, otherwise where would the shells fly? I remember that I wondered where would all those bullets fall? We were firing them into the sky and they would fall on the ground, although German ground, but densely populated by people. How would they avoid hitting the ones who fired them, and also peaceful German civilians? Of course, I did not want anyone to be killed by those fireworks on that sleepless night of peace.

At dawn, having spent all our ammo, we started to gather at the HQ. Baturin and Kazakov walked out to the officers and the *kombat* announced that at noon, Moscow time, a Victory lunch would be served to the entire battalion. He ordered to arrange a separate table for the *shtrafnik* men.

Everyone made speeches. Some were short, some were long, but all the speeches expressed both the joy of Victory and the pain of loss, as well as hope for a peaceful future and happy life. Every speech ended with a toast and everyone drank a full cup after it. Apparently, that was the reason why we did not have tea-cups on the table, but rather 'hotshots', just as in peacetime. Where did they find so many of them? Nevertheless, some officers got really drunk. Apparently, Baturin also had a good time. All of a sudden he called to me and privately told me what I had suspected for a long time.

It turned out that General Batov had indeed ordered that my company would attack across a minefield. Although I was quite sure about this in my assumptions, I was tortured by the thought. Had the General made that decision on the proposal of Baturin? The news shocked me. I was again taken by an awful headache and I fainted. Again I thought that this came from several drinks that I had, although Rita strictly observed that no one would pour *vodka* into my glass. She poured out only some weak wine, which was given to her especially for me, by our doctor Stepan Buzun. It seemed that many men were not getting drunk at all. Their speeches were sensible and full of hope.

We had dreamt about the peaceful life after the war, quite often even before the Victory. We painted the most optimistic pictures about the future. I think that the main thing we all were dreaming about was going back home, those who still had homes left after the war. Even these days, so many years after that bright and sunny Victory Day, we look back at our past after the war, and the present day. We had both children and grandchildren, nursed great-grandchildren and worked hard after the war. It is so horrible to realise that our great Motherland was destroyed and broken into pieces, in 1991, without a *Nazi* invasion! Motherland, Independence and Honour, for which so many lives were sacrificed in the Second World War!

Thus, that awful, long and most terrible war was over. What would be next? What was our destiny? Not all were supposed to go home, we still needed an army. Some of the officers, almost all who remained in the battalion were officers, had to continue their honourable military service. Staffs of all ranks and levels had already received orders and numbers for the officers. Some would be dismissed, some would remain service. Some of them still had to fight and win Japan!

Later I learnt that our *kombat*, Colonel Baturin, gave a rather positive evaluation of my battle qualities, in a recommendation for further service, writing, however, that I "did not have a good connection to the mass of Red Army men". Apparently, he meant that I was spending some of my time with my wife! Although it was I who got the warm nickname 'dad' from the *shtrafnik* men, he came to such a conclusion. Among other things, there were the following words in his character reference.

"He is a brave and determined officer. He reads the battlefield well, takes hardships well, and is physically fit. He can organise co-ordination of a small unit with attached units, is morally and psychologically stable and works hard to improve his theoretical knowledge. Recommendable to keep in the army as a commander of a rifle battalion".

So my future was already decided, although Baturin did not bother to hear my own opinion. I was not mad with him, as his recommendation to leave me in the armed forces suited me well. Even when I, a young Red Army man, was sent into the academy, I told myself, "Right! I will serve like a 'copper pot', i.e. 'as long as I last!' So I served in the army for forty years, from 1941 to 1981, faithfully and honestly.

CHAPTER 11

Victory!

The first days of peace, despite everyone's happiness, were clouded for me by that admission of Baturin that he had deliberately sent my company into a minefield. I felt so devastated and sad for the men who were killed there. They were now lying together in foreign soil, under a foreign grey sky, just as they fought against the enemy, leaving only an eternal memory and limitless sorrow, for us, their battle friends and their relatives. Yes, we all knew that orders were given, and had to be followed without discussion, especially in wartime. But we also understood that exactly because of this, any order should be logical, reasonable and above all, humane, even in war.

The German population gradually got used to the new reality. They got used to the fact that their "thousand years *Reich*" collapsed, and would never return. We gradually started noticing their habits and customs, some of which were completely incompatible with our own understanding of culture and morals. For example, though accustomed to all the inconveniences of life at the front, we still considered it out of order to piss in front of everyone, either next to a tree or just in the open. Strangely enough, we saw both German men and women doing just that.

In another case, the owner of the apartment where we stayed knew about the pregnancy of my wife. One night he knocked on the door of our room and after we said "*Ja, bitte,*" walked into the room with his two teenage daughters. He said that "*Frau* Major" was tired and needed to sleep, while I should have spent a night with one of his daughters. Probably, this was an attempt to provoke us, but we were so outraged by this incident that we moved out first thing the next morning.

In general, the Germans amazed us with their lack of morals and their shamelessness. On one warm sunny day our friends, who had already explored the area around Leipzig, invited us to go to a beach in order to swim and sunbathe. When we came there, we realised that the beach and the lake were beautiful and decided to stay. There were a good many people on the beach, especially many young Germans. We saw small tents here and there. I guess they were for keeping out of the sun, or changing clothes after swimming. But we noticed that there were feet sticking out of many of the tents. From their position and rhythmic movements we knew exactly what the German couples were doing, almost openly in public. We felt disgusted and we left the beach immediately. That was about one year after the Victory.

Some of our officers in the suburbs of Berlin, in May 1945, did not show their best side either. For example, one time when we were walking to our new apartment, whose new owner was a cameraman from the famous German Defa studios, we heard loud barking in the hall. We knew that there were no dogs in the house and were amazed. When we walked into the house, we saw our Nick Slautin, by then a Major, standing in front of the entire German family and servants, very drunk and barking. I shook him up, put him on his feet and before I managed to ask what sort of a show it was, he himself started explaining that he was demonstrating to the Germans what a 'dog' their Goebbels was.

Speaking of the reserved and scared attitude of the German population towards us, I cannot help mentioning a movie, which was the best example of Goebbels's propaganda. Our political officer Kazakov got the copy of the movie from somewhere. It was a disgusting movie, made according to the rules of the *Nazi* propaganda ministry. The idea was that the more disgusting the lie, the more people would believe it. It has been a long time since then, but both my conscience and morals do not allow me to tell all the details of what we saw in that movie, which was in colour.

Firstly, all the Soviet soldiers in that movie had huge red stars on their hats and had horns on their foreheads. They showed in the movie how they butchered and killed German civilians with bayonets, and smashed their heads on the corners of buildings. Everything was shown in a very realistic manner in the movie. There were many other far more horrendous things in the movie. That twenty-minute movie was full of such horrors that it became clear why the German population fled beyond the Oder in such panic.

Soon after the Victory, when a group of Russian officers was celebrating something, one of them asked the landlady for a small plate, calling it, in his 'broken' German, a children's plate. The landlady screamed and threw herself towards her baby. She thought that the officer asked for her baby on the plate. Unfortunately, there was nothing funny in that episode. The woman must have seen that awful movie, or someone had told her about it. It took us a lot of politeness and tolerance, in order to destroy the effect of such disgusting *Nazi* propaganda on the minds of Germans.

Referring back to the night of May 1, when I fainted at Baturin's party, I then had a fever that tortured me for three days. By the day of our trip to the *Reichstag* it had faded. But on May 9 I had a fever again, although I did not faint, but I was delirious for almost a day. Two or three days later all came back to normal. Such attacks of fever lasted two or three days, although I did not drink a single drop of alcohol. Such attacks started repeating themselves every seven to nine days. Rita recalled that when she was searching for me, even the doctors told her, "a head wound, he has fever, and this is most likely sepsis. You should rather look for him in a morgue … " Our doctor could not understand what was happening to me either.

I tried not to provoke those attacks and I thought that their intensity could not depend on alcohol. Even when we, the Oder's men, received our decorations for crossing the Oder, I did not drink a single shot at the dinner dedicated to that event. All my platoon leaders were awarded with Orders of Alexander Nevski or Bogdan Khmelnicky[1], while I and Nikolai Slautin who replaced me, received

---

1 These "officer" orders that were founded during the war were named after outstanding Russian and Ukrainian military leaders. Alexander Nevski, a saint and patron of the Russian army, defeated Swedish crusaders on the Neva river in 1240 and Teutonic knights on the ice of Peipus lake in 1242. Bogdan Khmelnicky lead the Ukrainian army in its war for independence from Poland and defeated the Polish armies several times.

orders of the Battle Red Banner[2]. Everyone wanted their orders to shine, so they covered the black oxidized parts of their orders with mercury from an ordinary thermometer that they broke for the occasion. But the Order of the Red Banner only had two such oxidized parts, a small plough and hammer against the white enamel background, all the other parts were gilded. Some men who received other decorations, decided to make their orders more beautiful, too. But the mercury when it made contact with the gilded layer immediately turned the thin layer of gold into an amalgam of silverfish colour, so my order became silver-covered, and not gilded.

I covered those silver parts of the order with bronze paint, for the order to look as it should. It was only when I studied in Leningrad military academy, that someone advised me to write to the Supreme Soviet of the USSR with a request to replace the worn out order for a new one. To be honest, I was not hoping to get any replacement, but one week later I received a government letter signed by the Chairman of the Supreme Soviet of the USSR, Nikolai Mikhailovich Shvernik. The letter recommended me to turn in my order to the Mint of Leningrad, while the director of the Mint was ordered to repair my order "spending precious metals from the stock of the Supreme Soviet". I turned in my order and received it back five days later. The order looked brand new, even with the restored gilding and the black plough and hammer. I even doubted whether this was my order, but when I looked at the number on the back of the order, I saw a barely noticeable scratch that was on the original one. It was my 'dear' order from the Oder. Since that time it has been shining with its gilding on my uniform.

Our battalion doctor Buzun reported to the *kombat* that I had to be urgently hospitalised with an unknown disease. They took me to the town of Neu-Ruppin, to a hospital there. After several days and yet another attack of fever, they discharged me with a diagnosis of post-coma inflammation, which meant, as they explained to me, inflammation of the brain cover as the result of concussion after the wound. As life demonstrated, this was still not the main reason of the strange attacks! June came. Exhausting attacks of the unknown disease wore down my noticeably weakened body. The battalion started releasing *shtrafniks* who were given amnesty on the occasion of the Great Victory, even those who had not taken part in battles.

I reported to the *kombat* that I wanted to take my wife either to Leningrad, her previous place of living before the war, or to Rembertuv at Warsaw, where her former hospital was located, and her mother, senior lieutenant of medical corps, was still serving. Passenger trains were already running and there was an express Moscow – Berlin – Moscow that ran precisely on schedule. The *kombat* approved my suggestion, probably because it would mean one burden less for him coping with my strange disease. They issued all the necessary papers quickly and the next day the *kombat* gave his Willys Jeep to chief of staff Kiselev in order to take us to the Silesian station of Berlin. Valery Semykin and Vasily Tsigichko volunteered to see us off to the station, but the *kombat* did not allow more people in his jeep.

---

2   This is often the name of the Order of the Red Banner that was used to stress its difference from the Order of the Labour Red Banner (established in 1928) for exceptional achievements in industry, science, state administration or social life.

We were again driving through Berlin. Not much had changed in the city since May 1945, but most of the streets had been cleared of debris. There were no white flags in windows and there were more pedestrians on the streets. Quite often we could see our field kitchens serving food to elderly people and children. "Well", I thought, "the Red Army does not really 'fry' German children, but feeds them. They are starving, and they are shouting and pushing each other at our field kitchens".

Philip found his way in this huge city amazingly easily, and decided to drive past the Brandenburg Gate and the famous *Unter Den Linden,* but soon we reached the station and went to the commandant. It turned out that all the tickets were sold, and only booked tickets remained. Those tickets were booked by staff of Marshal Zhukov, and if they were not needed, they would be sold one hour before the departure of the train. There were several junior officers standing in front of the ticket office. The announcement on the window of the ticket office stated that generals and holders of the Golden Star of Hero of the Soviet Union were served ahead of the line[3], while senior officers were served after them. There were no Heroes or generals in sight, so we were the first in the line! If there were at least two places we would be on the train! However, several minutes before the ticket office opened, a Sergeant-major of artillery arrived with the Golden Star over two rows of order bars on his breast. My heart sank into my stomach, what if we could not get tickets? But everything worked well. The Sergeant-major bought his ticket first, then we and two or three other officers. We were so happy! The train was already standing at the platform, and boarding was almost over. The guys quickly took us to the train and we said goodbye to them, maybe forever. So we started our journey.

The train quickly gained speed, while we were standing in the corridor. At an open window we could not get enough of the air that seemed to be full of the scents of our Motherland. We were near to meeting our own country. The Sergeant-major with the Golden Star was standing at the next window. All of a sudden I noticed that when everyone was in their compartments and no one was watching, the Sergeant-major undid the Golden Star and the upper row of bars from his tunic, and threw them out of the window! When he saw our amazement and bewilderment, he walked up to us and told us his story, straight. "Even you, Major, probably would not get tickets to this train, and so many officers would also remain without tickets. To get a ticket for myself, just a Sergeant-major, would be completely impossible, meanwhile my wife is about to give birth in Moscow. I am an artillery blacksmith, so I made a fake Golden Star and a bar for the orders one of which was designated the Order of Lenin[4]. It is good that no one asked for my papers for those decorations at the ticket office. So, here I am, in a direct train home. I don't care now, if they check my papers they are in order. I can deal with my conscience myself on this cheating". I could understand his excitement and decision, even more so that I was myself taking my wife to give birth.

3   Heroes of the Soviet Union and persons awarded with Order of Glory of all three classes still enjoy wide privileges in Russia, including service without queuing in all shops and offices.

4   Order of Lenin (the top military order of the Soviet Union) was awarded simultaneously with the first Golden Star (Star of Hero of the Soviet Union).

Massive transportation had started, of troops by train to the Far East for completion of the War against Japan, as well as demobilisation to Moscow and other cities. Many remember those events from documentaries and movies, for example *Belorussian Station*[5], while we, who were firsthand witnesses to all this, saw a lot of free-riders, even on the roof our Berlin – Moscow train. Those free-riders were unwilling to pay the ticket fare and wait for the next train, as they were in a hurry to get back home after so many years or war. One should mention that the railway network in Germany was well developed. In most cases railway crossings were replaced by bridges, so that roads carried vehicles over the railways. Those bridges were dangerous for those who were travelling on the roof. A tragic case happened on our train, too. A soldier was travelling on the roof our wagon, wanting to get back home faster, but apparently did not pay attention to the approaching bridge. He was either standing or walking on the roof. His head was smashed against the bridge and his body was thrown from the roof the train. The soldier was killed. Apparently, the train conductor noticed this as the train stopped. But, we travelled on, with traces of blood on the sides of our train. It was an extremely hard feeling to realise that the soldier survived the war but did not make it home alive, and the feeling depressed us for a long time.

Soon we crossed the Oder and then the border of Germany. What a contrast between the populations of defeated Germany and liberated Poland! At any station where our train stopped for at least several minutes, the train carriages were literally surrounded by swarms of traders of all sorts. They were selling anything from food and drinks, to watches, lighters, footwear and all sorts of German military uniforms. From the choir of voices one could hear "*mleko zimne, kawa goronza*" i.e. cold milk, hot coffee "*zapalki, bibulki*" and lighters, and paper for rolled cigarettes. One could hear "*bimber*" and "*Monopolka*" more seldom. The Poles offered everything for trade and sale. It seemed that the entire population of those stations, villages and towns turned into traders. It is hard to say which group was more numerous, children, teenagers, men or women. It seemed that everyone was captured by the hunt for fortune and profit. They used all sorts of currency in that area, Polish *zloty*, German marks or *Reichsmarks*, and Soviet *roubles*. That continued all the way to Warsaw.

We learnt in Warsaw that the train would stop in Rembertuv for only one or two minutes. We did not need more time to get off, as back then we did not have many belongings. Rita had only a few new dresses that fitted her during her pregnancy. We crossed the Vistula, which looked majestic and calm, over a restored bridge, and entered Praga, a suburb of Warsaw on the left bank of the Vistula. After several minutes we reached Rembertuv, the final destination of our journey.

It was a sunny day in mid-June. We asked the station's commandant about the location of the hospital, and he even ordered his military patrol to take us, so we did not have to look for it at all. Before we even approached the large building of the hospital, we were spotted, and a crowd of Rita's girlfriends ran to meet us. I immediately recognised Lusya Pegova and Zoya Farvazova who witnessed our front line wedding. The surgeon Mira Gurevich was there and some other girls, but Ekaterina Nikolaevna was nowhere to be seen. That happy group of girls volun-

---

5   Trains with returning soldiers came to the Belorussian Station in Moscow.

teered to see us off to *meshkanne*, as they called accommodation in Polish. It was a very exciting meeting; everyone had tears in their eyes.

Apparently, Rita's mother knew about our arrival from Rita's letters, and there was a nicely furnished room ready for us in the house where Ekaterina Nikolaevna stayed. Rita's brother Stas was no longer there. He had turned 18 in May, and was drafted into the Army by a field army recruiting office. Somewhere in Germany he changed from horse driver to truck driver, as he learnt to drive a car during his free time from the hospital. During the last days of the war, somewhere at the Front, near the Elbe, several days before the meeting of the Western Allies on that river, he was already a driver of a *Katyusha* rocket launcher truck. He drove his rocket launcher to the firing positions to launch a salvo. As he told us later, he was really scared, but that very salvo that they fired gave him a right to be considered a participant of combat in WWII!

At the family council we decided that Rita would stay in the hospital as long as her mother served there. When the time came, she would also give birth there, under the supervision of familiar doctors and the grandmother-to-be herself. I was again attacked by fever on the third day of our stay in Poland and I was put into the same hospital. But no doctor could find out the nature of the disease. Again, after two or three days of delirium my temperature came back to normal. My body was exhausted and every subsequent attack was harder to take.

There was another hospital, not a surgical one, but a therapeutic one, in a town not far from Rembertuv. I think the name of the town was Vesela Gura. They invited a consultant from that hospital who was called Pilipenko. He was an elderly lieutenant colonel with grey hair that looked almost white, and a large grey moustache. He examined me thoroughly and asked for all the necessary blood samples, which he took with him. After a couple of days the doctor came back with the conclusion that "the patient is suffering from frequent attacks of tropical malaria". The news was quite amazing. Where on earth could I have caught the disease, if the most southern place I had ever been to was Ufa? The version about sepsis was altogether gone. Thank God, they then knew the name of my disease and started treating me properly.

I had to go to the therapeutic hospital where they started intensive treatment with some injections from the mysterious malaria, and against the strong anaemia that developed as its result. They brought military personnel with all sorts of diseases into that hospital. I can very well remember how they once brought a group of officers and men with methanol poisoning. The consequences of that were tragic. Several men went completely blind, while several died. That was about one or two months after the end of the war. It must have been extremely bitter for the surviving blind, and the relatives of the ones who died, because they had not refused the temptation to drink something strong.

When my condition allowed for it, between attacks of that exotic and barely curable disease, I visited Rita who was preparing to become a mother. My condition started to get better little by little, the attacks became lighter and even rarer. I got to know the workers of the hospital quite well, while Rita was again formally working in the hospital. She received all her rations from there, which was quite important in those days.

A Polish military school was stationed next to our hospital. Our concerts took place there, too. Apparently, following the tradition of *Woisko Polsko*, they were determinedly studying ballroom dances and often arranged dancing nights. Rita begged me to go there sometimes. Of course, I was caring for her and resisted, but to my amazement her mother was always on her side in the matter, and I had to agree. At one of those dancing nights a rather old Polish officer invited her for a very special *mazurka* dance. He knelt on one knee in front of her, with his sabre in front of him, while his female partner had to dance by stepping or jumping over the blade of the sabre. You had to see the joy on Rita's face when she completed the dance with great elegance. Her dance partner bowed to her at the end of the dance, kissed her hand and told her that it was a long time since he had danced with such a skilful partner. Rita was extremely happy and proud, she blushed, but when she came back home she realised that the birth was starting, although it was too early according to our calculations.

The same night, Rita gave birth to our first son, in hospital at Rembertuv. We had to walk to the hospital through the whole town. Her mother, Ekaterina Nikolaevna, was the doctor in charge of the birth, the assisting doctor was Mira Gurevich. The baby weighed a bit over one kilogram. Of course the early birth was not the consequence of the *mazurka* but rather all the things that Rita and the 'small man' inside her had had to experience during the war, especially on the battlefield. A war is not the best midwife.

At first we wanted to call our son Arkadi to commemorate my first and best-loved front line *kombat* Osipov. However, the next day Rita told me, with tears in her eyes, that she saw her father in her dreams at night. He had died of hunger in besieged Leningrad. She wanted to call our firstborn son Sergey, to honour and remember her father. Well, I had no reasons to object. Our son gradually gained normal weight and height. At the same time, soon after the birth of our son, they had to perform surgery on me and extract the German bullet that had remained in my body for over a year, after I was wounded at Brest. They had to do it, as the bullet reached the most uncomfortable spot, my buttock, so I could not sit or lie down. They cut out the bullet relatively easily, under local anaesthesia, but my body was weakened by persistent malaria and reacted in a strange way. When I walked out of the hospital into the yard, I almost fainted. My forehead and face were covered with sticky cold sweat, and I could barely stand upright. It was good that there was a bench next to the exit and I sat down on it. Hospital workers who were passing by gave me liquid ammonia to smell and some pills, so soon I was back to normal.

Gradually the malaria left me, the attacks became less frequent and less exhausting, fever no longer took me into delirium, and I could and had to return to the battalion. Then I was facing a task. I had to register our son and legalise our marriage. I went to Warsaw to the commandant's office, hoping to process all the papers quickly, but they explained to me that the Consular Section of the Soviet Embassy was already present in Warsaw and I had to register all civil matters there.

I found the office and found out that the presence of both marrying persons was necessary for registering a marriage, while for registration of a baby it was enough to bring a birth certificate. Several days later we went to the Consular Section in our best uniforms, with shining decorations on the car of the chief of the hospital. The marriage registration procedure was simple and fast. There were no wedding rings, nor Mendelssohn's "Wedding March!" We simply received marks on our papers, about marriage, and were given a certificate of marriage and of the birth of our son. In that birth certificate they wrote our son's place of birth as "Warsaw, Poland".

It was already mid-September 1945. I knew that due to the end of the war our Penal Battalion would cease to exist and I was in a hurry to go to Berlin. I did not find the battalion there as it had already been disbanded. I went to Potsdam, to the HQ of GSOTG, the Group of Soviet Occupation Troops in Germany. I found the personnel section there, where Colonel Kirov explained the situation to me, and read out the recommendation that my former *kombat* wrote about me, "Major Pylcyn is a promising officer. It is advisable to leave him in the Armed Forces". That Major was then almost 22 years old.

Kirov dug up some papers, shrugged his shoulders and told me that for some reason I was not recommended for a decoration on the occasion of the end of the war. I observed that I had just received an order for crossing the Oder and for participation in the Battle of Berlin. But he replied that there was an order to recommend only officers who had spent over twelve months in the battalion, or on the occasion of Victory, or on the disbandment of the battalion. I already had four orders and a Medal for Bravery and I was not too sorry. I just thought that the saying "out of sight, out of mind" is indeed true. Baturin had in that way managed his revenge on me for my stubbornness.

There, in the staff office, I met Vasily Nazykov. He had served as Sergeant-major in charge of personal files in our *shtrafbat* and had been promoted to a lieutenant and served in the staff of the Group. He confirmed my assumptions, telling me that when Major Matvienko, my former company commander, gave recommendations for a decoration for me, Baturin put the recommendation aside, saying that I had just received a very high decoration. When we former *shtrafbat* officers gathered to celebrate the Victory, 45 years later, General Kiselev, our Philip that used to be chief of staff in the battalion, told a story of our political officer Kazakov. When Kazakov received his Order of the Patriotic War on the recommendation of the *kombat*, he went to the Political Department of the Front and pestered them for another Order of the Great Patriotic War, which outraged everyone in the battalion. He did not care too much about it. He left the battalion the next morning to go to his new place of service, without saying "goodbye" to any of the officers.

In the meantime, Colonel Kirov told me in Potsdam, "there is no point in me promoting you a rifle battalion commander, as it is not unlikely that this battalion might be disbanded the next day. You are already too late to go to the Far East to fight the Japanese. I guess you have had enough of war, here in Europe". The Colonel proposed me for the office of deputy battalion commander in a detached security battalion attached to the commandant's office in Leipzig, one of the largest cities in the Soviet Zone of Occupation of Germany. As I learnt later, before the German government was formed with all its functions, the entire administration of Germany was in the hands of the Soviet Military Administration of Germany (SMAG) at the staff of GSOTG, and was subject to the department responsible for Federal Land in Saxony.

Some time later, I learnt that most of my battle friends received offices as military commandants of towns and villages, railway stations and station villages. Their tasks were to carry out political, administrative and economic leadership of the civilian population. Namely, they had to act as local authorities. I did not have any objections to being appointed into that battalion, even more so that it was a Detached Battalion, just like a Penal Battalion. It meant that we enjoyed the rights of a regiment, while I as a deputy battalion commander had the rights of a line battalion, which fitted my recommendation. I went to Leipzig the next day and spent several years in that office.

The Detached Security Battalion was responsible for guarding former military and industrial plants, and the power supply stations of Leipzig. They also had to guard the commandant's office, as well as patrolling the streets and the railway station of the city. Jointly with regular army units they had to take part in search operations for individual *Waffen-SS*, SD[6] and *Wehrmacht* soldiers who were still wandering in the forests. I should mention one typical case when captured Germans pointed out a secret warehouse of weapons. It took twenty Studebaker trucks to take away weapons from that storage. After about one year of service in the security battalion, I was promoted to senior officer on line and operative matters of the city's commandant's office.

I was under the direct command of the military commandant of the city, Colonel Borisov. I don't know if the rumours were true, but we were told that he was a former Army commissar 1st rank and was demoted to a junior officer after the disaster at Kerch. But later he was again to become a Colonel. He was a very attentive, extremely just and good-hearted officer, who enjoyed the respect of all his subordinates. In the summer of 1947 he was urgently summoned to Moscow, where he was again put on trial for something and sent to a camp in Siberia for a long term. It may have been a continuation of the Kerch case. The mechanism of terror and repressions continued to function. Six months later, in early 1948 when I was serving in the Moscow Military District, I found Borisov's family and his wife who remembered me from Leipzig. They told me that he was stripped of all his ranks and that he served as a clerk for the camp administration. I don't know about the rest of the life of that former Army commissar, former colonel, and military commandant of one of the largest cities of defeated Germany.

I was given new accommodation, closer to the commandant's staff, in a rich mansion on Montbestrasse 24, that had belonged to some rich *Nazi* businessman who had fled to the west. I also had a car, an Opel Super 6 with a driver. One of my new responsibilities was receiving and escorting famous guests in Leipzig. It allowed me to get to know such famous persons of that time as Marshal of Armor Pavel Alekseevich Rotmistrov, Marshal of the Soviet Union Semen Mikhailovich Budenny, and "Marshal of Victory" George Konstantinovich Zhukov.

I saw Zhukov for the first time when he came to Leipzig for a deer hunt. I was still deputy battalion commander in the security battalion. I was ordered to guard the part of the forest where Zhukov's car and the cars of his escorting officers would be parked. I saw the Marshal at about 10–15 metres distance. He was not a giant, as I had imagined, but a rather short man, of just medium height, strong, tough and quite fast at the same time. He was dressed not in a Marshal's uniform, but in

---

6 *Sicherheitsdienst,* the SS Security Service.

leather jacket and trousers, and army long boots, if memory serves me well. On his head he had some sort of a leather cap or non-regulation visor hat.

We did not see the hunt itself, but it was somewhere close to us. We heard several shots. Then all the hunters gathered on the same spot, where the cars were parked, and brought two dead deer. One of the hunters, my *kombat* Major Milstein, came and reported to the unhappy Marshal. The latter blushed, looked at the Major and clearly and loudly, so that we too heard him, uttered a strong Russian curse and said, as I remember well, "I came here for a hunt, not for meat!" The *kombat* told me later that Zhukov's shot was unsuccessful, as he fired at the running deer and hit a tree, behind which the deer ran at the moment of the shot. Other officers who were merely assisting in the hunt killed two deer. Then my *kombat*, Leonid Milstein, was commissioned to offer one of the deer as a gift to the Marshal. It was clear that he failed his task!

Commander of the GSOTG Marshal Zhukov was soon replaced by Marshal of the Soviet Union Vasily Sokolovski. He had just been promoted to Marshal. Previously he was Zhukov's Chief of Staff. The sudden discharge of Marshal Zhukov, and the appointment of Sokolovski gave birth to a lot of rumours. Portraits were urgently removed of the then holder of three Golden Stars of the Soviet Union, Marshal of the Soviet Union G. K. Zhukov. But it was like a storm out of a clear blue sky! We were told something unclear and vague about his so-called 'wrong' attitude towards the Western Allies. However, the meeting that I soon had with Marshal Sokolovski convinced me that he was a good replacement for Zhukov himself. I also met the former chief prosecutor of the USSR Andrei Vyshinski. He was going to the final part of the Nuremberg trial of the main *Nazi* military criminals. I also got to meet the son of Joseph Stalin himself, General Vasily Stalin. I had heard much about him from one ex-pilot *shtrafnik* who had served in the air force division under the then Colonel Vasily Stalin.

Less than a month after the discharge of Colonel Borisov, I was transferred to the same office of a second-rank commandant in a small town called Debeln, on the order of Leipzig District. Most of the military commandants of the city's districts were also replaced. I don't know what sort of influence it had on the fate of Borisov, but I think that the main reason for those changes was the new military commandant of the District, Colonel Litvin. There were immediate tensions between us. Once I was invited to a meeting of the district commandants, and the *kombat* that I replaced during his leave. I do not remember why, but I had no time to change my uniform for my trousers with long boots, and I arrived in just straight uniform trousers. I was also stupid enough to sit down in the first row. Colonel Litvin held that meeting in the club, on the stage, which had a large table covered with red woollen material. A huge portrait of Stalin was in the background. Litvin noticed that I arrived in the wrong uniform and started berating me, without caring for his language. He told me that I was not an officer as I did not wear long boots, that only idiots wore straight trousers, and so on. I got interested to see how he would complete his reprimand if he looked at Stalin's portrait, in which the latter was depicted in tunic and straight trousers over his boots, although in most cases we were accustomed to portraits of Stalin long boots. Then I started to gaze not at my superior, but at the portrait of the Generalissimo. Finally, the Colonel traced my look and suddenly stopped his long moralising, and then angrily ordered me to "Sit down!"

He hated me after that incident. Even when he received an order to make recommendations to the Polish government, for officers who took part in the liberation of Warsaw and other Polish cities, Litvinov personally crossed my name off the list. That was how he revenged himself, depriving me of the Polish *Virtuti Militari* order that was issued to many of my friends.

For a long time I did not serve after my transfer to Debeln. It turned out that Rita's brother Stanislav was serving in the nearby town, as a driver of the *Katyusha* regiment commander. We often had dinners either at our place, or at the place of regiment commander Major Gilenkov, who became a good friend of ours. As early as December 1947, an order for transfer to Moscow came, and soon our familiar train "Berlin-Moscow" was taking us east, to our dear native land of the Soviet Union.

Stackpole Military History Series

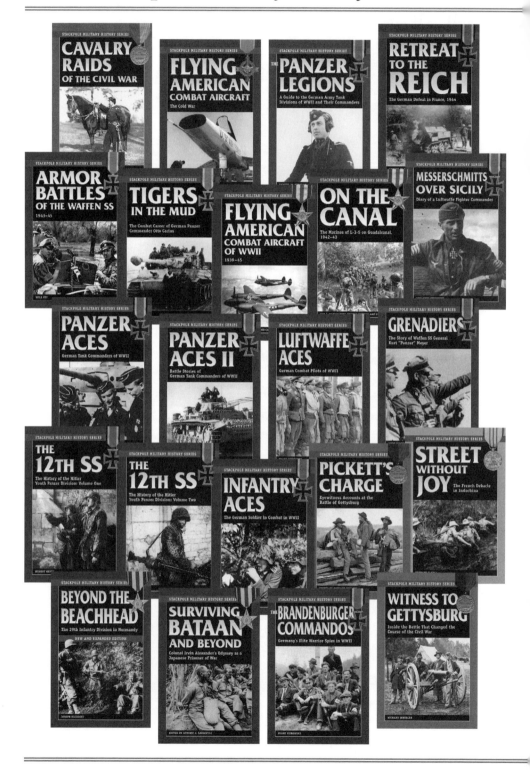

Real battles. Real soldiers. Real stories.

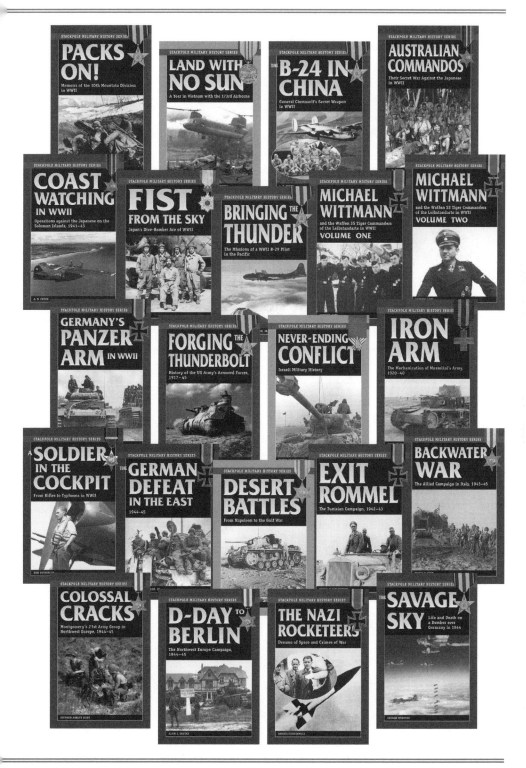

Stackpole Military History Series

Real battles. Real soldiers. Real stories.

Stackpole Military History Series

Real battles. Real soldiers. Real stories.

STACKPOLE MILITARY HISTORY SERIES

GOODWOOD
The British Offensive in Normandy, July 1944

IAN DAGLISH

STACKPOLE MILITARY HISTORY SERIES

DESTINATION NORMANDY
Three American Regiments on D-Day

STACKPOLE MILITARY HISTORY SERIES

EXPENDABLE WARRIORS
The Battle of Khe Sanh and the Vietnam War

BRUCE B. G. CLARKE

STACKPOLE MILITARY HISTORY SERIES

D-DAY DECEPTION
Operation Fortitude and the Normandy Invasion

STACKPOLE MILITARY HISTORY SERIES

RED STAR UNDER THE BALTIC
A Soviet Submariner in WWII

NEW for Spring 2009

STACKPOLE MILITARY HISTORY SERIES

HITLER'S NEMESIS
The Red Army, 1930–45

WALTER S. DUNN, JR., WITH A FOREWORD BY DAVID GLANTZ

STACKPOLE MILITARY HISTORY SERIES

PENALTY STRIKE
The Memoirs of a Red Army Penal Company Commander, 1943–45

ALEXANDER V. PYL'CYN

Stackpole Military History Series

SOVIET BLITZKRIEG

THE BATTLE FOR WHITE RUSSIA, 1944

Walter S. Dunn, Jr.

On June 22, 1944, the third anniversary of the German invasion of the Soviet Union, the Red Army launched Operation Bagration, its massive attempt to clear German forces from Belarus. In one of the largest campaigns of all time—involving two million Soviets and nearly a million Germans—the Soviets recaptured hundreds of miles of territory and annihilated an entire German army group in two months of vicious fighting. Bagration crippled the Germans in the East and helped turn the tide of the war.

$16.95 • Paperback • 6 x 9 • 288 pages • 18 b/w photos • 12 maps

WWW.STACKPOLEBOOKS.COM
1-800-732-3669

Stackpole Military History Series

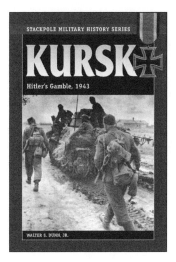

KURSK
HITLER'S GAMBLE
Walter S. Dunn, Jr.

During the summer of 1943, Germany unleashed its last major offensive on the Eastern Front and sparked the epic battle of Kursk, which included the largest tank engagement in history. Marked by fiery clashes between German Tigers and Soviet T-34s in the mud and dust of western Russia, the campaign began well enough for the Germans, but the Soviets counterattacked and eventually forced Hitler to end the operation. When it was over, thousands lay dead or wounded on both sides, but the victorious Red Army had turned the tide of World War II in the East.

$16.95 • Paperback • 6 x 9 • 240 pages • 9 photos, 1 map

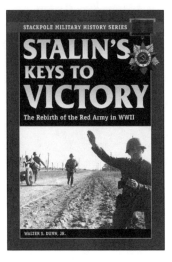

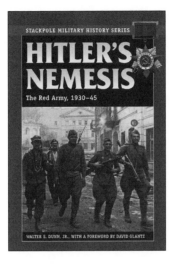

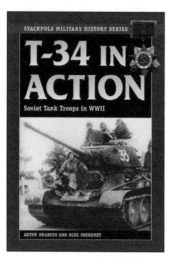

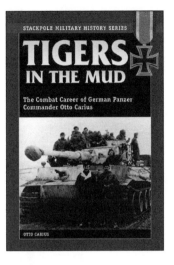

Stackpole Military History Series

GRENADIERS
THE STORY OF WAFFEN SS GENERAL
KURT "PANZER" MEYER

Kurt Meyer

Known for his bold and aggressive leadership, Kurt Meyer was one of the most highly decorated German soldiers of World War II. As commander of various units, from a motorcycle company to the Hitler Youth Panzer Division, he saw intense combat across Europe, from the invasion of Poland in 1939 to the 1944 campaign for Normandy, where he fell into Allied hands and was charged with war crimes.

$19.95 • Paperback • 6 x 9 • 448 pages • 93 b/w photos

Stackpole Military History Series

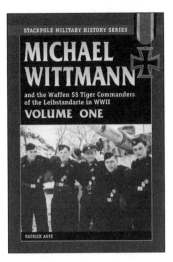
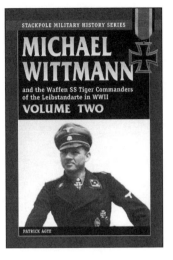

MICHAEL WITTMANN AND THE WAFFEN SS TIGER COMMANDERS OF THE LEIBSTANDARTE IN WORLD WAR II

Patrick Agte

By far the most famous tank commander on any side in World War II, German Tiger ace Michael Wittmann destroyed 138 enemy tanks and 132 anti-tank guns in a career that embodies the panzer legend: meticulous in planning, lethal in execution, and always cool under fire. Volume One covers Wittmann's armored battles against the Soviets in 1943–44 at places like Kharkov, Kursk, and the Cherkassy Pocket. Volume Two picks up with the epic campaign in Normandy, where Wittmann achieved his greatest successes before being killed in action. The Leibstandarte went on to fight at the Battle of the Bulge and in Austria and Hungary before surrendering in May 1945.

Volume One: $19.95 • Paperback • 6 x 9 • 432 pages
383 photos • 19 maps • 10 charts
Volume Two: $19.95 • Paperback • 6 x 9 • 400 pages
287 photos • 15 maps • 7 charts

WWW.STACKPOLEBOOKS.COM
1-800-732-3669

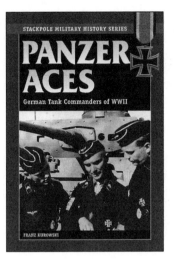